Illinois History of Sports

*Series Editors*
Benjamin G. Rader
Randy Roberts

Books in the Series

The Olympics: A History of the Modern Games
*Allen Guttmann*

Baseball: A History of America's Game
*Benjamin G. Rader*

The World's Game: A History of Soccer
*Bill Murray*

# The World's Game

# The World's Game

## A History of Soccer

## Bill Murray

University of Illinois Press
Urbana and Chicago

*This book is printed on acid-free paper.*

Library of Congress Cataloging-in-Publication Data

Murray, W. J. (William J.)
    The world's game : a history of soccer / Bill Murray.
        p.   cm. — (Illinois history of sports)
    Includes bibliographical references and index.
    ISBN 0-252-01748-X (cloth : alk. paper).
    1. Soccer—History.   I. Title.  II. Series
GV942.5.M88   1996
796.334'09—dc20                                    95-13742
                                                        CIP

To the folks in Adelaide

# Contents

# Acknowledgments

This book has been many years in the making, beginning with a child-hood in Scotland and emigration to Australia, where the World Game was played in microcosm among migrants who arrived, like me, from all parts of the world—a different experience from the streets and parks of Glasgow. It was a few more years before these experiences took shape in written form, but since then my thoughts on soccer have spread out from a book on the religious warfare of industrial Scotland as conducted through its two big teams, Celtic and Rangers, to an initial attempt to explain soccer's appeal throughout most of the world.

All those who helped me with these works have played their part in this book, in particular, colleagues and friends from the Australian Society for Sports History, especially: Roy Hay, who was ever ready to answer my many queries and supply books from his vast library; J. Neville Turner, who assisted me with a particular problem at a key moment; and Braham Dabscheck, Philip Mosely, and Bob Stewart. As ever, La Trobe University provided an understanding environment in which to work, from Beryl, Carol, and Heather in the history department office to John Horacek and the staff at the Borchardt library who were, as always, unstinting in their help in securing new books and others on interlibrary loan. From our German group Heidi Zogbaum was once more ready to help out with many linguistic problems. Don Ferrell not only discussed many sports issues with me but was always on hand to help with the mysteries of electronic communication.

In Germany Ulrich and Elke Matheja provided help in more ways than one, and *Kicker* magazine allowed me access to its marvelous resources. Arnd Krüger offered much food for thought. Tony Mason corrected some of the text and most kindly air-mailed a copy of his new book on South American soccer, allowing me to make some late adjustments. It is with pleasure that I thank the staff of the football associations of Brazil, Uruguay, and Argentina who allowed me to visit their libraries and trophy rooms, as well as Roberto Faria, a former player in Brazil and Europe, who took me on a tour of the main stadiums of Rio. Working with an American audience in mind has been a fascinating experience, and it has been a delight to have such a meticulous and knowledgeable copy editor as Bruce Bethell to render my text more accessible. Once more Pat Woods has been of inestimable help and read the penultimate draft with his usual care and critical comment.

# Introduction

On 8 December 1991 the draw for the opening rounds of the 1994 World Cup in soccer took place at New York's Madison Square Garden Paramount Theatre. This epic international sports competition involved nearly every country in the world, and its finals, which have been played every four years since 1930 (except during wartime), were to be played in the United States in the summer of 1994. Normally the draw would have been made in Zurich, home of the game's governing body, the Fédération Internationale de Football Association, better known by its acronym, FIFA, but it was hoped that having the draw in the United States would publicize the event in a country notorious for its disinterest in the game. The draw, made in New York, was shown live in many countries across the world but failed to attract those at whom it was aimed. The American sports public was a virtually untapped market for the world's most popular game, and commercial motives were to the fore in FIFA's determination to have the cup played there. But there were other reasons for FIFA's wanting the United States to host the game. In the expansion of soccer around the world, to become the ruling passion in virtually all of Europe and Latin America, as well as in most of Asia and all of Africa, only the English-speaking nations outside Great Britain remained unconquered: FIFA's penetration into the United States was also a missionary expedition to spread sporting light into soccer's darkest corner of the globe.

From the FIFA "family" of 168 nations at the time of the draw at Madison Square Garden, 143 entered. By the time the competition ended the "family" had grown to 191, the increase stemming mainly from the collapse of the former communist empires, for the newly autonomous nations made affiliation with FIFA one of their first priorities. Soccer has always been caught up in the big issues of world politics, and the 1994 World Cup was no exception. Although the Soviet Union and Yugoslavia were in the process of dissolution, their teams were in the draw, but the team from the newly independent Russia, with the blessing of the new Ukraine, took the place of the team from the Soviet Union and eventually qualified for the finals. The Ukraine itself, which had provided some of the best players for the Soviet Union, was too late to make a separate application, as was Georgia. The Baltic countries of Latvia, Lithuania, and Estonia, however, entered teams in the competition for the first time since 1938. Yugoslavia had to withdraw, and the new state of Croatia argued in vain that teams from the former members of the federal republic should play one another to decide which should represent the former Yugoslavia. The violence in the Balkans put an end to that.

The Middle East entrants posed particular problems for the U.S. organizers: the Iraqi team, as desperate to score political points off the field as to score goals on it, was in the draw, carefully kept clear of those from Kuwait and Saudi Arabia, although it was not allowed to play on its home territory. The ban on games in the recently war-torn countries of Lebanon and Kuwait was lifted. Israel was included with the European nations, its team having wandered around Asia and Oceania in the most recent qualifying tournaments, battling against the political hostility of the Arab nations and their supporters in Asia and Africa that refused to play against them.

The sports side of this vast international competition soon got under way. As host nation, the United States qualified automatically for the finals, as did the holders of the cup, the recently reunited Germany. The fate of the other twenty-two finalists remained undecided until the last minute. After nearly two years of knock-out competitions (see the glossary for this and other soccer-related terms) in regional leagues on a home-and-away basis, the last round of qualifying games was held on the evening of 17 November 1993. At that time twelve European teams still had a chance to qualify for the seven remaining European places, while in Buenos Aires, Argentina, one of the game's giants, struggled to a 1-0 victory over Australia, which had held them to a 1-1 draw in Sydney in the first leg. Prior to that hectic evening the representatives of the other regional confederations had been decided: Mexico was to represent North and Central America; the three South American places went to Bolivia, Brazil, Colombia, and Argentina, which qualified on a convoluted rule that also sent the Oceania winners across the globe to play against the runners-up in the two American confederations; Africa was represented by Cameroon, Morocco, and Nigeria; and Asia was represented by Saudi Arabia and South Korea.

The Asian qualifiers were decided in Qatar, where the winners of the various Asian and Middle East sections met in play-offs between 14 October and 28 October 1993. These games pitted Iraq against its bitter enemies Iran, with which it had fought a long and bloody war, Kuwait, and Saudi Arabia, which had faced Iraq's expansionist ambitions after Saddam Hussein called off the war with Iran. The explosive potential was obvious. The enmity between South Korea and North Korea, which were also among the twelve qualifiers, was more long-term. Fortunately, however, all the tensions were played out safely on the field in tight encounters whose outcomes, like those in Europe, were in doubt until the dying seconds of the last games. These games were played simultaneously, for goal difference (i.e., the number of goals scored minus goals allowed) looked likely to decide the qualifiers, and that was how it turned out. South Korea beat North Korea 3-0, and Japan was leading Iraq 2-1 with a minute to go and qualification at the expense of South Korea beckoning when Iraq tied the score: South Korea and Japan finished on equal points, but South Korea advanced on a two-goal difference. Saudi Arabia, which spent more on team preparation than any other country, qualified, earning the players massive cash bonuses and gifts of cars and land. Despite his team's success, the Saudis' Brazilian coach was dismissed for refusing to accept a royal family member's advice to substitute a goalkeeper during one of the games (he had previously incurred the ruling family's wrath for telling his players to treat the Iraqis politely and for speaking on friendly terms with the Iraqi coach). The U.S. organizers could breathe a sigh of relief, for although it had been agreed that the teams from North Korea, Iraq, and Iran would have no problems entering the United States should they have qualified, their potential to cause diplomatic embarrassment was enormous: Iraq in particular made it clear that it would have taken every opportunity to do so.

There was also relief, not unmixed with sadness, when the final European qualifiers became known. England failed when the Netherlands beat Poland, so that its 7-1 victory against San Marino became irrelevant. The country that with Scotland was the cradle of the game was out, but so was its notorious hooligan following. The other results were less fraught with political or social undertones, and the main concern was that the large ethnic communities of the United States be represented. The prayers of the Italians and the Irish, as well as of the organizers, were answered, in games that had to wait until the final minute to be decided: the Republic of Ireland held out for a 1-1 draw in Belfast against its northern neighbor, and in Milan the Italian team qualified at the expense of Portugal, which it beat 1-0. Greece had already qualified, thanks in part to its competing in a group weakened by Yugoslavia's withdrawal.

The biggest sensation of that final night was the elimination of France, which surrendered a safe lead in the last minutes of its game in Paris against Bulgaria—as it had done in the previous game against Israel—and so squandered what at one time looked like a certain entry to the finals. Spain beat Denmark 1-0 to qualify, although the Danes needed only a draw to advance. In Cardiff a missed penalty deprived Wales of a finals appearance and their young star Ryan Giggs of a world stage for his scintillating skills, as Romania went on to win 2-1. Scotland, bereft of a talent they once had in abundance, had already failed to qualify in a group that Switzerland won. The failure of Scotland and England, the founders and guardians of the laws and morality of the world's game, showed the distance the sport had traveled since it was organized as a leisure pastime for privileged private school alumni in London in 1863.

The large number of smaller nations among the European qualifiers was remarkable. Norway made the finals for the first time since 1938 and Greece for the first time ever, and they were accompanied by Sweden (runners-up in 1958), Switzerland, Romania, and Bulgaria. The Netherlands is a small nation in terms of geography but a major power in soccer; its team was second in the World Cup in 1974 and 1978 and was the European champion in 1988, but it went to USA 1994 weakened by the defection of its star player (nor was that the first such defection). Spain has provided some of the world's greatest club teams, but its national team has never reached the same heights, nor had the USSR team, now appearing as the Russian team and plagued with the problems that had all but ruined the domestic game since the onset of glasnost.

Latin America has shared the spoils of world soccer power with Europe, and despite domestic crisis being the norm in most of the countries there, the continent still has managed to produce teams of startling quality. Brazil's team, the only one to have appeared in every World Cup and the favorites of everyone who was not playing against it, had a rather rocky progress to the finals. Brazil was accompanied by Bolivia, which had never won a game in the competition, and Colombia, which arrived later to soccer but excelled in 1990 and qualified in 1993. Colombia's 2-1 victory against Argentina at home was followed by an unconfirmed report of twenty-eight deaths in the celebrations that followed, and there were seventy-eight confirmed deaths when it won 5-0 in the return game in Buenos Aires. None of these was to make the impact that a single death made later, however, when one of Colombia's star players was assassinated for scoring a goal against his own team in the finals. A World Cup without Argentina would have been unthinkable—above all to the Argentines—but it had to progress through the back door, as South American runners-up in a play-off against the minnows from Australia. A single goal in Buenos Aires spared the Argentine capital from an uncertain fate.

From Africa came Nigeria, Cameroon, and Morocco, the additional third place coming courtesy of the brilliant performances of Cameroon in Italy in 1990. Missing were Ghana, which is one of the original powers in African soccer but which has never appeared in the World Cup finals, and Zambia, whose dreams were shattered in the sea off Gabon when a plane carrying its team (minus its European stars) crashed shortly after a refueling stop on the way to a match in Senegal. There was no need for official mourning when the news was announced, for the grief among Zambians of all walks of life was spontaneous and universal. Astonishingly the team recovered from this catastrophic setback to come within an ace of qualifying, losing 0-1 to Morocco in Morocco, although it needed only a draw to qualify ahead of Morocco. The Asian qualifiers were no surprise: it was South Korea's third qualification since 1984, and the Middle East countries had been spending oil-derived fortunes on soccer since the 1970s. For Japan a dream that had begun barely a couple of years previously did not come true, but the country soon picked up the pieces, vowed that it would fight to win the rights for the 2002 World Cup, and minus the platform of the world stage, went back to its new domestic league, which has been one of the most remarkable success stories in soccer of recent years. China, rivals with South Korea and Japan for the 2002 World Cup, failed once again. From the Central and North American zone came Mexico, as usual, thanks to its geographical situation between the soccer lightweights of Canada and the United States, and the small, volatile, yet soccer-mad nations to the south. Canada's team was the runner-up, but it lost in the subsequent two-leg match against Australia. Completing the finalists were teams from the countries holding automatic entry; Germany, one of the most successful nations in the tournament (along with Argentina, Brazil, and Italy), and the United States, the vast bulk of whose citizens were blissfully unaware of the dramas shaking households around the world in the weeks leading up to and culminating in that dramatic evening of 17 November 1993.

As it turned out, the United States provided the stage for one of the best World Cups ever held, and although it effected no major revolution in the tastes of the U.S. sports public—that was never likely—it did give many Americans some insight into why soccer is the world's most popular game. The United States, like Australia, has developed its own code of football, but of all the football codes, that designed in the United States is the furthest removed from soccer; it is a game where kicking is almost an irrelevance, one that is expensive to equip and complicated to organize. Soccer, on the other hand, is the simplest game and from all points of view the most democratic. It is known as "the people's game," played mainly before the less-privileged sections of society, often by participants from poor backgrounds whose skills might elevate them to otherwise unattainable financial security and social esteem. In the United States baseball and basketball most often fulfill this role. Although basketball shares with soccer its economic democracy, soccer can be played at the highest levels by people who are not giants or in other ways physically advantaged; it is a game in which the small can outwit the large and the powerful. Indeed, most of soccer's superstars are well under six feet tall, and although most of them have muscular thighs and legs, others appear to be quite fragile. It is probably the most quickly expanding sport for women, above all in the United States, whose team won the first FIFA World Cup for Women, which was held in China in 1991.

Soccer is above all a game of skill, the only football code in which handling is banned for all players except the goalkeeper. As such, its skills are difficult to master, and some of them, most notably heading, appear outlandish to those who have not been brought up with the game. It is the simplest game to organize, however, for it can be played on any surface, in almost any climate, and with the most rudimentary of materials. Two players can start a game between themselves, and even a solitary player can practice his or her skills alone, bouncing the ball against a wall or simply keeping it up ("keepie-uppie"), seeing how many times the ball can be manipulated by head, thighs, and feet without it touching the ground. Unlike American football, soccer relies on spontaneity rather than programmed plays, the survival skills of the street urchin.

Soccer has evolved in a host of social and political cultures, invariably reflecting them not only in the style but also in the spirit in which the game is played. On-field brawls, assaults by fans on players and referees, and battles between rival supporters have all been part of the culture of soccer. Inevitably these have been given more publicity than have the thousands of games played in peace and harmony. They are part of the game's history, however, and for some people, above all in the United States, soccer is best known as a game played by foreigners that invariably ends with a riot. That the game itself did not produce these consequences was amply demonstrated as packed crowds in locations around the United States reveled in the spectacle played out before them in USA 1994. Americans were seeing the other side of what Pelé called the "beautiful game." This game has its dark side and has no solutions to a world where life is harsh and miserable for many; nevertheless, the world would be just as harsh and miserable—if not more so—without the joy and simple pleasures that soccer provides.

Of the great comforters of humankind, at least among males, soccer is less dangerous than drink, less illusory than religion, and it provides a closer sense of community than any political party does. The illusions of the faithful may become lost or the ecstasy of victory prove to be ephemeral, but with the start of each new season the hope eternal that fills the soccer fan's heart beats anew. Politicians can abuse this simple faith, the moneyed men defile it, and the cynics mock it, but soccer has survived them all to become the world's biggest and most firmly established institution. It all began in England with the Challenge Cup in 1872, but since then a host of trophies have been transformed into manifestations of the Holy Grail, all leading, however unwittingly, to the greatest of them all: the World Cup.

# The World's Game

# A Very British Beginning

When Americans celebrated the centenary of their national football code on 6 November 1969, the game they commemorated was in fact closer to soccer than to either rugby or what came to be known as American football. That first game was barely noticed at the time, for it was only one of many kicking games being played in the 1860s by young, mainly middle-class males throughout the English-speaking world. Played in New Brunswick, New Jersey, between Princeton and Rutgers Universities, however, it was the first intercollegiate football game, and although it was played on a large field with twenty-five men on each side, the ball was round and points were scored by players putting the ball through the goal; above all, running with the ball, which is a key feature of what became known as "rugby," was banned. There were so many young men playing football in the 1860s that some order had to be brought into the proceedings, and in England and Australia, as in the United States, the laws designed to impose that order evolved into the codes of football that we know today. The first of these codes was drawn up in London toward the end of 1863, and the game it regulated was called "association football." Nonetheless, football in various forms had been played throughout the world long before the nineteenth-century middle-class mania for rules and regulations. In America it had been popular among native peoples before the Europeans arrived, and it maintained this popularity as the Europeans brought their village games with them to the New World. By the nineteenth century most U.S. colleges, like those in Great Britain, played football, and the Oneida Football Club of Boston was said to have played soccer on the Boston Common in 1862. Since "soccer" (or association football, from which the name *soccer* was later derived) was not codified until 1863, the Oneida claim is somewhat fanciful. The rules for rugby football, which was played for decades in its distinctive form before codification, were finally drawn up in 1871. The American game progressed from rules close to soccer and then to rugby before Walter C. Camp set about finalizing the rules of the uniquely American game. In the state of Victoria in Australia another form of football was codified in 1866 and soon took root, so confusion over the "first" game of football is understandable.

In reality there was no first game of football, for its origins go back to the beginning of recorded history: in preindustrial societies it was often a "mob" game of village against village, lacking written rules and celebrated as part of a fertility rite or to mark particular seasons of the year; more sophisticated kicking games were to be found in societies as diverse as ancient China (which boasts the oldest rules resembling today's game), Japan and other parts of Asia, and pre-Columbian North, Central, and South America. Football was an essentially popular game, and the name originally referred to any ball game played on foot rather than on horseback. It was never exclusively a game of the people, however, and it counted among its aficionados countless anonymous clergymen and other local dignitaries, as well as men as famous as Oliver Cromwell, Walter Scott, and kings of Scotland, England, and France. Nevertheless, its very simplicity meant that it was looked down on by those who could afford more elevated pursuits, especially equestrian sports. Moreover, it was variously condemned for its uselessness as training for the military and for its threat to the soul through its licentiousness and to life and property through its violence. Others considered it to be a harmless way to let off steam, however, and saw no reason to deprive the poor of a simple pleasure.

As Britain changed from an agrarian to an industrial society beginning about 1750, the games played in the open fields of the countryside were adapted to suit the narrow streets and hard surfaces of the new urban communities. The leisure time determined by sun, seasons, and feudal obligation was replaced by the much more restricted leisure hours decreed by the artificial light of the factories and the needs of their owners. Improvements in roads and transportation allowed games to be played outside the local village, and as steam trains started to link the ever-growing towns of Britain, it became possible to play on a national basis the games that the middle class favored and promoted. This expanding scope involved agreement on rules and the formation of a national governing body. The industrial revolution advanced most quickly in Britain, and organized sport was introduced there long before it was in most other countries, with national rules drawn up for horse racing in the middle of the eighteenth century and for golf and cricket soon thereafter (1754 and 1788, respectively). It was in the midnineteenth century, however, that new and modernized leisure pursuits were recognized on a nationwide basis: mountaineering in 1857, track and field in 1866, and swimming in 1869. By 1888 sailing, cycling, ice skating, rowing, boxing, hockey, and lawn tennis were governed by national associations. Important among these newly codified sports was football, by then divided into the two distinct forms of association football and rugby. Like those for the game played in the United States, these rules were devised by young men from colleges and universities who wished to play against each other and so had to compromise on the rules in use at their local schools.

The so-called public schools of England did not invent football, but it was their "old boys" (alumni) who, having entered business or professional life and being anxious to continue playing their favorite game from their university days, provided the impetus for the first national rules. Before that each school played by its own rules. The boys from Rugby School, with its large grassy fields and wide-open spaces, played a football that allowed hard tackling and running with the ball. At Winchester the field was narrow, dribbling was encouraged, and there were no goals: to score the players needed only to get the ball across a line. At Harrow, whose Old Harrovians were among the major pioneers of association football, teams were limited to eleven players, and a large ball had to be maneuvered over a frequently muddy field. At Westminster and Charterhouse the game was restricted to the cloisters, which discouraged long kicking and handling.

As long as the boys of these schools played only among themselves, there was no problem about the rules of the game, which were based on tradition: indeed, the famous story of William Webb Ellis of Rugby School picking up the ball and running with it, showing a "fine disregard for the rules" and so inventing rugby in 1823, as the memorial stone at the school claims, shows instead a fine disregard for the truth. The first combined rules were drawn up in 1846 by some Old Salopians and Old Etonians, one of which forbade kicking opponents with steel-plated boots. The first serious attempt to create a uniform set of rules, however, came at Cambridge in 1848. These rules were never officially recorded, but according to H. C. Malden, who organized the meeting, representatives from the various public schools were sat down in a room at Trinity College, provided with pens, ink, and paper, and told to write down their schools' rules. Out of this meeting, which lasted until nearly midnight, emerged the "Cambridge Rules." No copy of them has survived, but they continued to be revised and reappeared in published form in 1863. These rules provided the basis of the laws of association football, which were agreed on at a meeting of alumni from various public schools at the historic meeting in London's Freemason's Tavern on 26 October 1863 and at five subsequent meetings.

The main dispute was over handling and hacking (kicking). The Blackheath club wanted to retain hacking, claiming that its abolition threatened the essential "manliness" of football, and sneered that such sissy reforms would reduce the game to something more suited to the French. When Blackheath and others formed their own association in 1871, hacking was banned from the new code of rugby football, but handling and running became its main features. By then the limited handling permitted under the first Football Association (FA) rules had been banned.

The debate in Britain over the rules of different versions of football was covered in great detail in *The Field* and reproduced in the press of other English-speaking countries. In Melbourne, where respectable young men of the liberal professions were keen to continue their favorite leisure pursuit without having to appear before their clients the following Monday with black eyes or broken arms, a set of rules were agreed on in 1866 that were meant to make their game less rough. Thus was born Australian Rules football, a wild and uninhibited game in which black eyes and broken limbs are still part of the rough-and-tumble. In Ireland in 1885 the rules of Gaelic football were formally drawn up shortly after the founding of the Gaelic Athletic Association. By then the American game developed by Walter Camp had triumphed over other football codes in the United States. The rugby code in England was facing a crisis similar to that in soccer over professionalism and control by the southern amateurs, but this led to the split of 1895 and the founding of the Rugby League, which went on to develop a significantly different game.

At the turn of the century, then, various forms of football were flourishing in the English-speaking countries of what had once been the British Empire. With a few exceptions, only soccer would be taken up by non-English-speaking peoples, becoming the world's most popular sport: today the "people's game" not only is played in every country in the world but is the popular passion in most.

The alumni of the English public schools not only gave the world the rules of association football; they also fostered the spirit in which they hoped it would be played, that of an amateur game unsullied by material reward. The social origins of soccer can still be found in the peculiar offense of "ungentlemanly conduct," a category applied to-day to a wide variety of sins, from foul language and spitting to un-sporting play, such as calling for a pass from an opponent. The men of the 1860s lived in a much simpler world than that of today, and they made that world even simpler by refusing to take seriously those who were outside their class and nationality. These class assumptions and the right of those who ruled to continue to do so were clearly set out in an article in *The Field* of April 1864:

In the ethics of education, books and book learning are now uni-versally admitted to be far from everything. Writers of the day, who have brought great wisdom to bear upon the subject, have even gone so far as to declare these to be only subordinate items of the great system by which the youth of a nation is so trained that when the time arrives it is prepared to command a division, lead a cavalry charge, bear the brunt of battle, the hardships of the field, or accept the responsibilities devolving upon the men to whose hands is entrusted the government of the nation. The education of the playground, and the lessons learned from schoolfellows and college friends are, apart from the physical advantages gained in the former, of the highest practical value.

This highly loaded political statement was not seen as such by the men who preached the virtues of "sport for sport's sake," the essen-tial amateur ideal. It is a class statement by the nation's self-appoint-ed leaders, the men of the old school tie, setting down the rules and discipline by which they would rule the empire entrusted to their care. Sport, then, was not just for fun and games but for building charac-ter and leadership.

During the two decades after 1863 association football was orga-nized and largely played by young men of the public schools, but thereafter it faced both the incursions of new wealth from the north and the influx of players from working-class stock. These were issues of the future, however, and in the later 1860s and early 1870s the men of the Football Association extended their control over a few local London teams to take in most of England and enter into agreements with the other countries of the United Kingdom.

The main rival to the FA was in Sheffield, where a code of football involving dribbling was particularly popular and where the first football club north of London was founded in 1857. Like those at Harrow and Cambridge, the Sheffield club banned hacking and running with the ball but allowed limited handling. The Forest club, which played on the edge of the Epping Forest, was founded in 1859 and comprised mainly Harrow alumni. It was the first club to devote itself exclusively to the dribbling game, and after it disbanded in 1864, it reformed as the Wanderers Football Club, the most famous in the early years of the FA. Notts County also played a dribbling game. Founded in 1862, it is the oldest soccer team still playing in major competition.

The different associations played against one another, the London and Sheffield associations playing several times after 1866, until all these groups came to a compromise agreement in 1877. The London FA then emerged as virtually the sole authority for the game in England, and an increasing number of local associations affiliated to it. In 1867 it had a mere 10 members; four years later this had risen to 50. It reached the 1,000 mark in 1888 and the 10,000 mark in 1905. In 1880 the FA took up residence in its first permanent office, and six years later it employed its first salaried secretary. By then the London FA had dropped its regional qualifier. Known thereafter simply as the Football Association, it was the ruling body of football in the land—eventually throughout the world—and the acronym FA became the most easily recognized symbol of soccer to millions, regardless of the language they spoke.

The success of the London FA in establishing its control over the other dribbling associations came with the popularity of the Challenge Cup, which it instituted in 1871. Today this competition is more popular than ever, and it was not until 1994 that it was tarnished by a sponsor's name. The Challenge Cup was the idea of Charles William Alcock, a driving force in the early history of the game and the FA's secretary from 1870 to 1895. Fifteen teams competed in that first knock-out competition held in the 1871–72 season; the Wanderers won the trophy, which was valued at £20. As captain of the Wanderers, Alcock was the first to show off the trophy before a few family and friends—today it is brandished before millions. Until 1885 crowds for the final of the Challenge Cup, or FA Cup (later simply "the Cup"), never reached 10,000, but even before then its romance had begun to flower. Part of this romance is in the nature of soccer, where scoring is difficult and the goalkeeper is technically capable of stopping every shot. As a result, a resolute and inspired team of underdogs can hold much more favored opponents at bay. The romance is also in the nature of the competition, with its sudden-death encounters, the luck of the draw, and the home-field factor: only finals and semifinals are played on neutral grounds (except in the case of a second replayed game, each team then having had the home-ground advantage). It is open to every member club in the FA, and although the "rabbits," or rank outsiders, are usually eliminated early in the competition, some few have come close to the ultimate prize, the final in London. Today that prize, contested at Wembley, has achieved an almost religious aura.

Also helping to secure the success of the dribbling game was the regular match with Scotland, which began in 1872 and extended to a British Home Championship in 1883 with the addition of Ireland and Wales. There had been unofficial "internationals" between Scotland and England in 1870 and 1871, but that of 1872, played on the West of Scotland Cricket Ground in Glasgow, a well-organized and serious affair watched by 2,000–4,000 people and reported fulsomely in the press, was the beginning of the longest-lasting annual international competition in the history of sport, continuing until 1989.

Organized soccer began in Scotland in 1867 when some youths of the Young Men's Christian Association (YMCA) formed a team, naming it Queen's Park, and after a few debates on the subject decided to follow the rules of the dribbling game rather than those of the handling and running game. They entered the FA Cup on several occasions, were behind the founding of the Scottish Football Association in 1873, and provided almost all the Scotland players in the early internationals. By the end of the 1870s several rivals had appeared, but until the advent of professionalism Queen's Park was the premier club in Scotland. By the 1880s the craze for soccer had engulfed most of Scotland, and an observer noted in 1881 that "one cannot go into a single village or town in Scotland without seeing the practice grounds and goalposts of the now omnipresent football club."

The national association of Wales was formed in 1876, and that in Ireland in 1880. Rugby became the national game of Wales, even in the mining districts that were the natural breeding grounds of soccer talent elsewhere, and in Ireland the popularity of rugby and the antipathy of the Gaelic Athletic Association fought against the establishment of soccer. Soccer caught on in northern Ireland, especially in Belfast, but neither Wales nor Ireland could hope for more than the occasional soccer victory against their more powerful neighbors. The Scots, however, although they are far outnumbered by the English, nevertheless often defeated them, and these victories helped to sustain the Scots through much of the arrogance of their brother enemy. Scotland and England dominated the annual Home International tournament played between the four "nations" from 1883, but in the International Board, set up in 1882 to agree on the rules of the game, all four associations had equal voting power.

The influence of Scots and Scotland in the development of soccer is paramount, not only in England, which Scots entered freely without serious diminution of their anti-Englishness, but throughout the British colonial possessions and other countries where British commercial and industrial expertise was established. The "Scotch professors" changed the nature of soccer by adopting the passing game instead of the dribbling game. Prior to this development, the strategy had been to get behind the man with the ball and rush forward in a mighty mass, with the hope of forcing the ball through the goal. The Scots decided that the ball could travel faster and more efficiently than a man, so they kept more players in defense, spread their forwards to include two wingers, and learned to pass accurately to fellow players rather than rely on the almighty kick and the rush to catch up with the ball. "Kick and rush" is an insult that would frequently be applied to British soccer by more skilled continentals, but they themselves learned their game from coaches who believed in the Scottish game: short passing, frequent interchanging, and keeping the ball on the ground.

It was the Scottish emigrants, too, who are often credited with introducing professionalism in England. Such a claim is obviously overstated, but what cannot be exaggerated is the number of Scottish players playing in England in the 1880s, most of whom had come in search of work but for some of whom the job was secondary to their soccer ability. By the 1880s soccer had been taken up by the working classes, and games organized by towns, counties, or private clubs could almost bring industry to a standstill. W. Pickford, one of the earliest historians of the game (his history appeared in 1906) and later a member of the FA, recalled from the vantage point of the early twentieth century the days when Darwen was a power in Lancashire soccer. This was back in the late 1870s, when a midweek game between two local clubs, especially if one of them was Blackburn Rovers, could bring the mills to a halt. Workers refused to return to work after dinner (i.e., the midday meal), and as much as the bosses might rage about this, there was nothing they could do about it. The hills around Barley Bank were black with people enjoying not only an afternoon off work but also a free view of the game from outside the enclosure. It was a problem that would repeat itself in other times and other places. By the end of the 1920s employers in South America had given up hope of expecting their workers to turn up when a big game was on, and as Robert Edelman tells us (*Serious Fun*), a Soviet trade-union congress in 1927 complained that the big games attracted so many spectators that the mines in the Donbass were completely empty on the days of important matches. If it is true, as was often claimed, that factory output improved when the local team was doing well, then all was not lost by the bosses.

The FA Cup games attracted the biggest crowds in England, and they increased dramatically in the 1880s; in 1901 a crowd of 110,820 turned up at the Crystal Palace to see Tottenham Hotspur and Sheffield United contest the final of the blue ribbon trophy. In Scotland the international against England was more popular than the Scottish Cup and in the 1890s attracted crowds of over 50,000. These crowds were increasingly made up of workers, who during the latter decades of the century won a shorter working week, above all the free Saturday afternoon, which gave birth to the British weekend. By the 1890s, too, the average British worker enjoyed a slightly higher standard of living than thirty years previously, with enough spare cash to see his favorite team, traveling by train to important away games or by tram across the rapidly sprawling cities to see a local derby. The teams themselves grew more or less spontaneously, some formed by churches and some from cricket clubs, while pub teams occasionally went beyond a mere kick-around to countywide and then national success. A few teams were formed in the workplace, sometimes with the encouragement of the employer but as often as not simply by the workers themselves. Whatever their origins, the most successful clubs were made up of working-class players, and from the 1880s these were to be found in the industrial regions of the north and midlands of England and the central industrial belt of Scotland. In 1883 the FA Cup went north for the first time, won by Blackburn Olympic, and northern teams made up of "mechanics and artisans" rather than university graduates dominated the game until well into the new century; control of the game, however, stayed with the "old boys" of the south.

———

That London retained control of the game can be attributed to the good sense of men like Alcock and Lord Kinnaird, the latter an Old

Etonian and president not only of the FA but also of the YMCA and other Christian bodies. These men of broad social vision loved the game so much that they did not mind sharing it with those outside their class, and it was this spirit that prevented a split when the "terrible" truth that some men accepted money to play the game became inescapable. They believed that professionalism degraded the spirit of the game, but by recognizing it they sought to control it. Thus in 1885, after a series of complaints about athletes accepting money and the creation of committees to deal with them, followed by threats of serious punishments, the FA legalized professionalism under a welter of constraints, most of which they soon had to abandon.

The acceptance of professionalism meant that players had to be given a regular income. The FA Cup was still the main competition, and there were many other local cup competitions, but even the best team could be eliminated in an early round, leaving the team with nothing to do. The answer was the Football League, based on the English County Cricket competition (and not on the baseball league then operating in the United States). The league was made up of selected teams that agreed to play one another on set dates, on a home-and-away basis, and promised to field their strongest team and to give the league matches preference over all others.

The individuals engaged in the discussions about the new league were essentially self-made men, small-business owners and industrialists who came from a social category different from that of the men of the FA. With the FA watching anxiously, discussions were held by those in favor of the league. The debates were acrimonious, but in the end, at a historic meeting on 17 April 1888, the idea was accepted. On 8 September 1888 the new Football League kicked off competition with twelve teams, including Preston North End, the so-called Invincibles, made up mainly of Scots, which not only won the first League "flag" without losing a game but completed the "double" when it won the FA Cup without losing a goal. On 11 January 1889 a constitution was drawn up that determined the following issues: the league games' precedence over all others; details such as the points scoring system, where two points were awarded for a win and one for a draw (and not, as had been strongly argued, none); and the use of goal average to differentiate teams level on points (goal difference was not introduced until 1976). How to share the gate money would remain a constant bone of contention. In 1893 the League established conventions determining teams' promotion from and relegation to a second division, thus giving birth to that other institution so intimately associated with soccer leagues. At first a team's division status was determined by play-offs, as in county cricket, but from the 1898–99 season promotion and relegation were decided automatically: the top team(s) in the lower division was promoted; the bottom team(s), relegated.

The League hoped that Scottish clubs would join its competition and so did not call itself the *English* Football League. According to its founder and guiding spirit, the Scottish-born Birmingham businessman William McGregor, its aim was to protect the interests of the clubs taking part in its competition. McGregor openly declared that "the League should never aspire to be a legislating body . . . by the very nature of things the League must be a selfish body." Nigel Jackson, the high priest of amateurism, thoroughly agreed, but in a different sense. He despised the commercialism of the League and any competition for which there was a prize. In 1882 he founded the Corinthians Football Club, which was restricted to the socially privileged and which at first spurned any game in which the least bauble or pennant was at stake. The League conceded the right of the FA to control football in all areas but the organization of league competition. This meant that the FA was left to control the FA Cup and internationals (where professionals dominated) and amateur soccer. The FA also ruled on certain matters concerning the rewards and disciplining of the professionals. This led to many tensions, especially in the early days, but a common interest in keeping the players in their place prevented a major split—that would have to wait for another time and other standards.

Scotland formed its own league in 1890, and professionalism, its natural and intended outcome, came in 1893. In the two Glasgow teams, Rangers and Celtic, it provided one of the most fiercely contested local derbies in the history of sport. Celtic was founded by a Catholic Marist brother in November 1887; playing in green-and-white hoops, with a shamrock in its emblem, the team was supported mainly by Scottish Catholics of Irish origins. Rangers, founded in 1872, grew in strength by their successful opposition to Celtic, emphasizing their Protestantism by banning Catholics from the club after about 1910 and proclaiming their Unionism in the red, white, and blue of their official strips. Thus the two teams came to represent the sectarian undertones of Scotland and Northern Ireland. For the men who ruled the two clubs it was also a profitable business, for matches between what became known as the "Old Firm" virtually guaranteed sellout crowds. Rangers and Celtic displaced Queen's Park as the most powerful clubs in Scotland, which did not prevent the amateurs building a new sports stadium early in the century, Hampden Park, which until 1950 was the world's largest.

By the turn of the century England, Scotland, Ireland, and (to a lesser degree) Wales had their own national soccer organizations, with their own cup and league competitions. For a long time to come there was no country beyond the United Kingdom to offer them serious competition. This sports division within the one political union has caused much confusion to sports historians and others unfamiliar with soccer. Within the soccer world itself it became a major bone of contention from the 1950s following the introduction of several international competitions in which the four British associations were awarded four places instead of one, as the regions' political unity should have dictated. So far history and tradition have prevailed against political reality.

The professional teams of Britain were fed by a vast network of amateur leagues, which were run by various county, municipal, and local associations and other voluntary bodies. These amateurs, playing in parks for their schools and for various youth teams, made up the vast majority of those playing soccer. Churches ran leagues throughout Britain, as did Christian organizations like the YMCA and the Boy's Brigade. The Glasgow Battalion of the Boy's Brigade grew to provide what was claimed to be the biggest football league in the world, fielding 200 teams in the 1950s. The various educational authorities also ran leagues and cups, ultimately on a national basis. From such competitions young boys could join various "junior" or amateur leagues, in which they might be spotted by a scout from one of the professional teams. Universities and colleges remained the home of true amateurism. The Corinthians were the most famous amateur team and unlike Queen's Park refused to play in regular competition with professionals. Instead they engaged in friendlies—games in which neither cup elimination nor league points were at stake—with other amateur clubs, but above all they went on regular tours abroad, to Europe and even the Americas, helping to spread the virtues of the game at the same time as they enjoyed an aristocratic leisure pursuit that would soon be an anachronism. In 1907 the amateurs of the public school tradition split from the FA to form their own Amateur Association, but they were never more than a splinter group, and in 1914 they patriotically returned to the fold of the FA.

The professional game went its own way, blanketed by an ethos that was determined by both the amateur ideals of the FA and the proprietary paternalism of the League. Both organizations were based on a Protestant morality that may have helped capitalism to expand in the wider world but that in sport acted as a restraint. The official history of the FA published in 1953 proudly claims that the FA stood unflinchingly against the evils of violence, women's football, and the corrupting power of money. Many of the men who ran the FA and the Football League devoted themselves to what they took to be the good of the game with no thought of financial recompense, and they thought that the players should do much the same. Power, recognition, and perhaps a title were their reward. For the average player, however, power lay in his boots, recognition lasted as long as he was fit to play, and titles were what he used to address other people. His financial rewards—about double what he might have earned in the factory, down in the mine, or in the shipyard—were the envy of those who played the game for nothing, but they seldom lasted beyond a decade of uncertain employment.

Before the legalization of professionalism, good players used a variety of covert measures to extract big payments for their services, and some of the moneyed men from the north advocated professionalism primarily to restore the proper master-servant relationship. With professionalism the player would be tied to a contract, with set fees for his services. The FA detested the whole idea of men playing for money, and worse, being bought and sold on the transfer market, but it could hope to do little more than limit the trade. When the fees for transfers escalated to £1,000 with the transfer of Alf Common from Sunderland to Middlesborough in 1905, the FA tried unsuccessfully to impose a £350 maximum. Not only were such limits unworkable, but as the League pointed out, smaller clubs often sold their best players to gain income that helped to keep them afloat.

By then players in England were restricted to a maximum wage of £208 per year, with a ban on bonuses, which were said to be detrimental to sportsmanship. The bigger clubs would have liked to have been able to offer higher rewards, but this was resisted by those who wanted to maintain some form of equality. The player had little say in the matter. Worst of all, he was saddled with a "retain and transfer" system that gave the club virtually complete control over him. Once signed (for a maximum payment of £10), the player became the property of the club and could not be transferred except with the club's permission. As long as the club offered a player the same wages as the previous year's, he had no grievance in the eyes of the League or the FA. The player's only right under this system was to refuse to go to a team to which he was being transferred, but this could result only in loss of wages and a bad reputation.

In 1909 a threatened strike by professional players was averted at the last minute, and although the players made some gains, the authority of the League and the FA was reinforced. The English authorities made agreements with their counterparts in Scotland, Ireland, and Wales, as well as with the Southern League in England, which in any case joined the Football League after the World War I, and since there was no professional soccer outside the United Kingdom before the 1920s, the option of playing in another country was closed. For the star player who attracted thousands of extra spectators to the game, and for those playing in teams that advanced to the final of the FA Cup, the rewards were the same. It was a form of socialism that the game's rulers never would have tolerated in daily life, but it did create one of the most evenly balanced and efficient sports competitions anywhere in the world.

---

In the first decade of the new century the game's increasing professionalism could also be seen in the reduction of the protests that had plagued it in the amateur days and in improved crowd control and spectator behavior. Nevertheless, early in the new century soccer provided the context for the greatest tragedy and the worst riot in sports to that time. Both took place in Scotland.

The tragedy came in 1902 during an international match between Scotland and England at Ibrox Park, Glasgow, the ground of Rangers. Part of a new wooden terracing for standing spectators gave way, plunging twenty-five to their death and leaving over five hundred badly injured. The game continued with spectators clinging to the stand where many had recently fallen to their deaths. The riot took place in April 1909, when the authorities refused to play extra-time in a second-drawn cup final between Rangers and Celtic at Hampden Park. Supporters of both teams then invaded the field, tore down the goalposts, and set fire to the pay boxes. Firefighters who came to put out the fires were attacked and had their hoses cut, and many police officers were injured in fighting that went on into the night. Rangers and Celtic fans, inspired by sectarian hatred, would continue to fight each other for decades, but on this occasion they found themselves on the same side. There would be other outbreaks of violence, especially in the years immediately following World War I, and bad language, fights between individuals, and drunkenness were part of the game's working-class culture; nonetheless, through to the 1960s the professional game in Britain boasted sporting behavior on the field and disciplined good manners by the crowds that were equaled in few other professional sports.

---

By the turn of the century soccer was established throughout most of the British Isles, but it had failed to take root in the lands that had once been under British colonial control. In the United States ties with the homeland had long been cut, and for over a century its citizens had carved out their own destiny, free from the prejudices and animosities of the Old World. In sport as in other aspects of life, Americans invented their own games: baseball as the popular passion, American football in the colleges, and later basketball, the one American game that would come to enjoy significant international popularity. Soccer remained a backwater in the United States, the game of the recent immigrants, and as such one that was frowned on by parents who wanted their sons to become good Americans. The non-British immigrants to the United States before the turn of the century came from countries where soccer was still virtually unknown. There were some exceptions, however; in New England's industrial region around Fall River, Massachusetts, and in St. Louis, Missouri, soccer established a foothold that it never lost. Progress was sporadic at best, however, despite some surges of popularity after 1904 and above all in the 1920s.

The American Football Association (AFA) was founded in 1884, and a short-lived professional league was introduced in 1894, but the problems that would continue to dog soccer in the United States were already present: the league was organized by people with no real interest in the game (in fact, by baseball owners seeking a more capital intensive use of their sports grounds), and it was played by "foreigners." Another problem, familiar to sports in general and in some way showing the progress of the game, was manifested in the splits between those who wanted to ban professionalism and those who claimed to be more "progressive." The first major split occurred in 1890, when some New York City and upper New York State individuals broke away from the AFA to found the American Amateur Football Association (AAFA) and rid themselves of the taint of the industrial teams of New England.

The U.S. soccer enthusiasts struggled on into the twentieth century and had their efforts boosted by visits from such renowned English amateur teams as the Pilgrims in 1905 and 1909 and the Corinthians in 1906 and 1911. In 1905 Fall River beat the tourists 3-0 before a crowd of 8,000, and in that same year the first Intercollegiate Association Football League was founded, those behind it hoping to take advantage of the crisis then racking American college football, for that game's violent nature had resulted in several deaths. The league's first members were Columbia, Cornell, and Harvard Universities, Haverford College, and the University of Pennsylvania. By 1912 there were organized leagues in twelve states. In that year Harvard University's stadium committee looked forward to the day when American colleges would entertain crowds as big as those at the FA Cup finals in England. It would not be the last time that such empty predictions would be made, and above all in the colleges soccer remained a near total irrelevance.

In the meantime soccer struck some roots elsewhere. On the West Coast the Greater Los Angeles Soccer League was set up in 1902, and a San Francisco league formed two years later. In the Midwest soccer had some hold in Chicago, Detroit, and above all, Saint Louis, which had established the curious distinction, one that it still retains, of being the home of native-born talent: the Kensingtons of Saint Louis were founded in 1890 as the first all-U.S.-born team, and Saint Louis became the most successful U.S. soccer team and also contributed six members of the U.S. soccer squad that provided the sensation of the 1950 World Cup in Brazil. It was on the East Coast, however, that soccer had its firmest grip, and when the two warring bodies from that part of the country, the AFA and the AAFA, resolved their differences in 1913, the United States was accepted into FIFA, preparing the way for the game's brief "golden age" in that country.

Canada developed its own variation of American football, ignored soccer, and adopted ice hockey as its national game. Unlike the United States, Canada at the time of the various codifications of football still had strong British migrant communities, and the drive to establish soccer came from the immigrant Scots—and a handful of Ulster Irish. David Forsyth, born in Perthshire, Scotland, in 1852 but brought to Canada with his parents a year later, devoted a lifetime to the game, but he never saw it develop beyond an interesting hobby. An all-around sportsman, distinguished educationist, and visionary, Forsyth was a founding member of the Western FA (1880), which played an important part in Canadian soccer until 1940, four years after Forsyth's death.

Soccer spread as the railways linked up Canada's far-flung wildernesses, trading centers, and eventually the Pacific and Atlantic coastlines. Vancouver, Winnipeg, and Toronto were the main soccer centers, along with the sparsely populated province of Saskatchewan. Attempts to establish regular internationals with the United States in the mid-1880s and mid-1920s failed, but in 1888 Forsyth took a Canadian team on a very successful tour of Scotland and England. A return trip in 1891, however, with a team reinforced by players from

Fall River and Pawtucket, Rhode Island, in the United States, was a failure. These ventures can scarcely be justified as internationals, and that characterization applies even less to Canada's success in the 1904 Olympic Games in Saint Louis, where a team from Galt (now part of Cambridge, Ontario) won the soccer gold medal after having beaten the two other competitors, Christian Brothers College and Saint Rose, 7-0 and 4-0.

In Australia in 1900 the previously independent states gave up most of their autonomy to become part of the unified Commonwealth of Australia. To mark the event there was a vigorous attempt to create a nationwide football code under the slogan "One people; one destiny; one football code." The code, however, was Australian Rules football, and its main rival was rugby. Soccer was not in the reckoning. Australia's first football association, and one of the first outside the United Kingdom (along with Natal in South Africa), was founded in New South Wales in 1882; two years later it organized the first intercolonial game, against Victoria, the next most populous state. By then Australian Rules football was the passion of the Victorians and, thanks to their missionary efforts, of every other state except New South Wales, which was fiercely antagonistic to its southern neighbor, and Queensland. In these two states rugby became the most popular football code, with League gaining the popular ascendancy over Union after the split of 1907. Soccer gained significant support in parts of New South Wales and Queensland, particularly in the industrial areas to the north and south of Sydney, and New South Wales remained the dominant soccer power in Australia. Soccer was always the second-most popular sport in every state, but as in Canada and the United States, it remained the game of the recent immigrants: the British before World War II and Europeans (particularly southern Europeans) thereafter.

Rugby had established itself as the national sport of New Zealand by the turn of the century, despite the efforts of some Victorians to export the Australian game; although it had a promising beginning, "Victorian Rules," as it originally was called, never took root. Soccer barely managed a promising beginning. New Zealand is perhaps the most British country outside Britain, and some regions are said to be more Scottish than Scotland. Despite this, and the proverbial enthusiasm of the Scots for promoting soccer around the world, soccer energies seem to have cooled in colonial climes. A football association was founded in Auckland, New Zealand's largest city, in 1886, and three years later in the south island province of Otago. The first national football association was formed in the capital, Wellington, on 2 October 1891, and the following year competition began for the Brown Shield, put up by a Scottish whisky merchant from Glasgow. This remained the main national competition until the London FA donated a trophy for competition in 1925. The trophy that was to have the longest life, however, was the Chatham Cup, donated by the crew of HMS *Chatham* in appreciation of the hospitality they had received during their stay in 1922.

After New Zealand and Wales, the most fanatical rugby country is South Africa, but only among the white population: soccer is by far the most popular game with the nonwhites. In New Zealand whites and Maoris play rugby together in the ironically named All Blacks (the name comes from the color of their shirts, shorts, and socks). In South Africa, however, the social forces behind the system of apartheid that became official policy in the 1950s had long been in place, and the more popular soccer became with the nonwhites, the more the whites looked down on it. Nevertheless, South Africa supplied more professional soccer players for English and Scottish league teams before the 1960s than all the other former colonies put together. The South African FA was founded in 1892, and the Currie Cup became a hotly contested competition from that year on, but the story of soccer in South Africa is more closely linked to the history of colonialism and the fight against apartheid.

———

In those parts of the British Empire where the imperial links were with indigenous peoples rather than white settlers, soccer was part of the colonial baggage, either as a leisure pursuit for the expatriates or as a means, along with the Bible, to accomplish their "civilizing" mission. India was the jewel in the British imperial crown, and particularly in Calcutta soccer was played with great zeal by clerks in the Indian public services and soldiers in the British army. The locals were watching and forming their own teams, however, one of which, Mohan Bagan, wrote its way into the hearts of patriotic Indians when in 1911 it carried off the Indian Football Association Shield by winning against the best teams of the British colonial presence. Tens of thousands turned up to watch that game, the news of its progress being carried in waves by those who could see it reporting the events to the great many behind them who could not. The victory was greeted with unprecedented rejoicing, while enthusiastic locals compared it to Japan's victory over Russia in the war of 1904–5, as further proof, in the words of one nationalist speaking in an ironic vein, that "the rice-eating Asian" could hold his own with the European. Calcutta remained one of the soccer hot spots of the empire and supplied most of the players who toured South Africa in 1935. A couple of years later, in 1937, crowds of up to 100,000 came to see the visiting Islington Corinthians amateur team from London.

The European intruders in China had set up their elite sports in Shanghai as early as 1843, and in 1879 soccer matches were being played there. John Prentice from Glasgow became president of the Engineers team, and in November 1887 the Shanghai Football Club was set up as a separate section of the Shanghai Athletic Club. Four years later Prentice donated a trophy that resulted in derby matches between the Engineers and Shanghai FC. Many further trophies would be put up for competition in the region, including the Interport, between Hong Kong and Shanghai, and the International Cup (1907), where Scotland dominated other teams made up of English, Irish, Germans, French, Belorussians, Jews, and above all, Portuguese. A Shanghai football association was founded in 1910.

The Hong Kong FC was founded in 1886, and in September 1896 the Hong Kong Shield was set up for competition between military and civilian groups. Games were played in Singapore in 1889, and a football association was founded there in 1892. In northern China a Tientsin soccer club was founded in 1884, and the game flourished for a while before falling into abeyance. Soccer was strong in Beijing in the early years of the century, and although the British were dominant, the French, Austrians, and even Americans took part. By this time the railways were being driven into the mainland and ships of European commerce and war patrolled the seas, while Christian missionaries, particularly through the YMCA, used sport to win the "heathens" over to the "true god."

These heathens were more willing to accept the round ball than they were a European god, however, and ethnic hostilities were a constant in the spread of soccer and revolution in the region. Before about 1900 most Chinese held European sport (not to mention Europeans) in contempt, but students who had been to Europe and the United States came back with the realization that the only way China could stand up to the intruders was to adopt some of their ways. When Japan trounced Russia in the war of 1904–5, it was by adopting Western expertise, and in China a political step to modernization came with the overthrow of the Manchu dynasty in 1911. By then modernization through sports was underway.

In 1904 the South China Athletic Association (AA) was founded, with soccer included among other sports: it would become the flag-bearer for Chinese pride in the decades to come. In October 1910 the first National Athletic Games were held in Nanking, with soccer included alongside track and field, tennis, basketball, and baseball. The competitors were mainly the products of the elite schools, those involved in trade, and those under the influence of the YMCA. In May 1911 the Singapore Chinese FA was founded, and in February 1913 the South China AA represented China in the inaugural Far East Asian Olympic Games. It was defeated by the Philippines' team, which included (against the rules) British, Spanish, and American players. Thereafter China (through the South China AA) dominated this competition, which lasted until 1934, by which time as many as 90,000 attended the big games.

The development of the game in Asia was patchy, however, and as in Africa its progress would come with the end of colonialism. In the United States, Canada, Australia, New Zealand, and white South Africa soccer remained a poor second to another code of football. The qualities that were to take soccer around the world, its appeal to the poor and its organizational simplicity, were not necessary in these countries, where there was generally more open space and plenty of grass. Moreover, when soccer became an essentially working-class game in the 1880s, it gained an unfortunate connotation with migrants seeking social advancement and national identity in another country. The role of individuals is vital, and it was more often the rugby-loving public-school boys who spread their game in the former colonies, whereas in the countries affected by Britain's industrial and commercial expansion, its agents were usually products of the non-rugby playing schools. Where a locally invented code was established, as in southern Australia and the United States, it took precedence over all other codes. And in regard to those enthusiasts trying to establish the association game in foreign lands, the football associations of Scotland and England were as arrogantly indifferent to their needs as they were to those of the non-English-speaking countries.

# All around the World

It was in April 1901, on a Saturday afternoon, that the Yankees came to Scotland to play a match with our crack eleven. . . . Previous of the time I speak of, the Americans had beaten the Australians and Canadians, and were considered by their own friends invincible even to the extent of a couple of goals. The Americans had also beaten the Englishmen the previous year at New York, and, as their own newspapers had it, "Came over to crow in the Land o' Cakes." [The match] was the general topic of conversation all over Scotland several weeks before it came off and on the Friday evening, when the Americans arrived and put up at the Express Hotel, Glasgow, the excitement was great. . . . [With ten minutes to go in "the great International" the Americans were leading by a goal.] It would never do to allow America to whip creation even at football! One final effort; no two final efforts, and it was done [the Scots tied and then went on to score two more goals]. The crowd completely besieged the pavilion at Bruce Park at the close, and cheered lustily as the Scotch champions made their way up the steps. Nor were the vanquished strangers forgotten—they came in for a round of hearty cheers for their pluck. . . .

So it was that Scotland beat the United States at soccer and won the title of world champions. The event, however, took place seventeen years earlier and only in the imagination of a reporter for *Scottish Umpire,* one of Scotland's two leading sports papers of that time. Excited by the progress of modern technology, the writer told how the problems of distance were vanquished, on the one hand by the Universal Postal Service that spread letters all over the world at the cost of one halfpenny per ounce, and on the other by the new "electrics" that had replaced the steamers and provided luxury accommodations as they glided across the Atlantic without vibration at 100 knots per hour. Equally important was the moral progress of the game, which had eliminated some of the worst problems that had plagued it back in 1884: the "low and unmanly"—even degrading—practice of betting was now outlawed, and wives and girlfriends had come back to soccer now that it was free from coarse language.

Like most visions of the future, *Scottish Umpire*'s was a critique of contemporary problems enlivened by wishful thinking. The game would never rid itself of betting and offensive language, but it would eventually encompass the world—a world, however, totally different from that envisaged by the Anglocentric commentator, oblivious to the possibility that any non-English-speaking nation could be interested in the game. In the 1880s soccer was being played in Switzerland, Germany, and France, but mainly by students, and in Uruguay and Argentina by students, sailors, workers, and expatriate Britons. Even in the 1890s, however, by which time several countries had established regular competitions, the standard of play was not very high outside the United Kingdom. It was still very much a game for middle-class elites or itinerant British workers, played before a few dozen curious onlookers or the participants' friends and families. By 1900 soccer in Britain was so far ahead of the game played elsewhere that its progress in much of Europe and South America could easily be overlooked. Nevertheless, by then several of the more affluent and usually Anglophile or cosmopolitan communities of Europe and South America had adopted soccer as their favorite leisure activity.

---

The claim that soccer is Britain's "most enduring export" has been repeated so often that it inevitably has come under scrutiny, with revisionists working in languages other than English claiming that such claims can no longer be made. As is often the case, however, it is the revisionists who have the weaker case. When the seeds of soccer were sown, there was almost always a British connection somewhere, in the fine details as much as in the broad sweep. Certainly once the seeds had taken root and the game was firmly planted, the British influence became nearly—but never totally—irrelevant. It was the countries closest to Britain in commercial, economic, educational, or moral terms that first took to soccer: Argentina and Uruguay in South America and Switzerland and Denmark in Europe, followed by Belgium, the Netherlands, the Scandinavian countries, Germany, and France, and then, from the turn of the century, the cities of Vienna, Budapest, and Prague. In view of their later success, Brazil, Italy, and Spain were comparatively tardy in taking up the association game.

The Swiss connections with Britain were significant in the spread of soccer, and as early as the 1860s British pupils in Swiss private schools popularized a form of football, but it was in the technical colleges that multiplied later in the century that the British influence was most felt. In francophone Switzerland the Lausanne Football and Cricket Club was founded as early as 1860, and in the German-speaking region Saint-Gallen was founded in 1879. The most famous Swiss team was founded by students in a Zurich café in 1876: Grasshopper, named by Tom Griffith, an English student who was studying biology and supported Blackburn Rovers. The former gave the new team its unusual name, and the latter gave it its colors, for it was under the blue and white halves of Blackburn Rovers that Grasshopper-Club Zurich went on to become the preeminent team in Switzerland.

Denmark placed second to Britain in the 1908 and 1912 Olympic Games, and it retained a pure amateurism long after other countries' football associations had adopted open or veiled professionalism. As a result Denmark's major successes before the 1980s were at the Olympic Games; their carefully trained players were then plundered by teams from other countries. Denmark's first club, KB Copenhagen, was founded in 1876, and its football association formed in 1889. Among its famous amateurs who did well at the 1908 and 1912 Olympic Games were the Bohr brothers, from the University of Copenhagen: deprived of gold in soccer, Niels went on to win a Nobel Prize in physics. Denmark became a favorite destination for touring British teams, and just after the turn of the century games between a Copenhagen "select" and a visiting British club team could attract 3,000 spectators.

Pim Mulier, a Dutch student who had gone to school in England and brought the game to the Netherlands, founded the first Dutch club, Haarlemse FFC, in 1879, established the first Dutch sports newspaper, *Nederlandsche Sport,* three years later, and went on to guide the fortunes of the game in the Netherlands over the following decades. Some workers brought over from Lancashire to set up spinning mills at Enschede also brought their soccer to the eastern provinces. About the same time some Scottish riveters took the game to Göteborg and other shipbuilding ports in Sweden. Embassy staff played the game in Stockholm, but it was in Helsingborg, Norrköping, Malmö, and above all Göteborg that the game first flourished. The oldest surviving team in the Swedish league is Ogryte IS, founded in Göteborg in 1887. By then soccer had spread into Norway through the port cities. In Belgium the British colleges at Bruges, Brussels, and Antwerp played football in the 1860s, and the first association club, Cercle des Régates de Bruxelles, was founded in 1878. Like Denmark, Belgium was a powerful force in the early days of amateurism, and like the Netherlands, it provided some of the game's great servants on the world body, the Fédération Internationale de Football Association (FIFA). In France, at the forefront of some of the game's major innovations, soccer had to share its popularity with rugby for several decades. It prospered first in the Channel ports and then in the colleges of Paris, but its strength came later when it was taken up by the industrial centers of the northeast and the port towns of Marseilles, Bordeaux, and Nantes. Soccer was played in the Bois de Boulogne in Paris from the late 1870s, by British expatriates and local French boys, but it was not until 1892 that a purely French club was founded, albeit by students educated in Britain.

In Germany soccer was essentially a game played in schools and colleges until the 1890s, but thereafter its strength came from the trading regions along the North Sea, especially Hamburg, and from Berlin, where British commercial travelers and engineers were prominent in founding several teams and inspiring others: Football-Club Dresden and Fussball-Club Britannia 1892, for example, were run by Germans. Konrad Koch, a physical education teacher who spent a year in England, introduced the "English" game to his school in Brunswick, the Braunschweiger Martino-Katharineum-Gymnasium, in 1874. The first handbook in German explaining the rules of association football and including tips for beginners was published by F. W. Moorman, a former captain of the University of Wales AFC, then captain of the Strasbourg University AFC. The first president of the South German Football Union was the British clergyman Archibald S. White. The other pioneers of soccer in Germany were Walter Bensemann and the two Schricker brothers. Bensemann was a gifted linguist and educator who had spent many years in Liverpool, and it was through his British connections that the first team to represent England, made up of amateurs and some professionals, visited Central Europe in 1899. A German team visited England in 1901. The England team's tour was made possible by the sponsorship of Frau Schricker, who underwrote the costs of the touring English party. It was also carried out despite the protests of patriotic Germans who had their passions inflamed by newspaper reports of British iniquities in the Boer War, which was then being fought in South Africa.

In Germany the British sports tradition came up against the fiercely nationalistic attitudes toward gymnastics, known as *Turnen,* which were made famous by "Turnvater" Jahn and which looked back for inspiration to the Prussian "war of liberation" against the French in 1813. This conflict between the Germans and the British was encapsulated in Ferdinand Hueppe's attempts to reconcile them. Hueppe, who was born in Neuwied on the Rhine on 24 August 1852, went on to take a doctorate in medicine and to become the first president of the German football association, the Deutscher Fussball-Bund, in 1900. From an early age he shared his father's fanaticism for rowing, skating, swimming, and gymnastics. He went to the local Moravian Boys' School (Knaben-Erziehungs-Anstalt der Evangelischen Brüdergemeine), where the British majority infected their German schoolmates with a love of sports, winning Hueppe over to soccer and cricket. Neuwied claims to have staged the first "international" football match in Europe to be reported in German, an 1886 match in which a team picked by one of the masters from Hueppe's old school played a team from the local German gymnastic club. This was little more than a playground match between a few boys, and the newspaper did not even bother to record the score.

Hueppe saw in fresh air and sports a means to cure the body's ills, but he also sought through sports to soothe his compatriots' chauvinist passions. By 1898 he found this impossible and gave his preference to the broader games emphasis associated with the British. By then Hueppe's old school, which had been made up mainly of British pupils, was suffering from the prevailing Anglophobia, and in 1913 it had to close down. Hueppe died in 1938, but in 1951, on the eve of the centenary of his birth, a new sports stadium at Neuwied was named after him. By then there was no embarrassment that it was used mainly for soccer.

Nationalists in other countries were offended by soccer's English origins, but they also disliked it because, unlike shooting and gymnastics, it has no obvious military value. In Germany Turnvater Jahn's spirit prevailed over Coubertin's teachings about the moral value of sports as a means to bring about international understanding, but increasingly German youths found soccer's simplicity and spontaneity irresistible. For lovers of the game who resented the British, its paternity caused emotional conflict, but some of these tortured souls, Germans as well as French (who played a football game called *soule*) and Italians (who played one called *calcio*), tried to prove that soccer was not really British. Some even convinced themselves that rugby was more English than soccer and thus that they were acting patriotically by taking up soccer rather than the quintessential English middle-class game of rugby, which enjoyed great popularity in the 1870s. More typical was Karl Planck, a prominent leader of the *Turner* movement, who wrote a denunciation of soccer, which he claimed reduced men to the level of the apes. Called "Fusslümmelei" (Football loutishness), the essay was subtitled "über Stauchballspiel und englische Krankheit," the sarcastic reference to "English sickness" being to the rickets that were thought to be endemic among the malnourished workers of that country. Soccer, however, had too many advantages for young middle-class Germans over the mind-numbing, ultranationalistic *Turnen,* whose harsh discipline they found increasingly boring. In the few years before World War I the military lifted its ban on the game, as did the education authorities in Bavaria, and even the leaders of the German Workers' Sports movement gave up their attempts to lead their charges in more morally acceptable directions. When Germans of all political persuasion closed ranks in 1914 to enter the greater game of military expansionism, the various "Britannias" playing in German soccer had to change to more patriotic names: Britannia Hamburg, for instance, became FC Blücher. Unsuccessfully resisting the changed names was Ferdinand Hueppe.

From the early years of the twentieth century until the advent of the great Italian teams of the 1930s, Vienna, Budapest, and Prague dominated soccer on the European continent. None of these capitals owed its wealth to industry, and British influence was negligible in their school systems, but there was nonetheless a British influence behind the foundation and early growth of the game in these cities. Vienna in the late nineteenth century was home to a large population of expatriate Britons who conducted businesses in the Austrian capital ranging from the gasworks to shops and engineering firms; moreover, the force behind Vienna's first football association, founded in 1904, was M. D. Nicholson, who in 1897 had taken a position with the Thomas Cook and Son's travel agency. Nicholson was the association's first president and had a cup and a team called after him. The Challenge Cup, the first official competition in Vienna, was founded in 1897, the year Nicholson arrived there. The first official game in Vienna, however, was played on 15 November 1894, between members of the Vienna Cricket and Football Club and the Scottish gardeners of the Baron Rothschild. The "cricketers" became the Wiener Amateure SV in 1911 and then became the famous FK Austria in 1925. The "gardeners," who called themselves First Vienna

Football Club, are still known as First Vienna. In 1898 the third great Austrian team was born when some workers in Vienna founded the 1. Arbeiter-Fussballklub (First Workers' Football Club); they too changed their name a year later, when several British players joined the team, to Sportklub Rapid, better known as Rapid Vienna.

Soccer was played in Hungary in the 1880s within gymnastic clubs. The two most notable were both British inspired: the Ujpest Sport Club, which was formed in 1885 and gave rise to Ujpest Dozsa, and the Budapest Gymnastic and Athletic Club, which put out a team in 1888 under the name Magyar Testgyakorlok Köre (Hungarian Gymnastics Club [MTK]), largely supported by wealthy, liberal Jews. Other soccer clubs followed, the most famous of which was Ferencvaros Torna (gymnastics) Club in 1899. The first recorded match was played in May 1897 between two teams of the Budapest Gymnastics Club (Budapesti Torna Club [BTC]), with a ball made in Britain, as they all were at that time, but supplied by Ferenc Ray, who had just spent two years at Zurich University. Some of the public and press representatives who saw that game were appalled at its violence, but soccer progressed undeterred, and thirteen clubs entered the first championship in 1901. In that same year the Hungarian Football Association was formed. The rivalry between MTK and Ferencvaros (or Franzstadt; they originally used the name of the German suburb in which they were founded) developed early, along broadly religious, class, and national lines: MTK was open to all who could afford to join, which restricted the club to the rich, but Fradi, as FTC was more popularly known, was Catholic and had a more working-class social base. In 1911 FTC built the first modern stadium, but a year later MTK built an even bigger and more palatial one that held 20,000 spectators.

Whereas Vienna and Budapest were capital cities of the powers that ruled the Dual Monarchy, Prague was the capital of the Slavs who sought their independence from it. Like the *Turner* movement in Germany, which began as a means to equip young Germans spiritually and physically to expel the French occupier from Prussia, the *Sokol* movement was founded in Bohemia by Dr. Tyrs in the 1860s with the ultimate aim of freeing all Slavs from Austro-Hungarian dominance. Out of the cycling and gymnastic clubs that were part of this movement emerged two all-conquering soccer teams in Prague in the early 1890s: Slavia in 1892, dedicated to Slav independence, and Sparta in 1893. These teams would have to wait until 1919 to see their political ambitions realized in the creation of Czechoslovakia, but among some of the Slavia players who mixed political ambition with sport was Eduard Beneš, later a leading figure in and, in 1935, president of the nation he had helped to create.

The ailing and reactionary Russian and Ottoman Empires tried to discourage soccer among the ethnic minorities that were under their control, out of fear that it would be used not just to inspire nationalism but as a cover for revolutionary activity. In the Balkans, where the borders of the Russian, Ottoman, and Austro-Hungarian Empires met, Romania had gained independence in 1878, and the oil fields of Ploiesti and the industries that grew up around them attracted a large British presence. This in turn led to the formation of several soccer teams. The Romanians themselves remained somewhat impervious to the game, despite the efforts of Prince Carol, heir to the throne and a sports fanatic, who was so keen that he urged the formation, in 1910, of the Federation of Romanian Sports Societies and became first secretary of the soccer section. A national club championship began that year. Bulgaria, like Romania, had managed to free itself from imperial control in 1878 and, also like Romania, had nationalist ambitions that were not satisfied by the boundaries drawn up for it at that time. Soccer is said to have been brought to Bulgaria by a Swiss physical education teacher in 1894, but its first club, unimaginatively called Football Club, was formed in 1909 by Bulgarian students in Istanbul, the Turkish capital. They had to wait four years for an official game, when they lost 0-1 to Slavia, founded in 1913, in Sofia. In 1914 the more famous Levski was founded by a group of teenagers. These two Balkan nations, however, would have to wait until USA 1994 before making their impact on the world scene.

Legend has it that the famous Croatian team, Hajduk Split, took its name ("bandits") in 1911 from the exasperated response of a college professor to a group of overexcited students, recently returned from Prague, who burst into his office to tell him they wanted to form a soccer team. The students asked their teacher what they should call their proposed club, and he replied that since they had entered his room like "brigands," that is what they might as well call their team. In fact "hajduk" was a term of respect for all those, Serbs and Croatians, who fought against the Turks for independence. Hajduk Split became one of the most successful teams in the federation of "south Slav" states set up in 1919 and provided the basis for the team that represented Yugoslavia in the first World Cup in 1930. Yugoslavia went on to provide some of the world's great players, most of whom were to find fame beyond the borders of their homeland.

In Turkey itself, young Turks who wanted more of what the modern world had to offer had to be discouraged from taking up soccer. British residents played there in the mid-1890s, but when some Turkish boys met in a private house to discuss the rules and the formation of a team, the house was raided and the "conspirators" arrested, the latter caught redhanded with the incriminating evidence of corner flags, colored jerseys, a ball, and a pump; the prize evidence was the rule book, denounced as subversive literature. Even at this time students of the Galatasaray High School were playing the game, but in secret. In 1905 they formed a class team and played openly, adopting the national colors. The Istanbul Sunday Amateur League was founded that year, with Galatasaray the first official team, although it did not win the championship until 1909. Galatasaray went on to make up, with Fenerbahce, founded in 1907, and Besiktas, said to have been formed in 1903, the big three in Turkish soccer. The wars that were occasionally disturbed by peace from 1908 to 1918 left little time for organized games, and ethnic tensions were constantly at a flash point, nowhere less than in such vital matters as contesting a soccer match.

The Russian authorities tolerated soccer only as long as it was a game of foreigners and the elite, but despite this it became the most popular sport there before the Bolsheviks took over in 1917. Soccer was played by British sailors in the Black Sea port of Odessa in the 1860s, but the first real soccer had to wait until 1894, when a field was specially made for it at the mill owned by the industrialist S. Morozov, near Moscow, where Harry Charnock, the British manager, organized the Orekhovo Sports Club in the hope that it would keep their workers at the mills from drinking too much vodka in their leisure time. After 1904 there were as many Russian as foreign teams playing against one another, all of which were made up of middle-class Russians, who refused to countenance games with the workers' clubs. They came to resent the foreigners' control of the game even more, and the foreigners in turn disliked the rough play of the Russians, so that at one stage separate leagues were founded. Nevertheless, the games that pitted foreigner against local drew the largest crowds, estimated by the British diplomat Robert Bruce Lockhart to be as high as 12,000, of which a third were women. In fact, crowds before the war were sold out at 4,000, as in the three games played on successive days in Saint Petersburg by Corinthians of Prague in 1910 (one of which they lost) and by Bolton Wanderers in 1911, who also played three games in three days. Lockhart was also speaking more with the romance of his namesake than with cold reality when he suggested that if the Russian authorities had incorporated the workers into the bourgeois leagues, they would have countered on the playing fields of Russia the influence emanating from the British Museum in London. In 1912 the first All Russia Football Association was set up, to bring order into the way the game was played, to seek entry to FIFA, and to bring together the various leagues that were prospering across the empire: in Saint Petersburg and Moscow, as well as in industrial centers like Kiev and Kharkov, or Odessa, where the British influence was particularly strong, and the mining region of the Donbass. But they did not include the workers' teams, which continued to play in their own "wild" or "outlaw" leagues. Even then the desire to win led some bourgeois teams to entice workers to play for them, and in 1914 some workers teams were granted legal charter, but by then greater events of a less sporting nature were about to overwhelm the world as it was then known.

The Latin countries that were later to lead the world in soccer made little impact on the game before 1914. The game came early to Britain's oldest ally, Portugal, where it was played by university students as early as 1866. The first team, Lisbon FC, was founded in 1875, and in the 1890s the Portuguese themselves, particularly students who had been to Britain, formed their own teams. Soccer was played in Spain in the 1890s, encouraged by British mining engineers in the Basque provinces, where the first team, Athletic Bilbao, was founded in 1898. British military personnel fostered the game in Madrid and Valencia, but in Barcelona, the thriving commercial city where French influences were stronger, it was the Swiss Hans (or Juan, or Joan) Gamper who founded the first major team in the Catalonian capital in 1899. FC Barcelona was at first made up of foreigners, mainly British, but they were in turn challenged by Català, a team of locals who merged with Español a few years later. Spain's international debut had to wait until after World War I, for soccer served as a platform for regional separatism rather than national unity. In Catalonia most soccer contacts were with the French, and until 1918 the major competition was the Pyrenees Cup.

Soccer in the form of Roman *harpastum* and Florentine *calcio* has an ancient history in Italy, and so the British influence there has been muted by long indigenous traditions. Soccer first flourished in the industrial north, particularly in the Turin-Genoa-Milan triangle, often in gymnastic associations. The first organized game of soccer there is said to have been arranged in 1887 by Italian businessman Edoardo Bosio, an optical goods manufacturer who made frequent trips to

Britain. He encouraged the game among his employees and arranged matches with some of Turin's aristocrats. In 1891 the two groups came together as the Internazionale Football Club. The first official soccer team was founded in Genoa in 1893, the Genoa Cricket and Football Club. Made up equally of Britons and locals, it dominated the first championships, admittedly a minor affair, from 1898. The famous Milan and Turin derbies that have dominated Italian soccer date back to the turn of the century. The Milan Cricket and Football Club was founded in 1899, with British and Swiss dominant, and it was a split within the club in 1908 that led to the foundation of Internazionale (unrelated to the Turin Internazionale). The financial backing of the tire magnate Dr. Piero Pirelli ensured the financial stability of what became the famous Associazione Calcio Milan, better known as AC Milan. In Turin the Juventus and Torino derby also emerged from a split, this one in 1906. Juventus was founded as a team for boys under seventeen (hence the name) in November 1897. It became FC Juventus in 1899 and entered the Italian championship the following year. In 1906 Alfredo Dick, an industrialist of Swiss descent, was forced out of the club because the old guard thought that there were too many Germans and Swiss in the team. He took the best players and constituted Torino, and since he had control over the grounds, he forced Juventus to go and find one of its own.

Within the first decade of the twentieth century soccer teams and controlling bodies were to be found in every country in Europe, from Iceland and the Scandinavian countries in the north to Malta and Greece in the south. Although most countries had national competitions, many games were played across national boundaries: Belgian teams with Dutch teams and French teams from the northeast, Catalan teams with others in the Mediterranean basin, and the teams of the central European capital cities with each other. Select teams representing cities also played against one another, as in Berlin versus Hamburg or Paris versus Brussels, and the first Continental international, between Hungary and Austria in 1902, was essentially a game between the best players in the two capitals. This was the first of many regular encounters that would be played in the years to come. Of the other famous international rivalries, France first played Belgium in 1904, and the following year Belgium played the Netherlands. It was on the other side of the Atlantic, however, that the first international outside the United Kingdom was played, in Montevideo on 16 May 1901, when Uruguay beat Argentina 3-2. Within three decades the two neighbors would play almost 100 fiercely contested encounters.

In the late nineteenth century the economy and soccer boomed alongside each other in the coastal regions of southern South America, particularly in the urban conglomerations in the estuary of the Río de la Plata, Buenos Aires and Montevideo. There British sailors and workers, particularly on the railways, played soccer in the 1860s, and by the 1880s several teams were formed, some of them well known today. The British influence was displaced early in the twentieth century by the mass emigration of workers from southern Europe, above all Italy, but teams that had obviously British names refused to abandon them when the Italians took over. In Chile the port towns of the Pacific seaboard welcomed British sailors who brought their soccer with them, remembered in the names of teams like Everton, the Wanderers, and the Corinthians.

It was in the schools, however, that the game was first organized. The splendid library in the present headquarters of the Argentine Football Association in Buenos Aires is named after Alexander (Alejandro) Watson Hutton, the man most closely associated with the development of soccer in South America in the early days. Hutton arrived in Buenos Aires from Scotland in February 1882 to teach at the Saint Andrew's Scottish School, but after a dispute over their attitude to sport he left to found his own English High School two years later. A makeshift league was started in 1891 and won by Saint Andrew's, and when this was reorganized two years later by Hutton, the Argentine Association Football League set the game up on solid foundations—early in the new century it boasted four divisions, the most prosperous soccer competition outside the United Kingdom.

Hutton was first president of the Argentine Football Association, founded in 1893, and his team, Alumni, made up of former pupils from his English High School and the prestigious English-speaking Lomas de Zamora High School, dominated the first two decades of the league. Hutton remained an honored figure over the next few decades, by which time the game had expanded well beyond its British origins. This can be traced in the changes of official names from English to Spanish, but remarkably many of the teams founded under the auspices of immigrant Britons retained their English names. The most famous of these was CA (Club Atlético) River Plate, founded in 1901 in the Boca district of Buenos Aires, from the merger of two student teams, La Rosales and Santa Rosa. Later it moved across the city to build the nation's largest soccer stadium, the Monumental. By then it had set up an undying rivalry with another team born in the Boca, but one that remained there: Boca Juniors, founded by an Irishman named Patrick McCarthy in 1905 but made famous by the Italian immigrants and their families who made it their own. By the 1930s these two teams had established a dominance in Argentine soccer that they never lost. Racing Club, founded in 1903, was named after the French team of the same name, whereas CA San Lorenzo (1905) is of Spanish origins; CA Independiente (1905) was founded by the Argentine employees of a store called the City of London who did not want to play for the store's official team. Outside the capital successful teams were founded at Quilmes by British railroad workers in 1887 and at Rosario in 1889: Rosario Athletic represented the bosses in the Central Argentine Railway Company, whereas Rosario Central was the team of the workers, and it is the workers' team that has survived until today, under the English name. Even more English in name, and still famous today under its original name, is CA Newell's Old Boys, founded in Rosario in 1903.

Soccer in Uruguay followed a pattern similar to that of Argentina, although the dominance of the capital, Montevideo, and of the two top teams, Peñarol and Nacional, was much more complete than that of Buenos Aires and its two top teams. Organized association football came to Uruguay through the British college run by Henry Castle Ayre, where Angel Baezza, a professor of gymnastics, and a professor of English literature named William Leslie Poole encouraged the playing of soccer. Poole also founded the first soccer club in Uruguay, Albion, in June 1891, partly through the efforts of one of Poole's most enthusiastic pupils, Enrique Candido Lichtenberger. On 28 September 1891 the Central Uruguayan Railway Cricket Club was founded, but the first game it played was soccer. Of the 118 members at that first meeting, 72 were British, 1 was German, and the rest "*orientales*"; nominated president was Frank (Francisco) Henderson. It was under the name Peñarol that the club became world famous, that name taken from the suburb in which the club played—though if some Britons had had their way in 1888, the district would have been called New Manchester. England's famous soccer club Manchester United, formed ca. 1888 under the auspices of railway workers, won its first league title in 1908 (by which time its association with the railways was broken), two years after the railway company in Uruguay had severed ties with its soccer club. In 1913, when the Uruguayan team officially became known as Peñarol, the club had been taken over by immigrant Italians. Peñarol's eternal rival, Nacional, was not part of the four clubs that made up the first Uruguayan Association Football League in March 1900; three were British and one was German, and one of their strongest teams in the early years of the league was River Plate from Argentina. Club Nacional de Football, founded out of a merger between students of Montevideo and Uruguay Athletic on 14 May 1899, joined the competition in 1901 and with Peñarol soon set up a stranglehold that left other teams as also-rans. Soccer's popularity in Uruguay was unparalleled by that of any other sport, and the country's success in soccer in the early decades was astonishing for such a small nation. Today Uruguay is home to one of the finest soccer museums in the world, which is located in the 100,000-capacity Centenary Stadium, built for the first World Cup in 1930.

In Brazil, with its spectacular coastline and numerous inlets, sailing was the main outdoor leisure pursuit of the wealthy elites. By the turn of the century, however, some of the luxury sports clubs of Rio de Janeiro and São Paulo had formed a soccer section, and soon the game was so popular that separate soccer clubs were formed. Such were the origins that produced one of the most famous derbies in the history of soccer: Flamengo versus Fluminense, better known as Fla-Flu. Oscar Cox founded Fluminense FC in 1902 and was a driving force in the formation of the first Rio championship in 1905. Archrival Flamengo broke away from the Flamengo Sailing Club in 1911 to become a separate football club, and later it became associated with the poorer Cariocas (Rio inhabitants), largely blacks, many of whom had only recently (1888) been freed from slavery. The wealthy elites retained their supremacy until the 1920s, but thereafter the strength of the game came from the poorer sections of Brazilian society, especially the blacks. Fluminense managed to avoid signing blacks until the 1950s and for this retained a certain social cachet, and even when it signed blacks and working-class players, they were excluded from the club's socially more elite activities. This paternalistic approach to players of lowly origins has lasted down to the present time, most recently in the deplorable treatment of soccer's most popular player, Pelé, by the most powerful administrator the game has ever known, João Havelange, president of FIFA. Flamengo was quicker to welcome talent from all sections of society and became the most popular club in Brazil. The result was that "Fla-Flu" derbies came to attract regular crowds of over 150,000 and in 1963 set a world record for an ordinary league game, when 177,656 spectators packed the Maracanã Stadium. It was in São Paulo, however, that soccer was first organized in Brazil.

Charles Miller, whose father was British and mother was Brazilian, is usually credited with bringing soccer to São Paulo, where he was born. He was sent to England for his schooling, and after ten years in Southampton returned in 1894, age twenty, with a couple of balls, only to find that he had no one with whom to play. Undeterred, he founded a team at the São Paulo Railway Company, where he worked, encouraged the English Gas Company and London and Brazilian Bank to do the same, and then persuaded the São Paulo Athletic Club to add soccer as well as cricket to its sports pursuits. In 1898 the English-speaking Mackenzie College became the first true Brazilian team, and in 1901 Miller and the Swiss-educated Antonio Casimaro da Costa founded the São Paulo championship. Five teams of various ethnic flavors formed that first league. By the following year sixty to seventy teams had been founded, the best games were watched by two to three thousand people, and soccer's popularity was spreading to the villages. It was still an elite and mainly Anglo pastime, however, and postmatch celebrations were marked by the drinking of whisky, the singing of English songs, and even the toasting of the British monarch. A Rio championship was started in 1905, and when a league was formed at Rio Branca in the remote province of Acre in 1919, the last Brazilian soccer frontier had been conquered.

The strongest teams remained in Rio and São Paulo, however, and the games between Cariocas and Paulistanos, which began in October 1901, became intense local derbies. Vasco da Gama, formed out of the Lusitania Esportes Clube by wealthy Portuguese merchants and bankers, was the closest rival to the big two in Rio, while Botafogo and Bangu had their moments of glory, now all in the past. Bangu was formed when some British technicians at a textile factory in the suburb of that name persuaded the management to form a soccer team and were soon joined by the workers in the factory. In the São Paulo league the early rivalry of São Paulo AC and CA Paulistano gave way to the more plebeian encounters between the Corinthians (usually left in the English) and SE (Sociedade Esportiva) Palmeiras. The Corinthians were founded in 1910 by a group of workers and named after the wealthy amateurs who had just toured the country.

Before the 1930s, however, Brazil was no match for Argentina and Uruguay, whose teams frequently played one another. The friendly internationals that began between Argentina and Uruguay in 1901 were followed by competitions for trophies, the first of which was offered in 1905 by the Scottish sports philanthropist and tea baron Thomas Lipton. There followed the Richard Newton Cup and others presented by the ministries for education of Argentina and Uruguay, so that the two countries could find themselves playing each other as often as five times a year. In 1910 Argentina organized a competition with Uruguay and Chile, hoping that this would be the start of an annual South American championship, but this did not materialize. In 1916, however, when Argentina organized a soccer championship to celebrate the centenary of its independence from Spain, the idea was raised again. This time a controlling body was set up, so that a controlling body for the soccer nations of South America was established nearly forty years before a similar confederation was established in Europe: the Confederación Sudamericana de Fútbol, better known as CONMEBOL.

CONMEBOL's first major task was to establish the South American Championship on a regular basis. The first official championship was set for 1917, although that of 1916 was granted unofficial status. Thereafter the championship was organized as an annual event, although there would be a few gaps. It was to be played in the capital of a different host nation, on a league system, over a set period. Paraguay joined in 1921, Peru in 1924, and Bolivia in 1925; when Colombia joined CONMEBOL in 1945, all the big South American countries were included. Brazil, whose area is almost as large as the rest of the continent put together and whose inhabitants speak Portuguese rather than Spanish, did not always enter the South America Cup with enthusiasm, and it was dominated by Argentina and Uruguay.

Further north, in the Caribbean islands, Central America, and above all in Mexico, soccer fever was spreading, but decades would pass before attempts to create a controlling body for these nations succeeded.

---

In Europe a controlling body for soccer was established in 1904, but whether out of innocence or arrogance, it claimed to be a world body. Britain's leadership was sought in this venture, but when Britain spurned them the Europeans went ahead to found the International Federation of Association Football. The aim of this grandiloquently titled body, free from any "European" qualifier, was to resolve disputes within nations concerning the authority of national federations or associations and to organize regular international competitions. Seven nations, all European, were represented in Paris in May 1904 at the founding of the Fédération Internationale de Football Association, but this had grown to twenty-four by 1914, by which time Argentina, Chile, the United States, and South Africa had joined, giving the new body a world dimension. The four British associations remained aloof from the creation of FIFA, and the London FA joined only condescendingly in 1905, the other British associations joining a few years later. The British associations had some reason to believe that they knew more about the game than anyone else, but their in-

sular arrogance was merely the first of many rebuffs that would rile
the Europeans. Nevertheless, the soccer novices were prepared to go
to exceptional lengths to welcome the British: an Englishman, Daniel
Burley Woolfall, replaced the first president of FIFA, Robert Guérin,
in 1906; the (British) International Board remained the controller of
the laws of the game, with only two members from FIFA added to it
in 1912; the percentage of receipts that other countries paid to FIFA
from all international matches did not apply to the Home Internationals; and throughout the life of FIFA, most of which has been with
few English-speaking countries as members, English has been the language to decide disputes: it was the official language until 1928, when
French and German (and later, Spanish) were added. The French
delegates to FIFA, who were aligned with a republican and anticler-
ical but fiercely amateur French sports organization, unsuccessfully
attempted to rally anti-English feeling, but it was they who had to
leave FIFA. The German delegates who objected to the British control of the International Board in 1913 were no more successful.

Without seeking the role, Britain had become the mecca of association football. Few disciples were invited to make the trip to the
game's homeland, but their greatest joy was when an English or Scottish team came to visit them. The amateurs were the first visitors to
the Continent, and a team from Oxford University, playing some form
of the dribbling game, played in Bohemia in 1875. Clapton Orient
beat an Antwerp team 7-0 in 1890. In 1897 an Oxford University
team helped Slavia open its new ground, and over the next two years
Queen's Park came from Scotland for the first of its many visits to
Denmark, the London FA sent a mixed team of professionals and
amateurs to Germany and Prague, and Oxford University played in
Vienna. None of these teams had trouble running up big scores, and
they generally treated the games as picnic matches. An amateur team
from the south of England that came to be known as the Middlesex
Wanderers had a rule that no more than nine goals be scored, and it
punished anyone who took the game into double figures by making
him pay for the postmatch dinner. The team also saw itself as a missionary for the game and continued to travel the world until well into
the 1930s. The most famous of the amateurs, however, was the Corinthians, which like the Pilgrims, another famous amateur touring team,
and Middlesex Wanderers not only made regular trips to Europe but
also visited South Africa, as well as North and South America.

Southampton was the first professional team to tour the Continent: in 1900 it beat a Vienna select 6-0 and the following year beat
a Budapest select 8-0 and 13-0 on successive days. In May 1904

Newcastle beat Berlin's Britannia 1892 10-0, and when the two touring professional teams, Everton and Tottenham Hotspur, agreed to play each other in Vienna the following year, 10,000 fans turned up, more than double the record crowd until then. From Scotland, the amateur team Queen's Park made regular tours, and in 1904 Celtic and Rangers made the first of their many tours. An England amateur team played against Austria in Vienna in 1908 to honor the sixtieth anniversary of Franz-Joseph's accession to the throne and went on to beat Hungary. The following year it returned to administer further defeats, playing before 3,000 spectators in a midweek game in Vienna. Every year teams from Britain played before eager locals, who took the games much more seriously than the visitors did. In England the FA decreed that these trips be treated with true moral purpose and not just as an excuse for a holiday. In 1912 Newcastle United was fined £100 for overpaying its players, and subsequently all teams had to submit their proposals for tours abroad (and have their accounts checked on return). At the end of the 1913–14 season nine teams were granted permission to travel abroad, but Manchester City had its proposal rejected, for no games had been scheduled.

Although these British teams easily beat most of their opponents, the sheer distances traveled made some of the tours into fairly strenuous affairs, with games scheduled for every other day, fields that were frequently far below the standards of British grounds, and lightweight balls that the British found more difficult to control than their own. When Aberdeen toured parts of Bohemia and Poland in May 1911, it took along only twelve players and played eight games in twelve days, losing only the first to Slavia in the heat of Prague, 2-3. The enlarged schedule came from two teams along the route that found out that the team was on the train and persuaded it to stop for a game. These unscheduled games, against Prerau and Brunn, which were not part of the Austrian football association, led to a protest by Slavia, which had guaranteed most of the Scottish visitors' expenses.

The first British team to lose on the Continent was Celtic, going down 1-2 to a Copenhagen select in 1907, although Celtic won all its other games with convincing margins. In 1909 Sunderland lost 1-2 to Wiener AC in Austria, and the difficulties facing the visitors and the seriousness with which the games were being taken by their hosts were reflected in some of the unsavory incidents that were becoming rather frequent. As there were in the Olympic movement, there were optimists in soccer who hoped that sports rivalry would bring peace and friendship among nations, and although we can find many incidents of sporting play reminiscent of games in the schoolyard, streets, or parks, where injuries to one player result in teams being reorganized to restore some equality, there were just as many stories where the will to win had the opposite effect—and this long before the advent of the working classes and professionalism in the game.

The first foreign team to tour South America was Southampton, making the journey in 1905, when it won all five of its matches in Argentina and conceded only three goals. Nottingham Forest followed in 1905, winning all seven of its games and conceding only one goal. One of its games, against Alumni, was watched by 10,000 spectators. The professionals were followed by an amateur eleven from South Africa in 1906. They won all but one of their games, nine of which were played in Buenos Aires and the others taking place in Rosario, Montevideo, and São Paulo. The locals joyously celebrated the South Africans' solitary loss, 0-1 to Alumni, as a victory of South Americans over Europeans. The Corinthians, which lost five games in their twenty-five-match tour of South Africa in 1907, visited Brazil in 1910, 1913, and 1914, easily winning most of their matches.

Despite the four to six weeks of travel required for the round-trip voyage from Europe, professional teams could complete their end-of-season trips to South America at a profit. Everton made £300 in 1909 from a two-week tour in which it played five matches. Tottenham Hotspur also toured that year; playing against Alumni before 5,000 well-dressed spectators, the British players had gravel and dirt thrown at them, and one fan even assaulted a player with an umbrella—more serious weapons would be used in future games. Everton and Spurs played two exhibition games against each other on that tour, but in contrast to internationals on the Continent, where such games drew large crowds, these matches did not attract the interest of a game against a local club: already local pride was asserting itself against superior skill. Southern League club Swindon played eight games in Argentina in 1912, winning six and drawing two. It played before massive crowds, especially in the Sunday matches, which earned £8,000 in gate money, and brought back an order from a local firm for 5,000 soccer balls. Exeter City visited South America in 1914, but by then the locals expected higher standards than those of the comparatively humble visitors. In fact Exeter lost only one of its eight games, a record better than that of the visiting Italian team, Torino, which lost two of its three games, but already the more direct, physical game played by the British was coming to be less appreciated than a South American idea of the game that was spreading beyond Argentina and Uruguay to Chile and Brazil.

Some players stayed behind to coach in the New World: Walter Bull of Tottenham Hotspur went to Argentina, John Harley went to Uruguay (the Scot died there in 1959), and John Hamilton went to Brazil in 1907 as the country's first professional coach. When a Rio select beat Corinthians in 1913, the team included two British players, Harry Robinson in goal and Harry Welfare at center forward. The visit by Corinthians the following year was cut short by the outbreak of war in Europe, and while soccer in South America continued to surge ahead, in Europe it was put temporarily on hold.

On the eve of the outbreak of hostilities in Europe the vulnerability of the British was becoming apparent, and determination to win began to replace locals' wide-eyed wonder at the visitors' prowess. They might not have been able to attract players at their peak in the British leagues, but they could make offers to professionals past their prime to come and show them how to play the game. So it was that a cavalcade of British coaches crossed the English Channel to earn the money and respect denied them at home. Among the most famous of these were John Madden, who coached Slavia Prague from 1905, and Jimmy Hogan, who coached the Austria team for the 1912 Olympics and then offered his services with several clubs before forming the basis, with Hugo Meisl, of the Austrian Wunderteam of the early 1930s. Neither of these men was a great player, but they brought the Scottish game to the Continent; it was taken up in central Europe and became known as the "Danubian school" at a time when British (or more particularly English) soccer was being dismissed as "kick and rush." There were many others, not only professionals past their prime but run-of-the-mill players whose names have not been recorded. When British aliens were interned in Germany on the outbreak of war in 1914, a large number of them were British soccer players turned coaches, including Stephen Bloomer, one of England's all-time greats, and a handful of others famous enough in their day but now forgotten. Crowds coming to watch soccer in the major European capitals were growing: 12,000 turned up for the final of the German championship in 1911 between Victoria 89 Berlin and VfB Leipzig.

On the eve of World War I soccer was about to take off in most of the urban centers of Europe and South America. The four years of hostilities did no more than temporarily dam this upsurge, and from the 1920s into the 1930s the working class took up soccer, transforming the game from an amateur pursuit of the middle class to a professional game that appealed to all. This marked the beginning of the end of British dominance, which from every point of view was virtually complete in 1914. No other countries attracted such crowds to

regular games or had such well-organized competitions, professional in the best sense of the word. Indeed, British soccer was the only
form of football with full-time professional players at this time. Evidence of the British influence remains in the English names of those
teams that chose to retain them and in the use of English technical
terms. The stability of the British game was envied and the conduct
of its players and spectators admired: the expression "fair play" is left
in English in most languages, even if in Britain it was often interpreted
in essentially class terms. But there were other approaches to the game,
and when the nations of Europe and South America grafted their own
skills on to the British plant and fed the result with their own flair,
they created a game that the British ignored to their own detriment.

# The Booming Twenties

"Gallant little Belgium" was named to host the 1920 Olympic Games, and the war-torn land did its best to justify the honor it had been given. The Antwerp games were beset by many problems, but their financial success was ensured by the soccer tournament, for the host nation's team advanced to the final, where it met Czechoslovakia, the nation newly created out of the carnage of the recent holocaust. The game was due to start at 5 P.M., but the grounds were packed two hours before that, and although every ticket had been sold, those without tickets still found ways to get in, above all through the "Olympic trench" that some small boys dug under the fence. The crowd spilled onto the field, and before the game could be played the spectators had to be pushed back from the touchlines by a cordon of soldiers. The match itself was both a triumph and a disaster; a triumph in that the Belgian team won and a disaster in the way that it won. With only two minutes to go in the first half and Belgium leading 2-0, the referee expelled the Czech fullback Steiner for a brutal foul. Steiner left the field, but he took his teammates with him.

John Langenus, who was then a young man but would soon earn a reputation as the best referee in Europe, thought that the Belgian team had shown itself superior in play and that the Czechs' protest against the referee was a pretext to avoid their likely defeat. He also admitted that the Czechs had been unhappy with the referee before the game began—as well they might, for the man in charge was the sixty-five-year-old John Lewis, a power in the Football League. The Englishman had been a good enough referee in his day, but that day was long past. Assisting him were two English linesmen, neither of whom spoke any language other than English. None of the Czechs spoke English. The British still knew best when it came to soccer, however, and this moral authority prevailed. Norway had eliminated the British team in an earlier round, so Britain's amateur predominance, which had been unassailable in the prewar era, was clearly shown to be over. Absent from the games were the defeated enemies, Germany, Austria, and Hungary; the same patriotic indignation that had them banned from the Olympics led the British football associations, supported by France and Belgium, to demand that they be expelled from FIFA. The Olympic ban on the defeated powers of 1918 was more successful than the soccer ban, which was lifted after a campaign led by Switzerland, whose French-speaking members favored some form of punishment but were overruled by the German-speaking majority. Switzerland was supported by Sweden and other neutrals, which refused to follow the British lead. The British associations then huffily left the world body in 1920.

---

Soccer had arrived in Europe, with its warring nationalities and culture clashes. It was already well entrenched in South America, and as it embraced the world, it embraced the world's problems, not only bringing the joy of sport but also encouraging the enmity of nations and individuals who could not leave their cultural baggage behind when they donned their athletic uniforms. Some sports authorities still tried to convince themselves that sports had nothing to do with politics, above all the British, whose overtly political act in leaving FIFA would not be their last attempt to use sports for political purposes.

Enthusiasts had continued to play soccer during World War I, not only in Britain (against the wishes of the upper-class enemies of the game) but also behind the trenches in Europe, in the lulls between artillery barrages, and on one famous occasion in no-man's-land, where combatants played during the first Christmas truce. In some tragically romantic incidents balls were kicked or dribbled into the enemy lines for the men to chase. Locals were astonished in 1914, as they would be in 1939, when one of the first acts of the British soldiers was to organize soccer matches. Thousands of balls were sent to the front for this purpose, from Britain and France but also from Germany. Many who at first looked on in bewilderment at this peculiar passion were won over to it. At the Ruhleben camp in Berlin, near the present site of the Olympic Stadium, the 4,000 British internees soon established a microcosm of British society in which soccer was by far the most popular activity, with leagues and elimination competitions, disciplinary boards, and appeals committees, all of which were reported in the camp journal. As many as 1,000 turned up to watch the big matches. Among these spectators were the guards, who scoffed at first but ended up supporting the game. Austrian prisoners of war similarly won over their Russian guards. French rural conscripts who had never seen the game were introduced to it by their British and Belgian allies, as well as by their compatriots who already played the game. At the end of the war a triangular tournament, the Coupe des Alliés, was founded by these three nations. The central powers played games with neutrals to try to win them to their side, which caused some anxiety among the British and French, who thought they were falling behind in this regard. Unknown numbers of players fell in battle, some of the better known won the highest medals, and the Jewish club Hakoah from Vienna emerged from the war having earned new respect through the role it had played in supplying the front-line troops with gifts and encouragement.

———————

When the hostilities ceased, some sought in soccer a relief from the nightmares that still lived with them and the misery that surrounded them. While political activists provoked revolution and counterrevolution in those parts of Europe being reshaped out of the old empires, record crowds flocked to games in Berlin, Budapest, Prague, and Vienna. Before the war most games were played before a handful of spectators, and the big attractions, such as a game between two British clubs, could draw 15,000—although 18,000 spectators are said to have attended an Austria-Hungary international in 1913. In 1919 workers in several European countries won the eight-hour workday, and attendance at soccer matches multiplied, with regular crowds of over 20,000 and often more than 50,000. In 1920, 40,000 came to see a Budapest select play against Berlin in the new democratic Weimar Republic, and in Budapest itself the Communist Revolution and the White reaction did not deter crowds of 30,000 from coming to soccer matches—the desperate political and economic situation, however, set in motion a massive emigration that included many soccer players who went on to star in Italy and elsewhere, first as players and then as coaches. A crowd of 85,000 fans turned up for an international in Vienna between Austria and Italy in 1923, many of them with forged tickets; the grounds at Hohe Warte in Vienna could not contain them, and a landslide resulted, but miraculously the worst injuries were broken bones. Internationals between Austria and Hungary produced crowds that numbered 65,000 and never went below 45,000. In Spain soccer was becoming more popular than bullfighting.

The numbers of people watching were paralleled by the numbers playing. In Germany in 1919 there were 150,000 registered players; by 1932 there were more than a million. In France there were 650 clubs affiliated with the French Football Federation in 1920, and four years later there were 3,983. In Poland in 1920 there were 36 clubs and 485 players, figures that almost doubled each year until 1924, when there were 402 clubs and 11,352 registered players; a year later there were 510 clubs and 17,558 players.

The soccer craze in the postwar years extended to women, and just as the war brought them to work in previously male strongholds in factories and essential war activities, so it brought them to traditionally male leisure pursuits on an unprecedented scale. For a few years after the war, teams of young English and French women in particular played before sellout crowds. In the early days women had been encouraged to come to soccer matches to lend an air of dignity to the occasion and to help to tone down the rougher aspects of male behavior. But some women wanted to do more than just watch. At Crouch End, London, in 1895, Nettie Honeyball organized a game between women from the north and south of England that attracted 8,000 spectators. Enough interest continued so that in 1902 the FA felt compelled to ban women from playing the game. The woman's game got into full swing in 1917, however, when the engineering firm of Dick, Kerr founded a women's team in Preston. In their time out from making the weapons of war to send to the boys at the front, Dick, Kerr's Ladies established themselves as a formidable soccer team. Other employers as well encouraged women to form teams, and the public flocked to their matches, often in such numbers that only League grounds were big enough to hold them. Dick, Kerr's was the all-triumphant team, however, drawing as many as 53,000 spectators to see it play St. Helen's Ladies at Everton's Goodison Park ground on Boxing Day 1920. As many as 14,000 were reported to have been locked out. In Ireland one match attracted 38,000 spectators, and tours of France and North America, where Dick, Kerr's Ladies played against men, attracted enthusiastic crowds. In the United States the exploits of Alfredda Inglehart and her long services to the game earned her the only place granted to a woman in the U.S. Soccer Hall of Fame.

In France the first serious women's sports clubs had appeared around 1910, and soccer teams were formed during the war. In 1920 there were even women's rugby teams. A French Cup for Women was founded, and under the banner of the French Federation of Women's

Sport, founded by Alice Milliat, a French women's soccer team toured England in 1920 and again in 1921. On that latter tour only Dick, Kerr's Ladies were able to beat them. In 1920, at Pershing Stadium in Paris, 10,000 spectators saw the French women draw with the English, 1-1. This was their only setback, and they returned to a rapturous welcome. French women were still playing soccer in 1926, but by then the women's game had died out in both France and England. In England the FA confirmed its ban on women's soccer in December 1921, declaring the game to be "unsuitable" for women and their participation "not to be encouraged": clubs were forbidden to allow their grounds to be used for such purposes. Despite the fact that these games raised an immense amount of money for charity, the official reason for the FA's ban was that the proceeds were not going to such purposes. The League raised no objections to this ruling, and in 1946 the FA reaffirmed its ban on the "evil" of women's soccer. The number of women playing the game was not reflected in those watching it, and as the working classes came to dominate the terraces, increasingly fewer women were to be seen there.

---

In the early 1920s soccer was the rage of the Viennese population, and players like Josef "Pepi" Uridil, known as the "Tank," became popular heroes. The son of a master tailor in a working-class district, Uridil became the chief goal scorer for SK Rapid with a direct style and power that left a string of vanquished opponents in his train. A song was written for him that became a great hit: "Heute spielt der Uridil" (Uridil is playing today), and he also starred in musicals and a film. His name was given to a variety of commercial products, from chocolates to soap, and artists sought him out to paint his portrait. He was just one of many stars who were becoming household names at this time. In Hungary the president of MTK was a wealthy Jew named Arpad Brüll, who lavished a fortune on rising young stars. One of these was György Orth, who became the hero of Hungarian soccer, a member of MTK when only fifteen years old and of the national team a year later, in 1917. (Hungary and Austria continued to play soccer throughout the war.) Orth was discovered by the English coach Jimmy Hogan (who escaped internment by being smuggled from Vienna to Budapest) and developed into a complete soccer player, but he had his career with the national team and MTK brutally interrupted in 1925 when a fullback broke Orth's leg in a game against FK Austria. He never fully recovered, and he played his last game for Hungary in 1927.

The 1920s were known as the "crazy years," and for George Bernard Shaw one of their craziest aspects was the passion for sports, which was increasing to such an extent that it appeared that one day no one would be interested in anything other than sports—above all, soccer. On the Continent Egon Erwin Kisch, the central European socialist writer, saw the cultural world undergo irreversible changes with radio replacing books, cinema replacing the theater, and phonograph recordings replacing live performances; he saw sports as a new force with which the politician had to come to terms. As a socialist he did not favor professionalism, but as a realist he recognized its inevitability.

One of the reasons that the top European teams did not fare well in the Olympic Games of 1924 and 1928 was that they were either in the process of becoming professional or had already done so. The first to make the move was Austria, which turned professional in 1924, followed by Hungary in the same year and Czechoslovakia in 1925. Long before this the best amateurs were well paid; Hungary's MTK accomplished this through the largess of its private sponsor, Arpad Brüll, who helped to stem the hemorrhaging of star players from Hungary to other countries. One of the reasons that France did not adopt professionalism until 1932 was the fear on the part of some clubs that the players would ask for even more than they were getting as amateurs. The crowds justified the salaries, which in Austria amounted to more than double a worker's wage, with large bonuses for special games such as the Mitropa Cup.

In South America the entry of working-class players into the game forced its middle-class controllers to decide whether to continue in a game whose social tone was being decidedly lowered. In 1930 the Buenos Aires weekly *El Grafico,* which was coming to depend increasingly on sports for its sales, commented on how the upper classes, seeing control of soccer slip out of their hands and the grounds being taken over by those outside their elite circles, were taking up rugby and cricket to retain what they saw as sport's essentially social function. For most South American countries, however, as for most continental European countries, rugby and cricket were not social alternatives, and even Argentines continued to follow soccer across class lines after it became professional. Argentine soccer was the first to become professional, which it did in 1931 after various splits over the issue prompted by the loss of star players to Italy. Uruguay followed in 1933, and Brazil did so between 1933 and 1936.

South American soccer made its explosive impact on the European scene at the Paris Olympics of 1924, when Uruguay won gold; this was followed by the spectacular success of three South American club teams that toured Europe in 1925. Uruguay then repeated its Paris triumph at the Amsterdam Olympics in 1928. These were the golden years of Uruguayan soccer, with the team following its Olympic triumphs by winning the first World Cup in 1930. The star of the Uruguayan team was José Leandro Andrade, its only black player, whose skills can still be appreciated in the frustratingly few seconds of film that remain of the 1924 soccer tournament. He was an idol in Uruguay, where he played for Nacional, and even Peñarol did not object when a plaque celebrating his exploits was placed in the Centenario Stadium, which that team shared with its eternal rival.

Many of the games at the Paris Olympics were played before sellout crowds, and 60,000 attended the final, with thousands left outside. Uruguay did not lose a goal until the semifinal, where it beat the Netherlands 2-1, that goal being the only one that it conceded as it went on to beat Switzerland 3-0 in the final. In Amsterdam in 1928 the South American dominance was even more complete: Uruguay and Argentina advanced to the final, where Uruguay won 2-1 after a 1-1 draw. Although these two teams were fierce rivals in encounters at home, the Buenos Aires press could still exult in this triumph of "Río Platense" soccer. It had reason to boast: two of the three club teams that toured Europe in 1925 were the Boca Juniors from Argentina and Uruguay's Nacional, which supplied the bulk of the players for the national team: the third was Paulistano from Brazil. All returned to rapturous welcomes.

European teams visited South America more frequently after the war. Third Lanark from Scotland, which added a few guest players so that the team could be called "the pick of Scotland," toured in 1923 and on the way home collected some Raith Rovers players who had survived a shipwreck off the Canary Islands. In 1922 Ferencvaros showed the South Americans a new brand of football, and Genoa played in Uruguay and Argentina the following year. The Spanish team Réal Club Desportivo Español traveled to Uruguay in 1926, beat Nacional, and then lost 0-1 to Peñarol, the scorer of that one goal becoming a national hero. In Peru so many came to see the Spanish team play that a new stand was built from the proceeds.

Barcelona had a much less happy tour of Argentina in 1928, however, and when England's Chelsea toured in 1929, it felt moved to send a letter of complaint to the London FA. Chelsea's tour covered Rosario and Buenos Aires in Argentina, Montevideo in Uruguay, and São Paulo and Rio in Brazil—nearly two thousand miles in a little over two weeks. It won nine of its fourteen games. Chelsea was impressed

by the speed and ball control of its opponents and by the sportsmanship of the crowds in Uruguay, Brazil, and Rosario in Argentina but
complained bitterly about the behavior of players and crowds in
Buenos Aires. Part of the problem came from the more physical British game and above all charges on the goalkeeper, which were banned
in South America, but some of it came from the pathological brutality of Luisito Monti, whose viciousness was excused on the grounds
that he was a great player (he would soon take both talents to Italy
to play for Juventus and the Italian national team). The touring party was astonished at the barbed-wire fences that were meant to keep
the crowds off the field but that did not always succeed, especially
when the home side scored and the crowds rushed onto the field to
"kiss and hug" the scorer; by the poor control of the games by referees who patrolled proceedings from the touchline and favored the
home team; and in Brazil by the floodlights and white balls that allowed games to be played away from the heat of the day. Chelsea's
players also noted the luxury of the facilities at some of the clubs,
Peñarol's grounds in Montevideo, River Plate's in Buenos Aires, and
Fluminense's in Rio, but also the poverty of others.

Brazilian soccer caught up with its southern neighbors in the 1920s,
and those in power could not ignore it as they had done in the past:
even when soccer was played by the social elites, it was considered
beneath the dignity of the ruling oligarchy. In 1925, however, Brazilian president Artur Bernardes made a point of congratulating the
Paulistano team on its return from its successful tour of Europe. Two
years later President Washington Luiz, a Paulista, told the captain of
São Paulo to take his players back onto the field after they left it in
protest against what they believed was biased officiating, but he refused to bow before presidential pressure.

That captain was a black. A few years previously he would not even
have been on the team; indeed, the Brazilian president refused to allow blacks to play for Brazil in the 1921 South American Championship in Argentina. The social transformation of Brazilian soccer came
in the early 1920s when the poor broke through. Since slavery had been
abolished only in 1888, Brazil's blacks were all poor, and racism was
added to the class bias that faced the game's controllers in other countries. As workers had discovered in Britain in the 1880s and were dis-
covering in Europe in the 1920s, soccer was an avenue to a better way
of life. One of Brazil's first sporting heroes was a mulatto named Arthur
Friedenreich, who was born of a German father and a black mother
but was accepted into the elite because of his upbringing as a European
and his desire to be seen as such. A reserve player for Fluminense,

Carlos Alberto, was also a mulatto, a fact that escaped the attention of his fellow players. When he was promoted to the first team he became more conscious of his color, so he took to rubbing rice powder into his face to conceal it when he entered the field and faced the crowd, the time at which he was most vulnerable to being "discovered." A black sailor nicknamed "Manteiga" was signed by FC América, and the club stood by him when nine members left in protest. Manteiga found the tensions too great, however, and eventually left. The first serious breach in the racial barrier came when Vasco da Gama won the Rio metropolitan league in 1923 and 1924 with several nonwhites. Several clubs refused to play against Vasco in 1924 and formed a separate league, but the popularity of Vasco led to it being invited to join the new league the following year. The elite had not entirely surrendered their social exclusiveness, however; they introduced a rigorously supervised literacy test for players in its member teams and carried out checks to see that players were working where they said they were. The desire for sports glory eventually won out over social pride, and when the literacy test was removed in 1929, the way was left open for professionalism. In the 1930s Flamengo outdid even Vasco and América in signing black players, while Bonsucesso fielded a team of eleven blacks.

One of the major figures behind the integration of blacks in Brazilian soccer was the journalist Mario Filho, honored today in the Maracanã Stadium, which was officially named after him. Filho was born into a family of journalists, but his father's paper suffered in the 1930 revolution that brought Getúlio Vargas to power. Filho wrote the sports page for O *Globo* and then at the end of 1931 founded the short-lived sports journal O *Mundo esportivo*. Appearing at the end of the soccer season and after the comparatively unpopular club América had won the Rio league, the paper survived both the dead season and the fans' disenchantment by moving into the favelas (slums), championing samba schools, and offering big prizes. Filho also encouraged supporters to dress up to support their soccer team, advocated the introduction of professionalism, and effectively integrated the two great joys of Brazil's poor, dance and soccer. Since then blacks, samba, and soccer have been the essence of Brazilian soccer success: infused with a mystical macumba (voodoolike rite) and a joyous samba rhythm, Brazil's soccer teams created a style of play that no other teams could match.

The debate over professionalism was bitter and divisive in South America. In the 1920s the European game was still blanketed by the amateur ethos as well. In most of northern Europe the middle classes managed to enforce their ideas and retain control of the game, albeit often with compromises and closed eyes. In Germany, which had the largest number of clubs and registered players in Europe, most of whom were from the working class even in the 1920s, the battle was dour. The attitude to paying players varied within the seven federations of the German football association (Deutscher Fussball-Bund [DFB]), but the DFB itself had no reservations on the issue: it banned all its member clubs from playing against any professional opposition. Among its federations its rigid amateurism was most tenaciously upheld by the Westdeutschland Spielverein (WSV), an attitude that was most severely tested by the rising fortunes of what was to become one of Germany's most popular clubs, Schalke 04.

Formed in 1904, as its name indicates, Schalke began as a street team, growing in strength as it attracted miners, factory workers, and skilled craftsmen from Gelsenkirchen, a village of about 600 people transformed in the last decades of the nineteenth century into one of the most heavily industrialized towns in the Rhineland. Many of the immigrants from east Germany who flocked into the area were of Polish origin, and Schalke's strength was in its players' proletarian and Polish origins. This also brought it into conflict with the bourgeois WSV, which went so far as to change its rules on promotion to prevent Schalke from entering the top division. Such moves were to no avail, however, and from fourth division in 1920 Schalke went to the first in 1926. The crowds continued to pour into the ever-growing stadiums of the Ruhr. By 1930 working-class membership of the WSV represented over 70 percent, and sometimes nearly 90 percent in some regions. These players did not share the middle-class scruples about being paid to be watched, and with the chronic depression that hit the region from 1930, teams made up of the unemployed formed themselves into midweek leagues whose players hoped to be bought by one of the "shamateur" teams (*Schein-Amateurismus,* or "amateur in appearance only"). Schalke was the major dispenser of perks and undercover payments, and in 1930 its indiscretions in this regard led the WSV to fine the team 1,000 marks. In addition eight working-class players were suspended. There was an immediate upsurge of sympathy for Schalke in the region, with one newspaper, borrowing a term more popular in the political language of the day, referring to the WSV's action as a "stab in the back." The WSV was forced to back down gradually, and when Schalke rejoined the league, it celebrated with a friendly against Fortuna Düsseldorf on the Monday evening of 1 June 1931. A crowd of 70,000 turned up, pressed against the touchline and crowding around the goals, with young boys perched on the top of the nets. The WSV finally bowed before reality and was about to introduce professionalism when the Nazis came to power. The new regime immediately abolished professionalism in most sports by removing the distinction between amateur and professional and soon set about bringing all private sports clubs under its control.

It is one of the ironies of sport that the amateur ideal of the English private schools was most faithfully followed by those dedicated to their destruction, socialists and communists, whose leaders nonetheless were helpless when the workers chose to follow their own pleasures and enjoy their soccer without the shadows of Marx and Lenin hanging over it. Nowhere was this more clearly demonstrated than in Schalke's willingness to join the bourgeois federations rather than those of the workers' sports movement, even though Schalke remained a club of the workers. Most workers saw nothing wrong with earning money out of sport, which the socialists condemned as exploitation, any more than they complained about paying to see professionals play, which the socialists denounced as bourgeois profiteering. The millions who followed the game in most of the countries of Europe, playing in park games themselves, watching it at the weekends, and reading about it in the press, were made up mainly of workers, but the teams they followed and the newspapers in which they read about their exploits belonged to the bourgeoisie. In Britain this was accepted as a fact of life, and during the General Strike of 1926 strikers and police played against each other in some well-publicized soccer matches—to the disgust of the more ideologically correct on the Continent. In Britain the workers' sports movement was a mere splinter group, but in parts of central Europe the organized workers' sports movements were quite strong, especially in Germany, Austria, and Czechoslovakia.

The leaders of the workers' sports movements in these countries would have preferred the favorite game of the workers to have been one more morally uplifting, but they found that they had to accept soccer. In the Soviet Union soccer had clearly established itself as the game of the workers, and in August 1928, at the first Spartakiad, a Soviet equivalent of the Olympic Games, soccer was the only sport that elicited the interest of the workers and soldiers, who were allowed in at half-price. The biggest attraction among the foreign teams, mainly made up of ordinary working-class players, was a team from Uruguay, not the class "amateurs" who had recently taken Europe by storm in Amsterdam but a team made up of some workers and a few journalists. It was eliminated in the semifinal, and a crowd of

50,000 people saw Moscow beat Ukraine 1-0 in the final. Outside the Soviet Union soccer teams of the Austrian workers made many trips abroad from 1928 and attracted crowds of up to 35,000 for the European Workers' Soccer Championship in 1932. At the second Workers' Olympiad in "red" Vienna in 1931, 65,000 attended the soccer final. The Soviet Union often sent teams to play against workers' teams, but more often than not these teams acted in a very uncomradely way, not only being more interested in scoring political points but insisting on comforts more appropriate to bourgeois professionals. The large numbers of people attending some workers' soccer games, however, cannot disguise the fact that much larger numbers were watching professional soccer. Moreover, the workers' teams succeeded in Austria partly because they did not give themselves obviously political names. The more serious idealists wanted to use sport to make good socialists or communists committed to the common good and so eschewing such bourgeois fetishes as the star cult: in match reports goal scorers were referred to as "number 9" or, more familiarly, "the center forward." In the Soviet Union itself "factors" were introduced emphasizing sporting conduct rather than scoring goals, but the players refused to have truck with such ideological baggage.

Under such circumstances it is hardly surprising that even the most dedicated socialists among the gifted soccer players should look to the bourgeois competitions, where their talents might better be appreciated and perhaps even rewarded. Schalke was unusual in that whereas it played in a bourgeois, albeit amateur, league, it remained a workers' club—but a workers' club without ideology. It went on to play under the Nazis as formerly it had played with the bourgeoisie, but it would be stretching things to say, as has been claimed, that in doing so it performed an act of resistance.

It was the totalitarian regimes, all claiming to be amateur, that were most successful in incorporating sport into their ideology, but this would have to wait until the 1930s. Before then the only team with an ideological commitment that reached the top ranks in the soccer world was the Jewish team Hakoah, the winner of the first professional league in Austria in 1925. Hakoah ("strength" or "force" in Hebrew) was formed in 1909 to combat the virulent antisemitism festering in the Austrian capital, as it was elsewhere in central and eastern Europe. Like the Muscular Christians of a few decades earlier, its organizers began as "Muscular Jews" to create healthy youths who might one day take up residence in Palestine. More immediately they set out to destroy some of the myths carefully nurtured by the antisemites: that Jews are weak, water shy, and more interested in making money than in playing games. The Jews' many championships in swimming made a mockery of the first two claims, and Hakoah on the soccer scene set out to show that it could mix it up with the most violent.

The strongest Jewish teams were in Hungary—for example, BTC—and a third of the national team and most of the famous MTK were Jewish. When the republic of Czechoslovakia was founded, one of the leagues was made up of Jewish teams. In the Netherlands, Ajax of Amsterdam was created by Jewish businessmen. FK Austria was regarded as the team of the Viennese liberals, where the Jewish influence was strong (it was even said that to play for the team you had to have a certificate of education), and it had the financial backing of wealthy Jews. The first exclusively Jewish soccer team, however, was Vivo es Athletikai Club of Budapest, and its visit to Vienna in May 1909 to play the reserve team of the "Cricketers" (later FK Austria) led to the formation of Hakoah four months later. Its members playing in blue and white with a Star of David on their chests, the new team roused the anger not only of the antisemites but of the liberal Jews who opposed Zionist activity because they feared it would encourage antisemitism.

The Hakoah club branched out to include many other sports, but soccer remained the most popular, and it retained a separate section. As the soccer team worked its way up from the fourth division to the top shortly after World War I, some of the Jews from the more successful teams switched to it. Hakoah played a bruising game that deliberately challenged the prejudices of its opponents, and many of its games ended in brawls. It also played a very skillful game, and West Ham was so impressed with its performance in a 1-1 draw in Vienna before 50,000 spectators in 1922 that it invited Hakoah for a return match in London the following year. Hakoah won 5-0, and its performance against a team that had reached the final of the FA Cup just a few months previously astonished the soccer world, at least in Europe. Although West Ham played several reserves, those English papers that deigned to report the match had to admit that Hakoah played with a class that was unknown in England. As the Austrian champion, it was invited by the German-American Soccer league to tour the United States in 1926, where it played before crowds of 25,000, 30,000, and 36,000 spectators. It returned the following year, inspiring the creation of notable Jewish soccer teams but also losing some of its best players to "the rich uncle from America." As a result it struggled and was relegated to the second division in 1929.

During the Great Depression some of the expatriates returned to help boost Hakoah's fortunes in the 1930s, and Hakoah was on its way back into the first division in March 1938 when the Nazis arrived in Vienna. Hakoah was stricken from the records, and its players had to flee for their lives.

———

Throughout the 1920s soccer prospered along with the cinema and dancing as the most popular leisure pursuits. It reigned supreme across Europe and in the Americas from the tip of Tierra del Fuego to the border between Mexico and the United States. At the Paris Olympics in 1924 representatives of the Central American republics got together to found a sports federation, which in 1930 gave rise to the Central American and Caribbean Games, which included a soccer tournament. In 1938 a separate soccer tournament that included Colombia and Venezuela was inaugurated, and over the years various other bodies were formed, bringing in the United States, Mexico, and Canada; it was not until 1961, however, that this took final form in the North American and Caribbean Football Confederation (Confederación Norte-Centro-americana y del Caribe de Fútbol, or CONCACAF).

The U.S. influence in this region has been overwhelming, and as in Taiwan, the Philippines, and Japan, the spread of American games was partly deliberate and partly incidental: the inhabitants of countries such as Nicaragua, Panama, Venezuela, and the Dominican Republic are baseball mad. But even in Cuba, where the love of baseball later proved too strong for Castro's anti-Americanism, soccer was the major team sport in the 1920s. Soccer teams were formed there as early as 1909 by some Spaniards and Cubans who had been to Britain, and in the 1920s several teams played in a well-organized league. When the game was at its height in 1928, one of its rich benefactors built a new floodlight-equipped stadium. As in most countries at this time, the top teams were sponsored by the rich, but the poor of Cuba and elsewhere made do with balls of cloth or stones wrapped in banana skins until the right thing came along.

Costa Rica, which has one of the area's more stable political regimes, also has been one of the most successful in terms of soccer, along with Honduras and El Salvador. Remarkably, in a region where the British sports influence is obvious only in the cricketing prowess of teams from the West Indies, the British influence in soccer can be found in the names of two cup competitions: the Great Britain Cup in Costa Rica and the Winston Churchill Cup in Honduras. Even in the West Indies, where international success came through cricket, soccer was the most popular sport at the local level. The strongest of the CONCACAF countries, however, is Mexico, whose major stadiums, the Estadio Azteca and the Estadio de la Cuidad Universitaria, both in Mexico City, are the largest in the Americas outside Brazil. Soccer came to Mexico with the country's modernization in the late nineteenth century, the game being spread by British, Spanish, and French technicians. A national league was founded in 1903, based on teams in Mexico City; its first football association formed in 1927 and in 1929 joined FIFA.

In the 1920s even the United States threatened to set itself up as a soccer nation to challenge its Latin neighbors, with crowds and financial backing that allowed its big clubs to entice top professionals from Europe, especially from Scotland. In 1914, the same year that the National Open Challenge Cup was contested, Charles M. Schwab of Bethlehem Steel spent freely on the construction of a soccer field and stadium and on raids on other clubs to secure their best players. In 1919 the Bethlehem team went on a fourteen-game tour of Scandinavia. In the Massachusetts factory town of Fall River a team was formed to rival that of the steel giant, and 10,000 spectators came to see these two teams in the 1916 final of the major competition. Bethlehem won 1-0 with the help of imported Scots, and this victory and the riot that followed the game convinced some Americans that soccer, riots, and foreigners were indistinguishable. The following year Fall River won the cup with nine native-born players, but soccer would struggle unavailingly to thrust off the burden of being seen as an un-American activity.

Several teams from Britain, the Continent, and South America toured the United States in the 1920s, and attempts were made to create national competitions. An American Soccer League (ASL) was founded in 1921 to make the game professional on a national basis, but the German-American Soccer League, founded in 1923 and surviving into the 1980s as the Cosmopolitan League, outlasted it. Tensions between amateurs and would-be professionals run through the history of soccer in the United States, bursting out every now and then when the game seemed to be progressing. One of the most significant of these occasions was in the 1928–29 season, when the ASL split from the amateur United States Football Association (USFA) founded back in 1913. Tom Cahill of the USFA denounced the professionals in the familiar language of such disputes, accusing the ASL of putting the dollar before disinterested administration and disguising its mercenary motives under the excuse of "modernization."

A compromise was finally patched up in October 1929, but in the meantime the "outlaw" leagues of the ASL and the Southern New York Association, which also left the USFA, tried to make a deal with the British football associations, which were not bound by FIFA regulations (they had rejoined in 1924 but left again in 1928). The British associations were already concerned about the loss of their players to the United States and ignored the rebels. Moreover, although they had left FIFA, they retained friendly relations with its member nations. There were no real winners, and philanthropic supporters of the game, such as H. E. Lewis of Bethlehem Steel and G. A. G. Wood of American Woollen Company, became disillusioned and withdrew their support. A more serious blow came with the effects of the Wall Street crash on the mill towns and the heavy industries, which were still soccer's strongholds.

Although the big U.S. teams relied on imported professionals, several local-born stars made names for themselves, such as Billy Gonsalves and Buff Donelli, both of whom were offered contracts with foreign teams. Joe Kennaway, Fall River's goalkeeper, was signed by Celtic after its goalkeeper, John Thomson, was killed in the course of a game against Rangers in September 1931. Indeed, there were enough quality soccer players who either were born in the United States or who became citizens for U.S. teams to take part creditably in all the major international soccer tournaments of the 1920s and 1930s: the Olympic Games and the World Cup.

At the Olympic Games in Paris in 1924 the United States contingent had to face the fury of a French public still angry at what they saw as their former ally's failure to support them in reparations claims against Germany. It did not help when the Americans beat the French in rugby, after which a riot broke out, but the soccer team managed to win over the crowd in its match against Uruguay. The U.S. was three goals down early in the game but then reorganized its defense in a "lock" or "bolt" system that would later become notorious as *verrou* (bolt) or *catenaccio* when perfected by the Italians, thus preventing the Uruguayans from scoring any more goals. At Amsterdam four years later Argentina dealt a quick blow to U.S. aspirations with an 11-2 thrashing. Nevertheless, at the World Cup in 1930 the U.S. team performed admirably, reaching the semifinals; once there, however, although the U.S. players were no blushing violets themselves, they were unprotected by the referee, John Langenus, and were kicked out (almost literally) by Argentina. That squad of sixteen had eleven native-born players. In the 1934 World Cup the U.S. team was eliminated by Italy, which won the tournament. Two years later, in Berlin, Italy cut short the U.S. team's progress before going on to win gold. The German crowd at the U.S. team's 0-1 loss to Italy was incensed at the poor sportsmanship of the Italians and the referee's failure to control them.

———————

Soccer in Canada and Australia, as in the United States, has forever remained a foreign game. Australia never reached the international success of the United States in soccer in the 1920s, but games involving foreign visitors drew massive crowds. A team of Chinese university students played before large crowds in 1923, including more than 47,500 in Sydney, but failed to attract the same interest on a return visit in 1927. The Canadian team, in one of its few ventures beyond the country's border, played before impressive crowds in Australia in 1924, and in 1927 the Bohemians of Prague toured the country, playing several closely fought games and attracting crowds of up to 18,000. They returned to Czechoslovakia with a nickname—the Roos—and a new emblem that they have retained until today: a golden kangaroo. The big attraction of the 1920s, however, was a professional England team that played to capacity crowds wherever it went in 1925: nearly 50,000 came to the game in Sydney, and 25,000 came to one in Brisbane. It won all its games comfortably. The large numbers of people who came to see the visitors only emphasized their refusal to watch the local teams. In South Africa crowds of 26,000 turned up to see Motherwell of Scotland play in 1931 and 1934, but well over twice that number came to see a visiting Indian team in 1935.

The biggest crowds in Asia were in Bengal, but the game was catching on in China, where South China AA carried the banner of the ethnic Chinese against the Europeans. In 1929 the Chinese won the Hong Kong Shield with a 5-0 victory over Kowloon, a team of non-Chinese that had appeared in the previous six finals. Most of the European clubs frowned on games against the ethnic Chinese, but they could not ignore the Chinese teams' growing strength and had to admit them to their leagues: after the 1926–27 season the Shanghai League had to admit the Three Cultures team. The Europeans were reluctant to include ethnic Chinese because, they said, the Chinese caused trouble, such as riots and attacks on referees, in interethnic matches. Certainly nationalist agitation added to an unwillingness to accept the referees' decisions, but games where no Europeans were involved were just as likely to end in riots. In 1931 the Kuomintang (the Chinese revolutionary party), in protest against the Hong Kong FA, which had suspended two Canton players for professionalism, instructed all Chinese clubs to withdraw from foreign competitions. That same year the Chinese founded an autonomous body, the Chinese National Amateur Athletic Association, whose soccer section was accepted into FIFA. The foreign-run Chinese football associations—Shanghai, Singapore, and Hong Kong—remained affiliated to the London FA. Despite anticolonial agitation, incipient revolution, and wars, games between Asian teams continued, and both China and Japan were represented in soccer at the 1936 Olympic Games. China's team was made up mainly of players from South China AA but also included six Malayan Chinese, an indication of the game's growth away from the more traditional centers. The Japan team had one player from Korea, the country they had conquered in 1908. It should have had more, perhaps, for the Korean team, Seoul Soccer Club, won the All-Japan Championship in 1935 and the Meiji Shrine Athletic Meet, but the Japanese selected only two Korean players, one of whom refused to play.

---

The spread of the game in Asia was patchy, however, and it was only in Europe and South America that regular leagues were set up, providing an infrastructure that reflected and then supported the growth of the game there. As we have seen, the first South American Championship was established in 1916, and others followed over the years. In Europe international championships began to proliferate in the late 1920s—in Scandinavia (1924), the Baltic (1929), and the Balkans (1921)—and in 1931 the Orient Cup was introduced with Egypt, Palestine, Turkey, and Greece the competing nations. The most prestigious competitions at this time, however, other than the Olympic Games and later the World Cup, were the two central European competitions, one for clubs and the other for national teams. Both were inaugurated in 1927. The first of these was the Mitteleuropäischer-Cup, or Mitropa Cup, instituted on 31 March 1927 and played annually on a knock-out home-and-away basis. The first competition was played by clubs from Austria, Czechoslovakia, Hungary, and Yugoslavia, each country represented by two clubs. In 1929 Yugoslavia, which kept losing its best players to France, withdrew and was replaced by Italian teams. Later Switzerland and Romania entered their champion clubs. Also in 1929 a competition for national teams was begun, with Austria, Czechoslovakia, Hungary, Italy, and Switzerland participating. It was played over two or three years, as a league, each team playing home and away. Called by various names, it was resurrected after World War II and called the Dr. Gerö Cup after the Austrian soccer president who had to flee his homeland after the *Anschluss* of 1938.

---

The potential for violence in games between teams representing nations whose political relations were tense was easily realized, and one contemporary observer commented dryly that no Mitropa Cup game was really decided until the final appeal had been heard by the appropriate foreign embassy. Throughout the 1920s foreign ambassadors pleaded with visiting teams to behave themselves, and well-won victories were applauded for doing more good work in ninety minutes than a team of ambassadors did in a week—or whatever amount of time the rhetoric of the moment justified. Visiting British teams were in constant trouble, mainly over the clash of styles but also over interpretations of the rules, especially the rule against charging the goalkeeper but occasionally rules governing more trivial matters. By and large, however, much of the violence came from teams desperate to win and spectators who could not accept a defeat. In Italy the on-field battles were satirized in the press, with cartoons showing games being played behind tanks and barbed wire and players knocking each other unconscious. The games across national borders brought out the worst, and the Mitropa Cup of 1932 was awarded to Bologna on a walk-over when both Juventus and Slavia were disqualified for crowd troubles at their semifinal game. Slavia beat Juventus 4-0 in Prague and on the return leg in Turin did all it could to hold its lead, body checking, obstructing, and wasting time. With Juventus winning 2-0, but unlikely to score the two more it needed to equal Slavia's four in the previous game, the Juventus spectators invaded the field, and 1,500 police were required to rescue the Slavia players, who were locked in the dressing room for hours.

In South America officials had to build moats and put up barbed wire in the 1920s to keep fans from the field. Some of this may have been because of simple crowd overspills and because South Americans loved to enter the field to celebrate with a goal scorer, but there were also instances of violence against players and referees. Even the first unofficial South American Championship in Buenos Aires in 1916 was marked by the enthusiasm that was to sweep the game along a passionate path, often at the cost of decorum or even simple fair play. On this occasion, when the Argentina/Uruguay game scheduled for 16 July had to be canceled because of the danger of overcrowding, frustrated fans set fire to the stands. On 4 January 1931 five people were killed in Arequipa, Peru, following a Uruguayan team's victory against the locals—a tally that would be overshadowed just over thirty years later in that country by the greatest tragedy in the history of soccer. On 5 February 1933, in a game between Argentina and Uruguay to celebrate the eightieth birthday of Alexander Watson Hutton, the pioneer of Argentine soccer, stones and bottles brought the game to a premature conclusion, and the police had to intervene to clear the field of spectators. The list could be continued. Brawling by players among themselves and by spectators against players and referees had been common enough in the game's early days in Britain, but in South America it seems never to have stopped.

British observers put these excesses down to "Latin temperament," while the socialist press blamed it all on capitalist greed, but in the Soviet Union itself violence on and off the field has been with the game from the beginning: a Moscow team playing in Odessa in November 1926 eventually responded in kind to the fouling it was subjected to, and the game ended in a riot; after an even more spectacular riot at a game in Leningrad in 1937, soldiers were ordered to ring the ground to keep spectators off the playing area, and this became the general practice, even when on some few occasions soldiers outnumbered spectators. "Hooligan" behavior was frequently denounced in the Soviet press, although what this means has changed through the years, from bad manners such as pushing and cursing to actual violence. The lectures in the Soviet press about the example players had to set has echoes of the Old Boy snobbery in regard to the workers in Britain from the 1880s, with the life of Stalin and the works of Marx and Lenin in place of the old school tie.

---

Were the game nothing but riots it could not have reached the popularity it has. Nor would it have been possible to organize a world competition that brings together on the soccer field all the tensions and frustrations of the world. Of all the football codes, however, only soccer has produced not only a genuine global competition but one that, despite the riots and battles on and off the field, progressed from strength to strength after 1930. It was the Frenchman Jules Rimet who carried out the vision of a world championship, energetically assisted in his endeavors by his compatriot Henri Delaunay, known as "Sir Henry" for his British airs, his pipe, and his cocker spaniel, as well as for his predilection for British names over the "Racing," "Olympique," "Stade," and "Union Sportive" favored by the French. Rimet and Delaunay began their campaign for a world competition at the Paris Olympics and finally won acceptance for their idea at Amsterdam in 1928. Uruguay was the obvious choice to host the first competition, to be held in 1930, not just because of its team's stunning success in the Paris and Amsterdam Olympics but because it was prepared to pick up the bill for travel and accommodation for all competing countries. Uruguay was particularly anxious for the honor, which it would celebrate in conjunction with that of the centenary of its constitution. It promised to build a special stadium for the event, the Estadio Centenario.

This first world competition open to amateurs and professionals alike faced some serious problems, despite the Uruguayans' generous promises to pay all major expenses. One that could not be foreseen was the depression that hit Europe and South America in 1930; the other was quite simply the time needed to take about twenty players on a four-week sea voyage for two weeks of soccer. The days of the Corinthians were over, of young men with independent incomes large enough to let them take time off when they liked and travel where they liked. In the case of the professionals, there was the need to provide their wages throughout the four weeks when they were at sea. The outcome was that none of the best European national teams made the journey. The four British nations had left FIFA in 1928, ostensibly over the issue of amateurism but in part over control of the game, and so there was never any expectation that they might come.

Romania and Yugoslavia made the trip, both with heavy political backing. King Carol had just come to the throne in Romania, and whereas in his younger days as a prince he had urged soccer and other games on his recalcitrant subjects, now he was in a position to impose his will. This he did by granting amnesty to all players under suspension and pressuring the British oil companies to release any employees who were needed for the team. In 1929 the king of Yugoslavia had declared the consolidation of the loose federation of south Slav states into one unified nation under his dictatorship. Success in soccer might help sugar the pill for those ethnic minorities that felt threatened by his ambitions—Yugoslavia in the 1920s was beginning to produce some of the world's best players and coaches, which it would export with a profusion equaled only by Hungary and Scotland.

Belgium went to Montevideo, in part because 1930 was the centenary of its own independence from the Netherlands, but also because of the influence of the president of their football association, Rodolphe William Seeldrayers, a pioneer of Belgian soccer who excelled in various sports but whose big love was soccer. He became vice president of FIFA in 1927 and in 1954 succeeded Rimet as president. Belgium was still amateur, and its silly rules about ownership of cafés and amateur status meant that it had to leave behind Raymond Braine, one of the greatest players of the era (those rules were later amended, but too late to prevent Braine from seeking his fortunes with Sparta in Prague). France went, but only at the last minute and with the help of three government departments that found reasons to excuse three of their employees who were picked for the national team.

The Uruguayans were furious at what they saw as an insult by the Europeans, and the competition began with thirteen teams instead of the anticipated sixteen: seven from South America, four from Europe, and Mexico and the United States from North America. They competed for the solid-gold cup crafted by the French sculptor Abel Fleur in the shape of the Winged Victory, a model of refined taste in an era when the trophy rooms of many successful soccer teams were being cluttered up with silverware of varying degrees of vulgarity. Uruguay had much to celebrate in that historic month: the date when its constitution was accepted (the tenth); the adoption of the national flag (eleventh) and its national holiday (eighteenth). The anniversary of the fall of the Bastille, 14 July, was also celebrated. Now they could add a new date, 13 July, when France kicked off against Chile in the first game of the first World Cup.

There were some strange refereeing decisions, and some games were kicking matches occasionally ending in brawls, but it would be wrong to give too much emphasis to such incidents in a competition that on the whole was played with admirable efficiency. Interpretation of the rules was always going to be difficult, with referees speaking different languages and trying to control players from different sports cultures, but some of the refereeing was eccentric, to say the least. In the France-Argentina game Marcel Langiller was on the point of tying the score when the Brazilian referee blew for time, with four to six minutes left to play. After scenes of complete confusion the teams were eventually recalled to finish the game, but the French had lost the edge and were scarcely mollified by the referee's pleas that his error had no base motive. The Bolivian referee in charge of the Argentina-Chile game awarded five penalties, more out of an air of insouciance than to please those who believe that a good game needs to have lots of goals; Argentina won 6-3.

Argentina advanced to the semifinal, where it beat the U.S. team 6-1 in a bruising encounter, and in the final met Uruguay, which had disposed of Yugoslavia in the other semifinal by the same score. For safety reasons a crowd limit of 90,000 was set in the 100,000 capacity Estadio Centenario, and the press of both countries played up the rivalry of the two nations, but according to John Langenus, the Belgian referee who controlled the game, there was no trouble on the field or among the spectators. Boatloads of Argentines crossed the Río de la Plata on the eve of the game, and thousands more in the capital complained that there were not enough boats. Those who could not make it packed the street outside the offices of *La Prensa* waiting for news of the game, while others paraded with placards and chanted "Death to Uruguay." The supporters were searched for weapons coming off the boat and before entering the ground, and there was no trouble when the home nation went on to win 4-2. It was later claimed that the Argentines had been cowed by death threats; however that may be, they gave an uncharacteristically tame performance, with even Monti being accused of playing in a sporting way. In Uruguay there was general rejoicing, and in Buenos Aires there were riots. The two countries broke off sports relations with each other for a few years. Shortly after the final the Argentine government of radicals was replaced in a coup by a less liberal regime. The new government has been blamed for the violence that racked Argentine football in the 1930s, but it is hard not to come to the conclusion that it was well established before 1930.

The next two World Cups were played in Europe, but with only lukewarm support from South America. Uruguay did not take part in another competition until 1950, and Argentina retaliated against the loss of its best players to Italy by sending a deliberately weakened team to Rome in 1934. They had lost the brilliant Orsi after the 1928 Olympics, and after 1930 Monti and several others were brought over with the promise of big money. It was the final factor that led Argentina to decide to adopt open professionalism. Brazil, like Argentina, underwent a change of government in 1930, and Getúlio Vargas's increasingly dictatorial ways were tempered by a populism in which he used soccer to help sustain his hold on power. It was in Europe, however, that the most deadly brands of fascism developed, as the dictators there used sports to win popularity at home and glory abroad. Mussolini's Italy led the way with two World Cup titles in soccer and a string of international victories at club level throughout the 1930s.

# The Decade of the Dictators

The Olympic Games of 1936 were a triumph for the Nazi regime, spoiled for Hitler only by Norway's elimination of Germany in the second round of the soccer tournament and, to a lesser extent, the victories of Jesse Owens and other black athletes in track and field. The Führer took no pleasure in the performances of the black athletes, and even less in the way the German crowds idolized Owens, but Germany's defeat in soccer could not be ascribed to some genetic freak of a race recently descended from the trees. Whereas Hitler snubbed Cornelius Johnson by walking out of the stadium before Johnson won gold in the high jump, he stormed out of the soccer stadium when Germany was losing 0-2 to its Aryan neighbors, with no chance of proceeding to the semifinals.

Although soccer boomed in the 1920s, in the 1930s it swept all before it as the most popular game throughout most of Europe and South America. As such it could not be ignored by dictatorships that prided themselves on their mass support, be they Fascist or some imitation of the Italian model. During the 1930s the dictators discovered sport, manipulating the masses with the aid of the latest technological developments and writing sports into the programs of national regeneration as a way of distracting the workers from more serious concerns. Sports were also used as a source of national pride and fitness for the average citizen and as a means of impressing other nations with victories in international competition. Mussolini's Fascist regime was the first to use sports as an integral part of government, and Hitler copied much of Mussolini's work in his Nazi regime; Stalin, on the other hand, reserved sports for national unification and defense preparation, unwilling to put the Soviet athletes to the test of international competition until he was sure that they would win. In each of these three dictatorships, and in the others that threatened to sweep democracy from the political map in the 1930s, soccer was the main cultural link between the government and the people.

———

Norway's victory over Germany at the 1936 Olympics has largely been forgotten—except in Norway, where it is still hailed as a feat to be cherished, along with the more familiar exploits of its skating and skiing heroes. Soccer at the 1936 Olympics is better remembered for the fracas at the Peru-Austria game: with the score tied 2-2 at the end of regular time, overenthusiastic Peruvians rushed onto the field and jostled some of the Austrian players. Peru went on to score two goals in extra-time, but Austria protested that its players had been upset by the spectators rushing the field. A replay was ordered, but Peru refused to participate. Instead, Peru's entire Olympic contingent retired from the games after trying to take along the rest of its South American compatriots. In Peru the two days and nights of celebrating that had greeted news of the victory quickly turned to anger when the crowds heard that the game had to be replayed. The German embassy in Lima was stoned, the Olympic flag that had been draped around it was dragged in the dirt, and dockers refused to work on the German ships in the port. In vain the Germans tried to point out that it was the International Olympic Committee that had made the decision: in ordering the return of the Olympic delegation, President Benavides of Peru claimed that "National-Socialist Germany could not bear to admit that a football team from a South American country, whose race they consider inferior, could carry out a victory over a team of aryan race."

By 1936 the soccer at the Olympic Games was no longer the major competition it had been in the 1920s. It was open only to amateurs at a time when the best soccer nations were professional, and although the new dictatorships redefined the concept so that they could send whomever they wanted to the great international amateur sports festivals, the future of the World Cup was consolidated after the success of Montevideo in 1930, with further successes in Italy in 1934 and France in 1938. Although the competition was an essentially European and American affair, Egypt, Palestine, and the Dutch East Indies represented Africa and Asia in the 1934 and 1938 World Cups. Japan and China made notable contributions to the 1936 Olympics, with Japan upsetting Sweden (3-2) in a game that had the sports press lost for words and China performing well but unsuccessfully against a U.K. contingent that was little more than a scratch team.

———

At its annual meeting in Stockholm in 1932 FIFA decided to hold the 1934 World Cup in Italy, and the Fascist regime quickly seized the opportunity to use the honor. Before the Fascists came to power in 1922, Italian soccer had been beset by several splits that retarded its growth, while the less industrialized south was slow to take up the game. By 1926 Mussolini had secured absolute political power; he then set out to create a new "totalitarian" regime with state control not just of politics and the workplace but of leisure activities: the *dopolavoro,* or after-work, program for the masses and intensive training for elite athletes. Soccer was not high on the Fascists' sports priorities, for it was too redolent of cosmopolitanism and "fair play," so they tried to popularize a recently invented Italian ball game called *volata.* The popularity of soccer could not be denied, however, and the Fascists had to make do with minor adjustments, such as changing British team names to Italian (AC Milan to Milano and Genoa 93 to Genova 93) and Internazionale Milan(o) to Ambrosiano-Inter before setting themselves up as the benefactors of the people's game.

Beginning in the late 1920s the head office of the Italian FA, which had variously been at Turin, Milan, and Bologna, was transferred to Rome, the Fascist salute became obligatory at matches, international victories were trumpeted as a triumph for the regime, and grandiose new stadiums were built to house them. By this time soccer had replaced cycling as the national game, and both soccer and the regime had the full backing of the nation's biggest sports journal, the daily *Gazzetto dello sport,* whose editor, Lando Ferretti, was a Fascist of the first hour. In 1923 the Agnelli family, which owned the Fiat works in Turin, bought its way into the Juventus soccer club and also became a whole-hearted supporter of the regime. Juventus was compared to Arsenal, the "Bank of England club," for its free spending on new players, but whereas Arsenal bought some of its best players within Britain—partly because Ministry of Labour regulations prevented them from signing continental talent—Juventus bought most of its players from Argentina: the *oriundi,* players of Italian descent who were accorded dual nationality. Raimundo Orsi was signed shortly after the Amsterdam Olympics of 1928 for a Fiat and £1,000 (100,000 lire), together with a monthly wage of 8,000 lire. The *oriundi,* more of whom were signed after the 1930 World Cup, played for the national team as well as the club teams, drawing anger from Argentina and leading to sarcastic comments that if Fascist Italy wanted to build up its prestige, then it should follow the British or Argentine example of raising homegrown players instead of buying ready-made products from other countries. The president of the Italian football association, Leandro Arpinati, opposed the policy of using *oriundi,* but he was overruled by Giovanni Agnelli and eventually was ousted as president by more committed Fascists.

In addition to draining marshes and building roads, the stock in trade of dictatorial regimes, the Fascists built modern soccer stadiums as monuments to their glory. The first of these was the Littoriale in Bologna, the hometown of Arpinati, who had the stadium built under his direction. It was opened in grand style on 29 May 1927 with a game against Spain, which Italy won before 60,000 spectators. Also at the game was King Vittorio Emanuele III, showing by his presence that he was an ally of Mussolini, even in sport. Two years later Italy had its first national championship and prepared to embark on a decade of spectacular sports progress under Vittorio Pozzo, who was appointed "commissario tecnico" of the Italian national team in 1929.

Pozzo, whose love of the game began in England and who remained an Anglophile, was not a Fascist, but he took advantage of the regime's adolescent authoritarianism to mold a team that was prepared to devote itself to the national cause. With his friend Hugo Meisl, another unregenerate Anglophile, he was the most powerful figure in European soccer before World War II. Pozzo was won over to soccer from track and field by some Juventus players, and when he went to England he became captivated by the soccer played at Old Trafford in Manchester, where United's Charlie Roberts freely discussed tactics with the young language student. To get him back to Italy, Pozzo's family tried cutting off his allowance, and when this failed they paid for a round-trip ticket to attend his sister's wedding. Pozzo never used the return portion of the ticket and kept it as a souvenir for the rest of his life. He never became the engineer his family wanted him to be; instead, his career path took a different direction in 1912 when he was placed in charge of the Italian soccer team for the Stockholm Olympics. His charges were beaten 2-3 by lowly Finland in a preliminary round but regained some prestige in the consolation tournament, where they beat Sweden 1-0 before losing 1-5 to Austria. Pozzo served with distinction as an *alpiniste* officer in World War I, and when he came back to soccer, it was mainly as a journalist, writing for the weekly *Il Calcio.*

When Pozzo took over the national team again in 1929, he built it around a core of Juventus players. His tactics revolved around an attacking center-half, and he found the man he needed in the Argentine Luisito Monti, who soon lived up to his reputation when he broke the leg of Bologna player Angelo Schiavio in a club match. It was also typical of Pozzo that he forced these two players to share the same room in the national team's preparation for the 1934 World Cup, an attention to individual players that was a key to his success. Schiavio was forced to overcome his resentment against Monti and went on to score the winning goal against Czechoslovakia in the World Cup final. Moreover, Schiavio would not have made it to that final if Pozzo had not managed to persuade the Fascist hierarchy to cease pressuring the young star to become a party member; he had sworn that he would give up the game rather than do that.

The 1934 World Cup took place between 27 May and 10 June, the final being played in Rome before Mussolini, who had promised rich rewards to the Italian players if they won the cup and dire punishment if they lost. Thus inspired, the Italian team fought its way to the final with a style that was a fitting tribute to the regime it represented. One of its most viciously contested games was against Spain, which ended in a draw, with so many players injured that seven Spaniards and four Italians were unfit for the replay. The star of that game was Spain's goalkeeper, Ricardo Zamora, whose agility and anticipation were first put on international show at the 1920 Olympics, when he was nineteen years old. In the meantime he had built up such a reputation that the Spaniards revered him as greatly as they did bullfighters. Against Italy he performed heroics, but the battering he received from the overzealous Italians left him unfit for the replay.

Other national heroes emerged from the 1934 World Cup, and thousands of supporters traveled many miles to see them, a new tourist market of which the transport firms and hotels were quick to take advantage: newspaper advertisements offered special train and hotel packages for fans who wanted to attend important games. They arrived in tens of thousands. At Montevideo in 1930, 20,000 Argentine fans had crossed the Río de la Plata for the final against Uruguay, and although no individual country could boast as many traveling supporters for the World Cup in Italy, the aggregate numbers were greater. A reported 7,000 came from the Netherlands, with a war cry telling everyone that they were headed for the finals. Their team did not live up to such optimism, however, and the Netherlands made an early exit from the competition at the hands of Switzerland. The Swiss brought 10,000 supporters for that match, as did the Austrians for their semifinal against Italy. France did not take many supporters, but there were 4,000 people at the Gare du Nord in Paris to welcome the team home after a brave performance and unlucky elimination. In its game against Austria France lost by a goal that was manifestly off-side—according to one report, it was scored while the Dutch referee was momentarily stunned by the news of Switzerland's victory against the Netherlands.

Thousands came from Germany, waving their swastika flags. Czechoslovakia made it to the final, and their supporters arrived for the game
against Italy in two special trains and three coaches, while gifts were
sent by air for the players, including special Czech food and silver rings
and amulets that the players were urged to sew onto their jerseys. The
Czech players also received more than 1,700 telegrams. Such encouragement was let down only by the result; the Czechs played superbly,
but Orsi scored a freak tying goal to take the game into extra-time,
where superior fitness and a desperate effort by Schiavio delighted Il
Duce and sent Pozzo into raptures.

---

   Newspapers had encouraged and in turn benefited from the growth
of soccer since its inception, but in the 1930s radio arrived as a new
branch of the media. Fears were expressed at first that this miracu-
lous means of communication might encourage people to stay at home
and listen to broadcasts rather than go to games, and some newspapers were worried that it might affect their sales, but these fears were
misplaced. Indeed, the opposite was true, for thousands were now able
to listen to broadcasts of games they had no chance of seeing, from
the blind and the sick in hospitals to the inhabitants of outlying rural areas. The first radio broadcast of a soccer match was for a league
game in England on 22 January 1927 between Arsenal and Sheffield
United, but the reactionaries of the League, and to a lesser extent the
FA, feared the effect of radio and banned live broadcasts. When ne-
gotiations to broadcast the 1929 FA Cup final, between Portsmouth
and Bolton, broke down, a newspaper arranged for land lines to be
laid from Wembley to the Southsea Common in Portsmouth and to
Bolton's ground at Burnden Park, with loudspeakers to relay a commentary by George Allison, later to manage Arsenal. 50,000 flocked
to the Southsea Common, and 12,000 paid to listen to the game at
Bolton.
   Belgium witnessed the trial of another means of bringing the game
to people who could not get inside the ground. As *Het Handelsblad*
of 4 November 1928 reported on its front page, complete with photo, a large stand was set up outside the grounds where Belgium was
playing Holland, from which a man with a stick pushed around
figures on a giant replica of a soccer field in an attempt to keep up
with the game being played inside the stadium. Variations on this
attempt to give visual representation to games that could not be seen
were tried out in other sports in other countries, all in response to
the desperate need many people have to follow the fortunes of their

favorite team. The success of Argentina and Uruguay at the Amsterdam Olympics of 1928 were followed feverishly by tens of thousands waiting for cables carrying progress reports of key games. In Argentina loudspeakers were set up outside the offices of the leading newspaper, La Prensa, through which the contents of the cables arriving from Europe by the minute were relayed to the crowds that packed the broad avenues and squares within hearing distance. As Tony Mason recalls (Passion of the People?), it was a foolish individual who interrupted the silence at the wrong moment.

This need has been ever present in the modern game. In the earliest days pub owners in Britain chalked up scores on blackboards as games progressed, the information being supplied by telephone and even, on a few occasions, by carrier pigeon. By the turn of the century newspapers could rush out editions with the scores of games in progress and a complete summary of all games less than two hours after they were completed. Radio never took over the job done by newspapers, but it did help to satisfy the fans' needs to share the fate of their team as it was being decided. In the early 1930s, when radios were still a luxury, crowds in Europe and South America would gather in public squares and hold parties in special locations to hear the broadcasts of the big matches, just as they had gathered outside newspaper offices to hear news of games being played abroad before radio was available.

The cinema was the most popular indoor leisure pursuit of the 1930s, and no newsreel was complete without extracts from the main soccer matches. On the Continent more than in Britain some cinemas specialized in showing entire games, but the atmosphere of soft seats and darkened halls could not replace that of windy terraces and the clamor of thousands of fans. In the press radiophotographs were wired across the waters, while "belinographs" allowed evening papers to reproduce a photograph from an event that took place in the country that same afternoon. Before television, however, radio was the main means to fill the needs of those who could not get to the games.

When Austria went to England in December 1932 for its first international on English soil, so many fans turned up at the central station in Vienna to see off the team that the railway authorities cordoned off a special area and charged a fee to enter it; when others tried to rush the area to see their heroes without paying, special reserves had to be brought in. While the game was being played, some followed its progress at parties in cafés or restaurants where a radio had been installed, and others followed it in the less intimate atmosphere of Vienna's main square, where it was broadcast over loudspeakers.

In Italy the new medium created a new sports hero: the soccer broadcaster. This was Nicolò Carosio, born in Palermo in 1907 of a Sicilian father and an English mother, who reigned over Italian radio for thirty years and was still commentating at the time of his death in 1984. His coverage of the England versus Italy game at Highbury in 1934 won him the gratitude of his compatriots as they listened, at home or in the public squares where loudspeakers were specially erected, to his passionate commentary on the drama being staged in London. Despite the crowds urging them on under the influence of Carosio's patriotic passion, the Italians failed to overcome the early three-goal lead taken by England. Carosio was welcomed back to Italy as a hero, along with Giuseppe Meazza, who scored the two goals that brought Italy to within an ace of leveling the game, and Attilio Ferraris IV, who earned the nickname "the lion of Highbury" for his performance. That loss was particularly strongly felt, for Italy went to England as world champions but aware that England's and Scotland's absence from the tournament took some of the luster off the title.

———

The absence of the British teams from the 1934 World Cup was disappointing but not surprising. The South Americans' performance in Italy, however, was both a disappointment and a surprise. Argentina's deliberately weakened team lost 2-3 to Sweden, and since it was a straight knock-out competition, this was the only game the Argentines played. Argentina also had the bitter irony of watching Monti, Orsi, and Enrico Guaita play in the colors of Italy. Brazil was also weakened by the split in the Rio and São Paulo leagues in 1933 over professionalism. It made the trip for only one game, losing 1-3 to Spain. Mexico fared even worse, for its one game was a preliminary, played in Rome against the United States, which it lost 2-4. The U.S. team in turn was thrashed 1-7 by Italy in Rome, and the scorer of its lone goal, Buff Donelli, was offered a contract in Italy.

For soccer lovers the biggest disappointment of the 1934 World Cup was the failure of the Austrian Wunderteam, which had delighted them over the previous three years. The creation of Hugo Meisl and Jimmy Hogan, who planned their strategy in the Ring-Café in Vienna, this legendary team was "born" in Vienna on 16 May 1931 when it overwhelmed Scotland, albeit without the latter's Rangers and Celtic players, 5-0; it lost only two of its following twenty-six games. Its brilliant run came to an end in the semifinal of the 1934 World Cup, when it lost 0-1 to Italy and then lost 2-3 to Germany in the play-off for third place. It was not so much the string of victories that captured the aficionados, however, as the inspired teamwork of a group of gifted individuals led by Matthias Sindelar, the "Mozart of football." Sindelar, so thin and unpredictable that his play was likened to a piece of paper wafted around by the wind, was nicknamed *"Der Papierene,"* the "Man of Paper."

The son of a bricklayer who died in World War I, Sindelar played almost his entire professional career with FK Austria. He starred in many memorable victories for club and country, setting up numerous goals and scoring as many. His fine skills were like a red rag to a bull for Monti, who successfully marked him out of the semifinal game against Italy in the 1934 World Cup, played in a mud bath that bogged down the free-flowing Austrian game. Disappointed at not making the final, Austria failed to lift its spirits for the play-off against Germany for third place and lost. Sindelar, still suffering from Monti's attentions in the semifinal, missed that game. It was the end of the "Wunderteam." Four years later Austrian soccer itself was dealt a death blow by the *Anschluss* with Germany.

One of the events organized to honor the "reunification" of Austria and Germany in March 1938 was a soccer match between "German-Austria" and the "Old Reich." The *Anschluss* celebration match of 3 April did not turn out as the Nazis expected, however, for 60,000 Austrian soccer fans turned it into an anti-Prussian, anti-German demonstration. Sindelar was picked for that game and was said to be under orders not to let the Germans lose. By one account he showed more skill in missing goals than he ever did in scoring, but the old Austria won, by two goals to nil, and Sindelar was one of the scorers.

Sindelar was past his best in 1938, but his well known anti-Nazi feelings would have kept him out of the World Cup team of that year in any case. When the Jewish president of FK Austria was deposed to make way for a more suitable "Aryan" replacement, Sindelar made no secret of where his loyalties lay. Personal problems complicated the professional, however, and in January 1939 Sindelar was found dead in the apartment above his recently purchased café, alongside his forty-year-old Catholic, some say part Jewish, mistress. The Nazis moved quickly to cover any suspicions of suicide on the part of the people's most popular son, and he was given what amounted to a hero's funeral service. Up to 20,000 turned up, in a ceremony previously reserved for statesmen, and for years afterward the anniversary of his death was remembered. It was also commemorated in a poem by Friedrich Torberg, the Jewish man of letters and football

fanatic who was also forced to leave the coffeehouse life in Vienna
that he loved so much.

The poem opens:

> Er war ein Kind aus Favoriten
> und hiess Mathias Sindelar . . .
>
> [There was a lad from Favoriten
> Whose name was Mathias Sindelar . . .]

Torberg then evokes his image on the field, concluding,

> . . . Er spielte lässig, leicht und heiter.
> Er spielte stets. Er kämpfte nie.
>
> [He played with gay and languid lightness.
> He always played. He never fought.]

Opponents had no answer to the unpredictable movements of a ma-
gician who played to no set plan. But nor had "Sindi" when

> [bis] eines Tags ein andrer Gegner
> ihm jählings in die Quere trat,
> ein fremd und furchtbar Überlegner,
> vor dem's nicht Regel gab noch Rat.
>
> [Till one day came another foe
> Who fell across his fateful path,
> A foreign and a frightful foe,
> Restrained by neither rules nor right.]

Unable to accept the new order, he sought release in the gas tap.
Despite what is said in most English references to his death, he was
not Jewish.

In soccer the two worlds made into one in March 1938 never
worked. At the World Cup in France later in that year the two styles
failed to blend, and Greater Germany failed miserably. When the war
began, matches between Austrian and German teams continued to
become the occasion for anti-German hatred. In November 1940
Schalke 04 visited Vienna for a game against Admira Wien and had
its team bus demolished, and the tires of former youth leader, now
*Gauleiter,* Baldur von Schirach's expensive car were ripped.

The German national team failed to bring off any notable victories on the soccer field, but the Nazi regime manipulated soccer for
some notable off-the-field successes. Germany's greatest triumph on
the international stage was winning third place in the 1934 World
Cup; in Berlin in 1936 and France in 1938 it suffered early elimina-

tion. There were other ways of using sports, however, and for the Nazis there was more to be gained by showing that regimes whose politics they despised were still happy to welcome them as friendly sports foes. The Netherlands caused them some consternation when after international encounters between the two in 1935 and 1937, the game to be played in Rotterdam on 11 December 1938 was canceled. When the team did play, the players resolutely refused to give the Nazi salute. The British authorities posed no such problems. In December 1935 Germany came to White Hart Lane, Tottenham Hotspur's grounds, to play England. It lost 0-3, but the conduct of the players and the behavior of the 10,000 Germans at the game won the praise of the press, and the after-dinner speeches applauded the action taken against demonstrators who had tried to have the visit canceled. In Scotland in October 1936 a 0-2 loss was overlooked as Nazi officials emphasized the racial bonds between the two countries in the post-match festivities. A comparatively small crowd (40,000) turned up because of misgivings about the regime, and the Scotland players did not give the Nazi salute. The England team at a game in Berlin in May 1938, however, was pressured by the British ambassador Neville Henderson, with the acquiescence of the FA but against the wishes of the players, to give the Hitler salute at the start of the game. For British teams that had nothing to do with the Continental practice of saluting spectators or even exchanging pennants before the game started, this was a significant gesture, and the game is better remembered for the salute than for England's 6-3 victory.

On the domestic front the Nazi regime's greatest coup was the support it received from Schalke 04 as the team bestrode the era with six German championships between 1934 and 1942. The Nazis were delighted to have the workers' most popular club as part of the new order, and it received their every support. For workers who had scruples about their relations with the new regime, the Nazis had ways of making them conform. Dietrich Schulze-Marmeling (*Der gezähmte Fussball: Zur Geschichte eines subversiven Sports*) tells the story of how the Nazis brought Barry Schulz, a star player from the former German Workers' Sports Federation (DAT), to their way of thinking. One day Schulz saw a Mercedes with four SS officers and one civilian pull up outside his house, raising the inevitable question of who was about to be arrested. It was in fact he whom they had come to see—to discuss his soccer future. The visitors asked Schulz politely whether he would turn out that afternoon for the wealthy SSC Friesen Cottbus club, and in case he had any hesitation about doing so, they pointed out that at twenty-three years of age, he was too young to have to give up the game. That afternoon he scored two goals for his new team in a 2-1 victory over Blau-Weiss Berlin.

During World War II playing soccer in Germany was one of the more pleasant ways to avoid the killing, and particularly after the defeat at Stalingrad in 1942, the threat of being sent to the front was used in soccer, as in other pursuits, to ensure that young men did what they were told. Proof that this was no idle threat came after the astonishing 1941 Greater Germany championship final in Berlin between the two "workers'" teams, Rapid Vienna and Schalke 04. At halftime the Austrians were losing 0-2, and shortly after the break they conceded another goal, only to come back and stun the 100,000 spectators with four goals in eighteen minutes, winning 4-3. For Franz "Bimbo" Binder, who scored three of these goals, the triumph was short-lived, but he survived his posting to the front, and after the war he returned to his career with Rapid Vienna, ending it in 1949 as Europe's highest ever goal scorer. One match played at the front is remembered in the Ukrainian stadium near Kiev where it took place: called the *"match smerti,"* or "match of death," it was played in April 1942 between individuals from Dinamo Kiev and officers of the Luftwaffe. Dinamo won 5-3, and all but three of the victorious team were said to have been executed for their effrontery. In fact games between the occupiers and their victims were not uncommon, and the execution of the Kiev players may just have been part of the normal Nazi treatment of "racial inferiors."

---

Some of the tragedy that lay ahead cast a shadow over the World Cup played in France in 1938, most notably in the absence of Austria but also in that of Spain, which was being torn apart in the deadly civil war that had erupted in July 1936. Soccer had flourished in Spain in the 1920s, and in 1928 Spain's team became the first from a Continental nation to defeat a professional England team, with a 4-3 victory in Madrid. National victories in Spain, however, were always muted by the separatist ambitions of the Basques and Catalans, whose leading teams were the most powerful in Spain before 1936. The main Bilbao team pointedly called itself Athletic Bilbao, and when its Basque offshoots set up a team in Madrid, it too used an English name, Athletic Madrid. Any expressions of Castilian centralism were derided by the fans, but when the civil war came, it involved class as well as ethnic enmities. Nevertheless, Basques and Catalans found themselves in bitter warfare against the rebel armies of General Franco, who ruthlessly applied his centralist policies when he came to power in 1939. Soccer continued to be played amid the massacres, and Catalan and Basque teams went on overseas tours to help raise funds for their cause.

In April 1937 Barcelona was invited to tour Mexico and went on to play in New York. At the end of the tour some of its players accepted offers to play in Mexico; none went back to the zone controlled by Franco. A Basque team began what became a virtual world tour on 24 April 1937, taking in Europe and North and South America. Playing to overflowing crowds in the Soviet Union, they were feted for their soccer and in return thanked their hosts for the aid they were giving in the fight against fascism in Spain. In their two-and-a-half-month stay they lost only once, 2-6, to a Moscow Spartak side that was helped by the referee but that nevertheless became the toast of the Soviets for the victory. While they were in South America, Basque players signed for Argentine clubs, most notably Angel Zubieta and Isidro Langara for San Lorenzo, which pushed the South American club's membership up from 15,000 to 35,000; three others were signed by "the millionaires," River Plate of Argentina.

As the world prepared for war, FIFA tried hard to hold together what it already referred to as its "family." Because FIFA included representatives from Germany, Italy, and Hungary, as well as from France and Czechoslovakia, major soccer nations on opposite sides of the ideological divide, it could do so only by maintaining a certain estrangement from reality, although even in the early 1930s FIFA's publications had come out with some vapid statements about soccer having nothing to do with politics. At the start of the civil war in Spain FIFA had banned all international matches there, but when Franco started to gain ascendancy, it changed its position and supported him. Franco then demanded that no games be permitted against the touring Basque team, and FIFA agreed. Several South American football associations then threatened to ignore the ban, above all Chile, supported by Bolivia, Paraguay, Peru, and Uruguay. A debate raged in the Argentine press, but eventually the Argentines sided with FIFA. The Argentine football association had been miffed that its (late) application to host the 1938 World Cup had been unsuccessful, and infuriated fans attacked its offices when it withdrew from the competition. When the Basques arrived, however, FIFA's power was confirmed. None of the five games scheduled was played, and Uruguay and Chile did not carry out their threat to secede.

In February 1939 Jules Rimet, the president of FIFA, made a special visit to South America to help solve the problems and allay the suspicion noted in FIFA's official publication, *Football World/Football*

*Mondial/Fussball Welt* (April 1939), regarding the "reproach sometimes made by South America, of [FIFA] being too European"—in fact, there was only one South American on the FIFA executive board, but that was said to be because of the problem of communications. It was too late for Rimet to get Argentina to enter the 1938 World Cup, but he did smooth a few ruffled feathers and in the end kept the malcontents within "the great football family." He was given a particularly warm welcome by the Argentina football association, which was itself in dispute with Uruguay and which had first issued the invitation to Rimet. The Argentine association's secretary proved with a few figures how much the game was loved in his country: there were 2,000 associations with 300,000 members, and 3 million spectators had gone to the games in Buenos Aires in the season just completed. Argentina's hurt at losing the 1938 finals to France was obviously forgotten, for it pledged its presence at the 1942 games, which Rimet suggested it should host if Germany pulled out. Rimet also raised the possibility of a game between Europe and South America, but FIFA decided more realistically that a game between the best clubs of Europe and South America would be a better idea.

Brazil was the only CONMEBOL country to send a team to the World Cup in France, and its football association was quick to pledge its loyalty to FIFA, although when the team was eliminated from the competition on a disputed penalty, the association in turn threatened to leave the "football family." Of the other American countries, Cuba qualified because Mexico withdrew and caused a sensation when it defeated Romania 2-1 after a 1-1 draw. But it was the Brazilians who were the center of attention, most notably their black stars, Leônidas da Silva (the "Black Diamond"), Domingos da Guia, and Tim (Elba de Pádua Lima). Their captain, however, was white, amateur, and a physician. The Europeans were also intrigued by the obvious interest in the game in Brazil, where Mario Filho, through his contacts in the cafés, publicity in his newspapers, and prizes for the most colorfully outfitted fans, had encouraged the popularity of the professional game. It was he who arranged for his newspaper, *O Globo*, to pay for telephone links to the players and trainer of the Brazilian team in France. The Brazilian Sports Federation promised the players houses and share of the receipts from the final if they won the cup, but because they were eliminated in the semifinal, they had to make do with the piles of gifts they took home with them. Back home in Brazil the crowds in Rio and São Paulo gave the players a rapturous welcome.

Brazil's failure to win the cup was due to an incredible act of confidence on the part of their coach, who dropped Leônidas in the semifinal, claiming that he wanted to keep him fresh for the final. It was said that Brazil had enough talent for two teams, either of which could have beaten any of the European teams—but only if it included Leônidas. His absence, also said to be because of racial prejudice, was certainly crucial, and Italy won 2-1. Before this Brazil played its first-round game in Strasbourg, overcoming the muddy conditions that some said would bring it down and winning 6-5 against a Poland team inspired by its greatest player ever, Ernest Wilimowski. Brazil next beat Czechoslovakia after a drawn game that degenerated into a brawl and was christened the "Battle of Bordeaux." Brazil had more reserves to make up for the injuries and suspensions from the first game, and it won the replay 2-1. In the play-off for third place Brazil defeated Sweden 4-2. Swedish soccer enjoyed royal recognition by this time, as King Gustav even forsook his beloved tennis to join 40,000 spectators (including 10,000 Norwegians) watching a match between Sweden and Norway in 1938, with English referee A. J. Jewell specially flown in to officiate.

The 1938 World Cup final was an all-European affair, but unlike those of 1930 and 1934, the host nation was not one of the finalists. Soccer in France had been improving since the adoption of professionalism in 1932, but it still relied on imported foreigners to bolster its club teams, and France's World Cup team included the naturalized Austrian Gusti Jordan and the black Raoul Diagne, the son of a deputy from Senegal. France beat Belgium in the first round but was then eliminated by Italy before 58,000 spectators at the Colombes Stadium, which had been specially renovated for the occasion. The French resentment against the Italians was expressed most vehemently, however, at the semifinal match between Brazil and Italy played in Marseilles, when a storm of abuse accompanied the Italians from the field after a victory gained by a controversial goal. Spectators invaded the field and had to be restrained by police. Two years earlier sports and other relations between France and Italy had been strained when Italy refused to send cyclists to the Tour de France and then in April 1937 canceled at the last minute an international soccer match to be played in conjunction with the Paris Exhibition of that year. Mussolini wanted to insult France's Popular Front government, but his excuse was the safety of his players. Most of them, however, were well used to playing before hostile crowds. When Jacques de Ryswick accompanied the French team to a friendly international against Italy in Naples in December 1938, he was appalled at the abuse showered on the French team but was told in consolation that this was nothing compared to the reception reserved for Italian teams from the north.

The final was played between Italy and Hungary before 45,000 spectators, and the Italians' fast, determined play proved superior to the Hungarians' individual, measured style. Goalkeeper Antal Szabo took consolation for the 2-4 loss by claiming that Hungary had saved the lives of eleven men; when pressed to explain what he meant, he claimed that the Italian team had received a telegram before the game saying "Win or die." The Italians doubtless took such a threat less literally, for they were used to playing for high rewards for winning and threats of harsh penalties for losing, including the threat of being sent on military service. Italy went on the following year to play England in a game that they billed as the World Champions against the Champions of Soccer. The game ended in a draw after a goal for Italy thanks to the German referee, Peco Bauwens, who ignored two blatant offenses, but more important was that the game was played without any serious incidents and was highlighted by the England team giving the Fascist salute to the four corners of the stadium.

Britain's soccer, like its politics, continued in the 1930s along the path of "splendid isolation" that other Europeans so frequently commented on sarcastically. When the British football associations left FIFA in 1928, they nevertheless continued to play games against FIFA teams. England lost eight games on the Continent before 1940, but the only games it took seriously were those played at home: in 1931 it avenged its 1929 defeat in Spain with a 7-1 thrashing in a return match in London; in 1932 the Austrian Wunderteam was unlucky to lose 3-4 in a game that most observers admitted showed that Austria played a better class of soccer. Then came the Battle of Highbury in 1934, the brutality of which the English blamed on the visitors, threatening never to invite Italy again. England beat Germany 3-0 in 1935, it defeated Hungary 6-2 in 1936, and the following year, although England's home record looked shaky against the Czechoslovak team, especially after the Czechs scored four goals, England went on to win 5-4, thanks mainly to the budding "maestro," Stanley Matthews. To celebrate the seventy-fifth anniversary of the FA, a team representing Europe was invited in 1938 to play England and lost 0-3. Manager Pozzo complained about not having the necessary three weeks to prepare his team, but the wonder on the English side was that their manager was allowed the luxury of having the team together for three days before the match.

Britain produced many superb players in this time, but British superiority over Continental teams was mainly in their fitness and firepower—with head or foot. In Britain, unlike in central and southern Europe, individualism was frowned on and artistry less prized than guts. Players were never allowed to develop swelled heads, and the stars were paid the same amount as the plodders. Herbert Chapman, a close friend of Meisl and Pozzo, was one of the few Britons who was interested in what was happening across the Channel. He had transformed Arsenal into the glamor team of the 1930s, highly sought after for tours on the Continent and the subject of a film that was made in the summer of 1939, for which players acting as themselves were paid nearly ten times their normal summer wage of £6 a week. Some of the "revolutionary" ideas he learned from the Continent included using floodlights for competitive matches, numbering players' jerseys, and giving the manager more say in running the team. What he considered his most revolutionary idea, however, was to have a squad of twenty of England's best players meet regularly under a selector, coach, and trainer to prepare for international matches.

Chapman's concern about his players did not extend to freeing them from the financial restrictions that not only bound them to a meager maximum wage and restricted their freedom of movement but limited their ability to make money outside the club. Alex James was the star of the Arsenal team of the 1930s and one of the great players of all time, but he got no sympathy from Chapman when he tried to improve his personal well-being. After voicing criticisms of the system in an "exposé" published in the News of the World in 1937, he was cold-shouldered by the British soccer authorities and ended his career as a coach in Poland on the eve of World War II. A few players took their talents abroad for bigger salaries, and when France adopted professionalism in 1932, it attracted several British professionals. One superstar the French nearly snared was Hughie Gallacher, who was as anxious as his compatriot Alex James to cash in on his soccer genius.

For the men running British soccer, the descendants of the "Old Boys" with all the smugness that was their hallmark, there were matters more pressing than the just rewards to professional soccer players—or even the morality of playing sports with Fascists or Nazis. The closest they came to a troubled conscience was when the game was threatened with the stain of money from a "tainted source": the football pools. Having faced the threat of women's soccer, greyhound racing, and dirt-track motorbike racing in the 1920s, the men running British soccer prepared in 1936 to put an end to their game's association with the millions of pounds that were being wagered on it through the pools.

Betting on the outcome of a group of soccer matches was common in the 1890s, but no player or official was allowed to take part in it. In 1910 any player or official who was convicted of taking part in coupon betting faced permanent suspension. Newspapers had offered their readers prizes for guessing the correct outcome of certain games, increasing their circulation as customers bought the paper to get the entry form, but the League asked the government to intervene. The government first and unsuccessfully sought to do this through its control of the Post Office, but in 1928 it managed to ban betting on games through newspapers. By this time pools companies such as Littlewoods and Vernons, which operated out of Liverpool, were making large profits, while the government raked in its percentage in taxes and the Post Office enjoyed a booming trade in sixpence and one-shilling postal orders, not to mention stamps. It is hardly surprising, then, that a royal commission into lotteries and betting in 1933 did nothing about the pools.

The pools offered a cheap form of gambling for those who could not afford to go to the races, and the outlay for those who bet on them did not jeopardize the family budget. By the 1930s they had become such a craze that sixteen and a half times as many people were said to follow the pools as followed football. Correctly predicting three draws, four away wins, or ten home wins from a selected choice of games was one way to win a reasonable prize, depending on the number of upsets on that particular day, since the prize money was shared. Bigger money was to be won on predicting eight draws, and even more on the "penny points," where for a penny a line you had to guess the results of a given twenty-four games, earning three points for a draw, two for an away win, and one for a home win. Maximum points could earn a fortune for the lucky winner. On days when there were few upsets the big prize had to be shared among many winners, but often there was only one winner—or no winner, in which case the prize money rolled over into the jackpot. In some countries dreams of wealth came from the lucky number in a lottery; in Britain they came from winning the pools.

For millions of people this was an innocuous pastime, and many were introduced to soccer in this way, for it encouraged an interest in the game. Some even claimed that it involved some skill, and most newspapers assigned a "specialist" to give prognostications on likely outcomes each week. Unlike betting through a bookmaker on the outcome of a particular game, and unlike betting on other sports such as racing and boxing, where the results could more easily be rigged, betting in soccer pools provoked comparatively little fear of corruption. For the owners of the pools companies, soccer was a gold mine, with Littlewoods and Vernons taking the bulk of the profit from the estimated £30 million spent each year in the mid-1930s, when 30,000 people, mainly women, were employed to check the coupons.

For men of the League like John Lewis and Charles Sutcliffe, however, the whole idea of gambling was iniquitous. Sutcliffe, like Lewis a high-minded Protestant, was born in Burnley in 1864, the son of a solicitor who could have made a fortune in that profession if he had not devoted so much of his time and talent to soccer. An indefatigable worker, driven by a Methodist upbringing and two unhappy marriages but supported by a daughter who shared his love of soccer and the work that went with it, Sutcliffe was opposed to gambling in all its forms: his vision was of a world of honesty and hard work, with the rich helping the poor and virtue its own reward.

The pools needed to know which teams were playing on a given date, and only the leagues, mainly the Scottish and English, could supply this information. The pools were prepared to pay for use of the schedules, and the League could have charged a fee or a percentage for providing them, perhaps for the benefit of the players. This was never one of Sutcliffe's concerns, however, and rather than touch a "tainted source," the League tried to put the pools out of business by rearranging all fixtures and keeping them secret. The plan was to come into play for games scheduled for 29 February 1936. Word of this was soon leaked to the press, and questions were raised about teams not knowing until the last minute who their opponents were to be. The whole thing turned out to be as big a fiasco as expected, and among the first to complain were the clubs whose representatives had given the League the right to act as it thought fit. The fans also demanded a return to sanity, and after one more week of mystery matches, the pools were left free to continue unhampered in their use of the League schedules. The bulk of the British public was then left free to discuss such lesser crises as Mussolini's continuing atrocities in Ethiopia and Hitler's reoccupation of the demilitarized zone of the Rhineland.

Not that the British political leadership showed itself to be terribly interested in such issues, and in September 1938 Neville Chamberlain justified the dismemberment of Czechoslovakia on the grounds that the people of Great Britain should not have to be troubled by the fortunes of people in "far away lands about whom we know little." His concern for Czechoslovakia was on a par with the British public's total disinterest in the World Cup that had been played in France a few months earlier.

France, Britain's partner in appeasement, came under attack in its own sports press for failing to take sport as seriously as the dictators did. On 24 January 1939 France's most popular evening daily, *Paris-soir*, denounced France's leaders for failing to appear at a France versus Poland soccer match that was watched by 40,000 people; in February it complained that France was losing touch with Europe, leaving Germany to make friends through its sports relations; and after the German invasion of Czechoslovakia in March, the paper changed tack to emphasize instead the sports relations of France with its empire in North Africa, claiming that the sons of fathers who had fought against France now represented it in sports and were prepared to live or die for it.

---

When war came this time, there was no talk in Britain of continuing its soccer program as normal. British soldiers sent to France soon organized soccer competitions with the locals, but these came to an end with the blitzkrieg of May through June 1940. The Nazis continued their program of games as usual, even after Stalingrad, in an attempt to keep up an atmosphere of normality. As late as 5 November 1944 league matches canceled because of massive air strikes were said to have been called off for "technical reasons." Germany also played against neutrals such as Switzerland and Sweden, allies such as Italy, Hungary, and Romania, creations such as Croatia and Slovakia, and friends such as Franco's Spain. The last game played by Mussolini's Italy was against fellow fascists, Pavelic's Croatia and Franco's Spain, in April 1942.

In the Soviet Union soccer continued to be played throughout the war. Even during the pitiless siege of Leningrad, amid the daily death and starvation, matches were played in 1942 before crowds of up to 8,000, broadcast throughout the Soviet Union to give heart to their fellow citizens and dismay the Germans. No sooner had Stalingrad been relieved than a scratch match, attended by 10,000 people, was arranged on 2 May 1943 between a team of local stars and some Spartak players. In 1942 and 1943 an artificial field was laid out on Red Square so that games could be played there on May Day and broadcast throughout the "Russian Motherland." Amid the heroism of the Russian people, the treachery of its leaders was still at work. In 1939 Lavrenty Beria became chief of the secret police; a vindictive and jealous individual with a long memory, his love of soccer set up some tremors of fear among those, officials and players alike, who had crossed his path when he was an average player with Dinamo Tblisi. Above all he had an abiding hatred of the Spartak teams, and one of his first acts was to try to arrest Nikolai Starostin, one of the four brothers on whom the success of Moscow Spartak was built. Family connections saved Nikolai on that occasion, but in 1942 he, along with Alexander, Andrei, and Pyotr, were imprisoned in Lubianka for questioning in regard to antistate terrorism and propagating bourgeois sport. Two years later all four brothers were sent to exile—Nikolai to Ukhta, where he met other players and soon became their coach, with even the guards listening enthralled to his team talks. All four brothers escaped death in exile because of their soccer reputations.

During the war some of the heroes of the soccer field proved themselves heroes in the grimmer battles for life and death, while others ended up as victims. Among the Jews who perished were the Hungarians Arpad Weisz, who played and coached in Italy in the 1920s, and Gyula Feldmann of Maccabi and MTK, who also went to Italy in the 1920s; Bela Guttmann, of MTK and Hakoah, escaped capture and went on to coach the European champion Benfica in the early 1960s. Among non-Jewish victims, Asbjorn Halvorsen, the star of Norway's Olympic team that beat Great Britain in 1920 and later secretary of the Norwegian football association, refused to collaborate with the Nazis and was tortured to death. Etienne Mattler, captain of France's team in the 1930s, survived imprisonment and torture for his resistance activities, but Eugène Maes, France's center forward early in the century, fell to the enemy; wounded in World War I, he did not survive the sequel. Carl Sturmer, who starred in Italy before World War I and went as a coach to Italy afterward, was shot by the Americans as a spy. Alex Villaplane of the 1930 French World Cup team was shot by the French as a collaborator, while Wilimowski, who went from starring for Poland before 1939 to starring for Germany thereafter, never went back to Poland. Raymond Braine had questions to answer for his role in Belgium under Nazi occupation. In Italy some, such as Dino Fiorini, died with the Fascists, while others, such as Bruno Neri, died with the partisans.

Countless others met similar fates, their soccer skills no guarantee of the choices they would make when faced by the supreme agony. Many would-be stars were killed in action, some established stars never played again, and others, especially in England, lived through their peak years decked out in khaki instead of their team's colors, winning medals on the battlefield instead of on the soccer field.

————————

The defeated Germans recovered in soccer as they did in the economy. Sepp Herberger, appointed manager of the German team after the "disgrace" of Berlin in 1936, continued his career after the war and went on to manage the German team that won the World Cup in 1954; the captain of that team was Fritz Walter, who began his career in 1940. Bert Trautmann was a dedicated soldier of the reich when, at twenty-two years of age, he was captured in the last stages of the war. Imprisoned in Britain, he survived the insults of those with hatred in their hearts to became a magnificent and much-loved goalkeeper with Manchester City.

Even before the guns had gone silent in Europe, arrangements were being made to resume soccer matches, and shortly after the victories in Europe and Japan, the British football associations made their peace with FIFA, returning to the fold in 1946. One of their first acts was to arrange a Great Britain versus "The Rest of Europe" spectacular that was played in Hampden Park, Glasgow, before 134,000 spectators in May 1947. The 6-1 victory to Great Britain reassured Britons that the world was back to normal. On the other hand, the match netted the depleted FIFA coffers £30,000, and soccer in Europe prepared to enter another boom period. When the question of the next World Cup's location was raised, however, South America was the only choice, and the honor fell to Brazil.

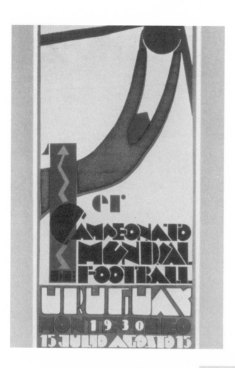

The changing style of World
Cup posters: (this page) Uruguay (1930), France (1938);
(following page) England
(1966), Mexico (1986).
(From FIFA Public Relations,
Zurich)

Reaching for the
moon: an attempt
to sell USA 1994.

Soccer at the service of commerce early in the century. (From A. Gibson and
W. Pickford, *Association Football and the Men Who Made It* [London: Caxton, ca. 1906])

The first World Cup, Montevideo, Uruguay, 1930. (From the *Official History of FIFA, 1904–1984* [Zurich: FIFA, 1984])

Mlle. Bracquemond, captain of Fémina-Sport, prepares to cross the ball. (From Thérèse Herckelbout-Brulé, "Football Is a Healthy Sport for Women," *Très-sport,* January 1926)

An artistic French view of women in soccer, used to advertise the 1924 Olympic Games in Paris.

Soccer and war: defending the goal. (From the title page of *Vie au grand air,* 15 December 1916.)

The final goal in a fruitful series, as the Nazis prepare to add Britain to those countries already in the net: Poland, Norway, Holland, Belgium, and France. The bottom caption reads: "How will he be able to stop this one?" (From Paolo Facchinetti, *Dal Football al Calcio* [Bologna: Conti Editore, 1989])

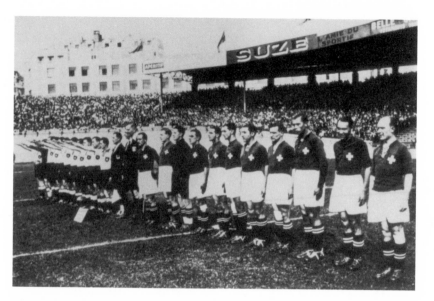

The Swiss team stands resolutely to attention while the German team gives the Nazi salute before the game in the 1938 World Cup in France. (From *FIFA, 1904–1984* [Zurich: FIFA, 1984])

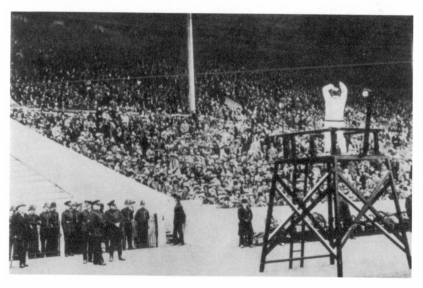

The traditional hymn singing before the English FA Cup Final in the 1920s. (From Rudolph Kircher, *Fair Play, Sport Spiel und Geist in England* [Frankfurt: Societäts-Druckerei, 1927])

Scottish supporters descend on London for the biennial Scotland vs. England international at Wembley. (From Alan Breck, *Book of Scottish Football* [London: Daily Express, 1937])

A French view of the World Cup in Mussolini's Italy, 1934. (From *Sport*, 13 June 1934.)

Despite scenes like this from a contemporary game in Africa, Europe, above all the United Kingdom, has been the scene of some of the world's worst soccer disasters. (From *Confédération Africaine de football, 1957–1987* [Cairo: Nubar, ca. 1987]; photo by Daniel Djagoué)

A clearing in the African jungle. (From *Confédération Africaine de football, 1957–1987* [Cairo: Nubar, ca. 1987]; photo by D.R.)

Pelé at the beginning of his
brilliant career. (From *FIFA,
1904–1984* [Zurich: FIFA,
1984])

Stanley Matthews, like Pelé
the undisputed king of his
generation.

More than most, the French have a feel for their history. Here, Delacroix's *Liberty on the Barricades* is used to parody the financial and other disasters at Olympique Marseille after 1993. (From *France Football*, 26 April–2 May 1994)

# New Masters for Old:
# Soccer in the Fifties

After nearly six years of war and no serious soccer, the sports fans of Great Britain would have been happy to watch any foreign visitors, but when that team came from the Soviet Union, glorious allies in the recent war but still men of mystery whose prowess in the world of international sports had not been seriously tested, the interest and curiosity led to packed grounds wherever it played. The conduct of the visitors' officials off the field and their players on it showed that any sports glasnost was still well into the future. The Moscow Dinamos, mischievously said to be the national team masquerading under a club name (in fact they had three "guests," one of whim was Vsevolod Bobrov), thrashed third-division Cardiff City 10-1 in Wales, drew 2-2 with Glasgow Rangers in Scotland, and in London drew 3-3 with Chelsea and beat Arsenal 4-3 in a game made farcical by fog. On the way home they beat Norrköping, a Swedish team bristling with talent, 5-0, but this game is often overlooked, even by the Soviets.

The touring Soviets made an impression with their well-drilled, short-passing game, raised a few eyebrows with their flowing shorts and the large "D" sewn on their jerseys, and provoked embarrassed hilarity by presenting flowers to the opposition at the beginning of the games. All this, however, was clouded over in a mist of political prejudice that the Soviet authorities did their best to promote. They made several demands that showed them to be as suspicious of British sportsmanship as they were of British capitalism, and by briefly playing an extra man in two of their games (allowing one substitute was one of the concessions made by the British), they showed to some that they were not to be trusted. The Soviet referee in the Arsenal game gave his decisions as though his future depended on them, but then the linesmen at the Rangers game in Glasgow, whose futures were not at stake, made some decisions that might generously be put down to patriotism. The Dinamo players were welcomed back by a sports public that had followed every step of their tour on radio, but then they fell under Stalin's paranoia. Individuals who had come under foreign influences were suspected of undermining the Soviet way of life, and several Dinamo players found themselves on the way "north of the Arctic circle."

The British knew nothing of the Soviet world of soccer and they were happy to leave it that way. Even when further vistas were opened in the years ahead, the British public clung contentedly to the world as they knew it. Monster gates that continued to rise until 1949 helped to confirm for the men who ran Scottish and English soccer that all was well in the best of all worlds: in England 41.3 million people went through the turnstiles to watch the first-division games of the 1948–49 season, and as many as 30,000 could be locked out for some games. In Scotland internationals with England and the annual cup finals were guaranteed a 134,000 sellout, and crowds of over 100,000 turned up even for important midweek cup games. Young and adult males in the postwar world of tightened belts and limited leisure choices found in soccer a cheap and exciting way to pass their free time.

In South America soccer continued to monopolize sporting interest. In Brazil the dictator Getúlio Vargas had nurtured for his own benefit the people's love of dance, popular music, and soccer, and when he left office in 1945 the soccer fervor continued, to be consecrated in the massive Maracanã Stadium, which was constructed for the 1950 World Cup. The stadium, which held more than 200,000 spectators, was finished just in time for the final. The competition was held between 24 June and 16 July, in venues so far apart that they had to be reached by airplane. The consequent schedules proved too much for some countries. France had been eliminated in the preliminaries but was then offered a place after numerous withdrawals; when it learned of its schedule, however, it withdrew—a slight embarrassment, in that the trophy had just been named after Jules Rimet, the FIFA president who founded the competition. Germany was still an outcast from the war, as was Japan, but they were not missed as a soccer power. Austria and Hungary had been allies of Germany in the recent conflict, but they were invited. Austria thought that it was not ready, and Hungary preferred to stay behind the recently drawn Iron

Curtain. So too did the Soviet Union, whose brief excursion into the soccer world was as short as it was startling. Czechoslovakia's future still lay in the balance, and it refused to send a team. Italy came with a drastically weakened team, and by ship, but for reasons beyond human will. The previous year, on 4 May 1949, the heart had been torn out of Italian soccer when the entire Torino team was wiped out in a plane crash on the way back from a benefit match in Portugal. "Il grande Torino" was on its way to establishing a reputation that might have equaled that of the Austrian Wunderteam when it met its tragic fate.

Other European nations had trivial reasons not to go; Scotland, for example, refused to go because it captured only second place in the Home International tournament. Thus the UK was represented by only one team, despite FIFA's generous offer of two. England came back from Brazil perhaps wishing it had not gone. Europe's other representatives were Spain, Yugoslavia, and Sweden. Spain was still rebuilding after the civil war, but Sweden, spared the devastation of World War II, and Yugoslavia had shown their potential when they played against each other in the finals of the 1948 Olympics in London. Sweden, coached by the Englishman George Raynor, won that game 3-1. Four of its star players were immediately signed to play professionally in Italy and Spain: the famous Gre-No-Li trio of Gunnar Gren, Gunnar Nordahl, and Nils Liedholm went to Milan, and Garvis Carlsson went to Atlético Madrid. Raynor claims that he turned down an offer of £1,000 to assist with their transfers. Sweden shouldered the losses and stuck by its principles not to play expatriate professionals, so it went to Brazil with a weakened team. Despite this Sweden still placed third.

Asia was to be represented by Burma or India, but both withdrew—India dropping out because FIFA insisted that its athletes play with soccer boots. Most of Asia was involved in some form of postcolonial upheaval at this time, making organized sports difficult. The first Asian Games were played in India the following year, and they clearly showed politics to be just as divisive in the absence of the colonial masters as with them: Pakistan, included in the soccer tournament, refused to set foot on Indian soil. Of the Middle East countries, Syria and the newly created Israel were easily eliminated in the preliminaries. No African nation was entered.

In view of all the withdrawals, it was perhaps not surprising that the first and second places in Brazil went to two South American teams, but even had the best of Europe been there, it is still likely that Uruguay and Brazil would have filled the top places. There were withdrawals from South America as well, most notably Peru and Ecuador, but Argentina's refusal to participate was partly because the Peronist government feared losing and partly to snub the organizers. The Argentine soccer authorities were in the midst of one of their perennial problems; poor relations with their northern neighbor and chronic discontent with their players. Argentine soccer continued to supply teams and individuals of the highest class but failed to match this with harmonious organization of their talents. Argentina justly complained that Italy plundered their best players, but Argentina in turn picked up talent from other South American countries, and in the late 1940s the bosses' mistreatment of the players, in particular their refusal to recognize the players' union established in late 1944, provoked a strike and mass exodus to Colombia, where a rebel professional league had been founded in 1948. Because the league was not a member of FIFA, its teams could lure players from other countries, including England and Scotland, with massive signing-on fees and perks that went straight to the players.

Boca Juniors and River Plate had emerged as the giants of Argentine soccer in the 1930s: Boca had the bigger support, but River Plate became known as "los millonarios" for spending freely on players. The 1940s belonged to River Plate, which towered over Argentine soccer until 1948 with one of the great teams of all times, its forward line, known as "the Machine" (la máquina), made up of Muñoz, José Manuel Moreno, Adolfo Pedernera, Angel Labruna, and Loustau. Deambrosi sometimes played instead of Loustau, and in 1946 a twenty year old named Alfredo Di Stéfano added his genius to the glittering talent. Like those of so many other Argentine players of supreme class, his talents were put on show abroad, in his case in Colombia and Spain.

Sports took over once the 1950 World Cup tournament got under way, and Brazilians of all walks of life prepared for the party they would have when the home team won the trophy. The carnival had to be canceled, however, when Uruguay came from a goal behind in the deciding match to beat Brazil 2-1. That the final match was also the deciding match was sheer chance, for the competition had been organized around leagues, even for the final places. Sweden finished ahead of Spain in the final pool of four, and when the final match kicked off at the Maracanã on 16 July, Brazil needed only to draw to win the league, for it was one point ahead of Uruguay. In previous games Brazil had crushed Sweden 7-1 and Spain 6-1, so all its confidence in winning seemed justified, especially when it went a goal ahead in the deciding game. Uruguay was not to be overawed by its giant neighbors or by the din from the 200,000 spectators, however; it played with flawless passing to tie and then score the winner eleven minutes from the final whistle. The crowd at the Maracanã fell silent, the preparations for the party were put away, and the samba written especially for the celebration, "Brazil the Victors," was not used. It was not the end of Brazilian soccer, however, and after a lapse in 1954 Brazil went on to achieve the potential that was always there, waiting to be unlocked.

Brazil's defeat was a much bigger surprise than that of the Austrian Wunderteam in 1934, but the biggest upset in the 1950 tournament—indeed, the biggest upset in the history of professional sports—was England's 0-1 defeat by the United States. An equivalent upset would have been if a representative U.S. baseball team had been beaten by England. The England team at the 1950 World Cup included some of its greatest players ever; the team from the United States was one of the most makeshift outfits ever to take part in the World Cup. In the United States the event passed unnoticed, although in Europe it was greeted with disbelief, and in England itself the news provoked only an indifferent shrug that owed as much to insular arrogance as to a stiff upper lip. England learned nothing from 1950, and it was not until its defeat by the Hungarian "Golden Team" in 1953 and a further defeat at the World Cup in Switzerland the following year that the complacency of the one-time masters was jolted.

England lost to Eire in 1949, but that Irish team was made up of players who earned their living in the English leagues; it remained undefeated at home in matches against Continental opposition until 1953. Easy victories against Portugal, Belgium, the Netherlands, and Switzerland—or more to the point, against Italy in Milan in 1948 (4-0) in a game to celebrate the fiftieth anniversary of the Italian football association—seemed to show that all was well in the world of English soccer. England then survived a series of close shaves before the day of reckoning. Yugoslavia held it to a 2-2 draw at the end of 1950, and the following year Argentina came to help celebrate the Festival of Britain and held onto a 1-0 lead, only to concede two goals in the last eleven minutes—the players were welcomed back as heroes to Perón's Argentina. England was lucky not to lose in games against France and Austria in 1951 (both 2-2), and a "Rest of Europe" team (minus the Hungarians) in 1953 (4-4). For François Thébaud, writing in *Miroir-sprint*, it was not so much luck as biased refereeing that had preserved the English record, and this he saw as the only obstacle to a Hungarian victory in its match at Wembley on 25 November 1953. England was outclassed 3-6 in a breathtaking

display of football, and to show it was no flash in the pan, the
"Mighty Magyars" inflicted an even more decisive victory in Budapest the following May: 7-1. The manner of England's defeat was one
thing; that it came from a team from a communist nation was another.
The tensions of the cold war, although more in evidence at the Olympics, where the two rival superpowers confronted each other from
1952, were felt as well in soccer, an area where U.S. influence was
irrelevant.

The Soviet Union never made any pretensions about sports being
merely a harmless pursuit for purely personal pleasure, and from the
start its soccer teams were organized into workers' clubs and given
more suitably proletarian names, glorifying the pillars of the new
society. Spartak represented the members of the producers' coopera-
tives; Torpedo, the automobile workers; and Locomotiv, the railway
workers. The Central Army Club and Wings of the Soviet were the
sports sections of the armed forces. These clubs encompassed many
sports, and their various facilities were open to the public throughout the week, even the stadiums, as long as the visitors kept off the
sacred turf. The Spartaks and Dinamos in Moscow and Leningrad,
as well as in Kiev and Tbilisi, produced famous ice hockey and volleyball teams, but they have more often been associated with soccer.
Soccer matches between Moscow Spartak and Moscow Dinamo developed into highly charged affairs, with Dinamo being the team of
the secret police and backed by the state.

Soccer's popularity survived the civil and foreign wars that accompanied the Bolshevik accession to power between 1917 and 1920, and
the new regime used it to help to create a nation out of the multieth-
nic states that made up the Soviet Union. It was also used, more ten-
tatively, to spread the virtues of the regime abroad. Before the 1952
Olympics the Soviet national team barely crossed the frontiers, getting only as far as Turkey in 1924 and 1925, where it had easy victories. Club teams and city selects occasionally played further afield,
usually against workers' teams, but they did not play against a professional team until 1934, when a Moscow select played Zidenice,
then heading the Czech league. It lost 2-3. In the partial glasnost of
the Popular Front period inaugurated in 1934, the Soviets sent a soccer team to take part in the Spartakiad held in Paris instead of Moscow in August of that year, beating Norway in the final before a crowd
estimated at 50,000. In September 1935 a Ukrainian team beat Red
Star, a professional team from the working-class district of Saint-

Denis, 6-1, and in January 1936 a Moscow select lost narrowly (1-2) to the very bourgeois Racing Club of Paris in 1936. Despite the loss, the local communists were delighted at the performance of the workers' team.

That game also brought about a change that the game's popularity had long called for, and in 1936 the first truly national Soviet league was established, with clubs instead of cities making up the teams. Tough times still lay ahead, not to mention the periodic purges, and Stalin's call for a "more joyous life" sounded even then rather sick; the worst days were over, however, and soccer spread even further throughout the vast empire. Players were urged to attend cultural classes, study Marxism-Leninism, and follow the example of their great leader, thus setting an example to the hundreds of thousands who followed their exploits. Whatever the players or the public thought of such sanctimonious humbug—and it seems to have done little to improve manners on the field or off it—soccer remained freer than any other cultural form from the prescriptions of Soviet taste. Unlike theater, literature, art, or cinema, it was played without a script, a free and unfettered celebration of spontaneity acted out in stadiums where people came not to be educated but to talk openly and indulge their feelings in a way denied them in daily life. In the late 1940s, in the time of the cultural repression associated with Andrey Aleksandrovich Zdhanov, when soccer itself became suspect for its bourgeois values and foreign influences, it was even more seen as an island of freedom. This, combined with the relief that came with the end of the war, led to even greater numbers coming to watch soccer. Other sports shared in this boom, but hockey remained a long way behind, with basketball the next most popular sport.

Although the spectators and most of the players could use soccer as a politics-free zone, the game as a whole remained tied to the regime. Spartak never recovered from the deportation of the Starostin brothers, and Moscow Dinamo suffered from the purge that followed soon after its return from the 1945 tour, allowing the Central Army team (ZDKA) to come to the fore. It was said that this team represented the Soviet Union in soccer when it first entered the Olympic Games in 1952, only to be eliminated in the first round after a preliminary victory against Bulgaria. This was no ordinary defeat, whether viewed from a sports or a political point of view. A few years before it Yugoslavia had fallen under the anathema of Stalin for Tito's refusal to follow the dictates of Moscow. One of the first sports-related victims of this sectarian squabble was the French communist newspaper *Sports,* a loyal Stalinist organ, which refused to make any mention of the Yugoslavia versus France World Cup qualifying matches of 1949 and as a result lost most of its readers. The game that eliminated the Soviets from the Helsinki Olympics was one of the strangest matches in the history of the game. Shortly after halftime the Yugoslavs were up 5-1, and with fifteen minutes to go reporters who had already completed their accounts of the game were deserting the press box. One of those who stayed behind was French reporter Jacques de Ryswick, who was also a radio commentator for Radio Luxembourg. An Italian colleague told him with more prejudice than knowledge that "these Russians always hide something," and a Polish colleague warned that the Soviets were inexhaustible. Perhaps they were, for with the score at 5-1, only a quarter of an hour remaining, and the Italian reporter's headline already telling his readers how the light cavalry of the Yugoslavs had smashed the Soviet steamroller, the Soviets powered on relentlessly to score four goals before the final whistle. It was not enough, however. No more goals were scored in extra-time, and Yugoslavia won the replay 3-1.

Yugoslavia went on to lose in the final to Hungary, and the Soviet team went home to an interrogation about being agents of Tito. The coach, Boris Arkadyev, was sacked for political incompetence, and one of the players, Konstantin Beskov, a star of the 1945 tour and later awarded the Order of Lenin in 1985 for services to sport, was suspended for a year for "irresponsible play and cowardly conduct in a match." As Robert Edelman has shown, however, too much has been made of the "team of the lieutenants" being the Central Army team playing to the orders of the hierarchy, and in line with his general argument that the conduct of soccer in the Soviet Union was not so terribly different from that in other countries, he claims that much of the furor was based on the myth and rumor that sports fans love to propagate. The problem was that the Soviet team had too many veterans in the forward line; these older players took longer to recover from the hard-won draw and the full training session forced on them in the one day before the replay.

Stalin had no interest in soccer and had astonished everyone back in 1936 when he not only stayed awake during an exhibition game played in Red Square in his honor but wanted to see it go beyond its allotted thirty minutes. The game was played between two Spartak teams after Dinamo withdrew, with prearranged moves and an agreed on 4-3 score in the hope that this feast of goals would help retain the Great Leader's interest. Stalin was still not won over to the game, preferring American gangster movies, but his son, Vasillii, was a soccer fanatic. He had a special interest in the Air Force team, which he built up in the late 1940s and to which he drafted some of the players disgraced in the Olympic fiasco. In 1948 he had even brought Nikolai Starostin back from exile under cover to coach the Air Force team, but Beria, whom he loathed as much as Beria loathed him, eventually had Starostin arrested leaving Stalin's house. He was sent to Central Asia, where he coached a second division team until his return in 1955. Stalin was dead by then, and although his spirit lived on in the crushing of the Hungarian uprising in 1956, the regime had opened up to the sporting world. In that same year at the Melbourne Olympics in 1956 the Soviets beat Yugoslavia by the game's only goal to win the gold medal before 100,000 spectators. (The Australian public had not suddenly discovered soccer, nor had it taken an unusual interest in communist sporting progress; the soccer final merely coincided with the closing ceremony.)

---

Hungary's victory at the 1952 Olympics announced to the soccer world that the "Golden Team," one of the greatest in the history of the game, had arrived. Between 1950 and 1956 it played forty-six international matches, lost only one, and scored 210 goals. It was the brainchild of the minister for sport, organized by Gustav Sebes, and built around the club team Honved ("Defense of the Nation"), formerly Kispest, the earlier name taken from a suburb of Budapest. As with teams in other communist countries, both Honved and the national team were nominally amateur, with the country's best players working in government sinecures so that they could practice whenever they wanted. Unlike other communist regimes, the Hungarians allowed the talent they inherited to flower without hindrance, and as the genius of the team, Ferenc Puskas, was quick to remind them, party hacks could be found behind any desk, whereas there was only one of him.

In most Communist countries Olympic success took precedence over soccer, where state interference, in any case, acted more often as a blight than as an incentive. Czechoslovakia never regained its glory days, although under the inspiration of Josef Masopust it placed second in the 1962 World Cup. Poland placed third in 1972, but generally the Soviet bloc countries found it easier to achieve success in track and field, for the state, through scientific selection at birth, rigorous testing in infancy, ruthless exploitation in young adulthood, and performance-enhancing drugs, could produce freak athletes in those sports more easily than it could star soccer players. Above all in East Germany soccer played second fiddle to the

regime's demonic pursuit of Olympic gold. In team games communist philosophy decreed that individual skills and spontaneity, the
essence of soccer, be submerged in the collective: in Czechoslovakia "bourgeois" teams like Sparta and Slavia suffered at the expense
of the new Army team, Dukla, and had to undergo political name
changes: Slavia became Dinamo Prague and Sparta became Spartak
Sokolova. In Bulgaria Levski Sofia had to give up the name honor-
ing its national hero in the war against the Turks to become the more
mundane Dinamo Sofia. As with other teams in other ideologies, the
fans did not take kindly to this violation of sacred traditions and
persisted in using the old names. By the 1960s most communist
states had given in to popular pressure and restored the old names.
In Romania, where Nicolae Ceauşescu ruled less as a communist
than as a self-obsessed monomaniac, soccer teams became his personal playthings. In the Soviet Union success in soccer on the international stage never matched the enthusiasm with which it was followed at the domestic level—when the Soviet team was eliminated
from the 1970 World Cup *Izvestia* received 300,000 letters, which
it followed up with a month of argument, recrimination, and suggestions. In addition to being constrained by the priorities of the
Soviet hierarchy, the soccer season was limited by the hostile climate,
which did not coincide with the peak competition time in Europe.
And unlike established soccer powers such as Czechoslovakia and
Hungary, the Soviet Union did not have a tradition of international
competition on which to build.

The one soccer nation to prosper under communism was Hungary. There the main victim of the communists was Ferencvaros, whose
antisemitism in the 1930s had won it the favor of the Hungarian fascists and their Nazi allies; for this tainted past its best players were
redistributed to Honved and the national team. Even in Hungary, the
great days of the past were never to return after the Golden Team
broke up in 1956. Before then, however, Hungary set the soccer world
agog.

Hungary's success was based on the country's sports resources
being channeled into Honved and the national team, which often
practiced against weak opposition. Other clubs lost their best players to Honved, and the national team was made up of a regular squad
of twenty to twenty-two players who did not have to fear that they
would be dropped for any temporary loss of form. Tactics were thus
perfected around the particular skills of a group of players of exceptional talent: above all Ferenc Puskas, but also Sandor Kocsis, Zoltan
Czibor, and Nandor Hidegkuti. These players received material re-

wards meager even by the standards of the 1950s, but they were compensated by the benevolence of the regime and the acclaim of the public, to which they returned as conquering heroes after their many victories. In November 1953, as Puskas and company lined up in preparation for the systematic humiliation of the undefeated English at Wembley, their every move was followed on radio by the whole of Hungary, whose streets were deserted for the ninety minutes of the game.

The regime equated the heroes of the soccer field to the heroes of more prosaic occupations. Puskas appeared in newsreels promising "future glories" and in turn had the thrill of two "Kossuth prize–winning Stakhanovites" (workers especially honored for their output) conveying the affection of the people and congratulating him and the team on their "unforgettable achievement" and "heroic deed." Hidegkuti's mother was selected from various groups of family members shown listening to the radio broadcast to express her pride in their achievement. Her comments were preceded by the reminder that she was "a Stakhanovite forewoman at the Ujlak Brickworks." Prior to the game members of the national team had been seen helping to build the Nepstadion (People's Stadium) with other voluntary labor, and hardly had the final whistle blown when stamps celebrating its completion were overprinted with the date, venue, and score of the Wembley game.

Hungary went to Switzerland in 1954 as the runaway favorite to win the World Cup, as had Brazil in 1950. Instead it lost 2-3 in the final to Germany, which it had beaten 8-3 in a preliminary round. This defeat had been deliberately planned by Sepp Herberger, the German coach, who took advantage of the weird qualifying arrangements—one of which was that goal difference would not be used to separate teams tied on points—to field a virtual reserve team against Hungary, knowing that Germany could lose by a large margin and still qualify for the elimination games by beating Turkey and South Korea, which he rightly judged to be pushovers. In this way Herberger gave away none of his strategies, and more to the point, Puskas was eliminated from the game with a nasty tackle. Puskas returned for the final, although still injured, but an overconfident Hungary surrendered an early 2-0 lead to lose 2-3, the Germans being helped by some good fortune and a bad off-side decision that deprived Puskas and Hungary of a clear tying goal in the closing stages. Luciano Serra, in his history of the game (*Storia del calcio*), refers to the cloud that hung over the German victory in a political climate that "decreed at all cost that no communist nation win" and the rumors of drugs that the

Germans were said to have taken. Drugs can never guarantee success to a soccer player, however, and as the Germans had shown earlier, there were more direct ways of ensuring victory. As for the crucial linesman's decision, this was not the only occasion in which a British official was embroiled in controversy, even where politics were irrelevant.

Germany's road to the final had been fairly simple, qualifying for Switzerland by defeating the Saar (not yet reunified with Germany) and Norway and then placing second in its pool with Hungary, which went straight to the finals when Poland withdrew. In the straight knock-out tournament, Hungary beat Brazil 4-2 in a quarterfinal that began with superb play but degenerated, under English referee Arthur Ellis, into a brawl reminiscent of that at Bordeaux in 1938—this one was entitled the "Battle of Berne." In the semifinal Hungary beat Uruguay 4-2 after extra-time in what was claimed to be the finest exhibition of soccer ever played. Germany beat Yugoslavia 2-0, and its 6-1 win against Austria in the semifinal was claimed with historical hyperbole to be Germany's biggest victory over Austria since the battle of Königgrätz (in 1866).

England and Scotland went to Switzerland hoping that their history might carry them through. Scotland lost its first home game to Continental opposition against Austria in 1950, and whatever reputation it had built up over the years was shattered as it was again beaten, first by Austria, 0-1, and then by Uruguay, 0-7. The British associations still did not take the World Cup seriously, and Scotland went to Switzerland without its Rangers players because the club thought that its summer tour of the United States was more important. England fared better but was no match for the superb Uruguay team that eliminated it in the quarterfinal (2-4).

The Hungarians were hardly disgraced by their defeat in the final, but they had to return from Switzerland in secret to avoid their disappointed fans, who called for the death of Sebes. The government had to cancel the issue of stamps it had prepared proclaiming Hungary World Champions, but before long Hungary and Honved took up where they had left off. It all came to an end in October 1956, when the tanks of the Warsaw Pact countries crushed the dreams of a Hungary free from Soviet domination. The tanks arrived while Honved was out of the country for a European Cup game against Atlético Bilbao. The players considered staying abroad, but most of them had families and eventually went home. Before they did so, they played the second leg of their home-and-away European Cup match in Brussels, where they came within an inch of victory in a display of football that turned the jeers of the anticommunist crowd into applause.

Hungary's glory days in soccer were over. Replacing Hungary on the international stage was Brazil, which won the 1958 World Cup in Sweden, a world championship previously denied it, at least in part, by its temperamental weakness: the indiscipline shown in 1938 and 1954 and made manifest at the Olympic Games in 1952, when in a game against Germany the players spent as much time trying to kick the opponents as they did trying to kick the ball and dissolved in tears when they were defeated. Now that was all behind them, and although they had a staff psychiatrist who did not disdain a bit of voodoo, their success rested firmly on a constellation of stars who were intent on playing soccer.

The worst incidents in the 1958 World Cup were comparatively minor. Sweden qualified for the final with a 3-1 win over Germany that owed a great deal to the referee. One goal was scored after blatant ball handling, and Germany's Erich Juskowiak was ejected for retaliating after deliberate provocation by Kurt Hamrin of Sweden, whose agonies suddenly disappeared when his opponent was expelled. Today he would have followed Juskowiak. Off the field the Swedish supporters behaved in a manner that many found obnoxious, a behavior that had been noticed at games in the 1930s but was passed over since the Swedes' numbers were so small. The Germans in particular were subjected to a barrage of hatred. None of this was overlooked in Germany, where restaurants removed Swedish dishes from their menus and cars with Swedish license plates were refused service. It was a defeat that many Germans considered a greater injustice than that still to come in 1966.

The Swedish team's success was due largely to the work of George Raynor, who had performed minor miracles in the late 1940s, his team winning the 1948 Olympics and placing third in Brazil in 1950. Constantly losing its best players to the professional countries, especially Italy, Raynor's team failed in Finland in 1952, and Raynor went to look for a job in England. Not wanted there, he was finally lured to the big time in Italy before coming back to Sweden to prepare for the 1958 World Cup. Raynor was helped this time by the Swedish football association's decision to lift its ban on expatriate professionals, and it was with these aging stars from the Italian league that Sweden went on to lose 2-5 to Brazil in the final. Sweden opened the scoring, but this Brazilian team combined the individual ball skills with which it had become synonymous with teamwork and tactics. It also had the seventeen-year-old Edson Arantes do Nascimento, about to be deified under the name of Pelé, as well as other stars such as Manoel Francisco dos Santos, better known as Garrincha (the "little bird"), and the veteran Valdir Pereira ("Didi"). All three were said to have had to overcome racial prejudice in some form or another to win their places, and it was the black players who were blamed for the 1-2 loss to Uruguay in the 1950 World Cup, particularly the goalkeeper, Moacir Barbosa. But Brazilian soccer, however paternal, was losing its racism, and even Fluminense was by then playing blacks. So it was that Brazil set out to startle the world with teams of unsurpassable quality through to the 1970s, teams that exhibited the best possibilities of a multiracial society. Unfortunately, they were also a cover for social injustice and political opportunism.

Third place in the 1958 World Cup went to France, which beat Germany 6-3 in the play-off. France proceeded to this stage with unprecedented expressions of support from the French public. Sales of television sets broke all records, thousands of telegrams and sacks full of postcards arrived at the team's training quarters, and *L'Equipe* arranged a special plane to take the players' wives and families to the semifinal against Brazil (a perhaps infelicitous gesture, for it was said to have distracted the players). Until then France's soccer stars had been in the shadow of its cyclists and boxers, for although soccer was the most popular game, most of its best players were foreigners or of foreign origins. Such was the case with the dual strike force at the World Cup in Sweden: Raymond Kopa (born Kopazewski) was the son of a Polish miner, and Just Fontaine, whose thirteen goals in the finals are still a World Cup record for an individual, was Moroccan. Supported by others such as Roger Piantoni, the French team played exciting soccer of which any nation would have been proud. France would reach even higher pinnacles under Michel Platini in the early 1980s.

The 1958 World Cup finals were the only ones in which all four British football associations took part. Scotland was as poor as it was in 1954, but Northern Ireland and Wales played well enough to reach the quarterfinals. The Irish team had some players of rare quality, and some of its biggest difficulties in getting to Sweden had nothing to do with their play. The upholders of the Sabbath tried to stop the team taking part in a tournament where it might have to play on a Sunday, and then, in a game against Italy that was declared a friendly when fog prevented the official referee from getting to the game, its fans went berserk in Belfast (yet another "battle of"). The authorities were more lenient about such matters in those days, and so there was no suggestion of the team being banned from the competition. Wales might have gone even further than it did had it not lost its star player, the "gentle giant" John Charles, through injury. England failed to make the knock-out stage, defeated by the Soviet Union in a play-off, but it played well and deserved some sympathy. Like Italy at the 1950 World Cup, England had lost a clutch of its best players earlier in the year when a plane returning Manchester United's "Busby Babes" from a European Cup game in Belgrade failed to take off at a snow-covered Munich airport and crashed into a house at the end of the runway. Eight players died, including Duncan Edwards, the most promising youngster of his generation, and several were injured. Matt Busby, who was himself brought close to death as a result of the crash, rebuilt a new team of stars, but it took him a few years to mold them into a match-winning unit.

Middle Eastern politics made their first serious entry into the competition when Indonesia, Egypt, and Sudan refused to play against Israel in the preliminary rounds. It looked as if Israel would qualify without playing a game, but FIFA decided that Israel would have to play one of the teams that had lost, and so Wales qualified. Uruguay was offered the chance to play Israel but dismissed this as a "gift." Uruguay was in a sense represented by one of its best players ever, Juan Schiaffino, the star of the 1950 and 1954 World Cups, but he was now in Italy's colors. Also playing in Italian shirts were the Argentines who had excelled in the previous year's South America Cup in Lima: Humberto Dionisio Maschio, Antonio Valentin Angelillo, and Enrique Omar Sivori, the "angels with dirty faces." Thus weakened, Argentina came home to a hostile reception, and the plane returning the players had to go straight to the hangar to avoid any incidents.

––––––––

Before the 1960s international matches were the highlight of the soccer calendar, but from the mid-1950s, with the spread of floodlights, improvements in air travel, and advances in television, new European club competitions were inaugurated and thereafter continued to grow in popularity. It was through the first of these, the European Cup, that a team emerged that showed itself worthy to take its place alongside the great club teams of the past: Argentina's River Plate and Italy's Torino of the 1940s and Hungary's Honved of the early 1950s. Réal Madrid, resplendent in all-white uniforms innocent of any markings but the player's number on the back of the jersey, won the first five championships in the European Cup. It was followed by Portugal's Benfica, under the guidance of Bela Guttmann, thus showing that the Iberian countries had finally arrived on the big stage. Both Spain and Portugal were governed by a form of clerical fascism, but whereas Salazar did not concern himself with any particular soccer team, Franco used the popularity of soccer as an instrument in his Castilian centralism.

Réal Madrid was formed in 1902, but the great team of the 1950s was begun at the end of the Spanish civil war and fashioned in the 1940s. Santiago Bernabéu was the architect of the team, as he was of the magnificent stadium that today bears his name. He was trapped in Madrid when the civil war broke out in 1936 but eventually escaped and joined Franco, in whose service he won a military medal. Franco, who shared Bernabéu's love of soccer, also rewarded Bernabéu by helping his friend when he took over as president of Réal Madrid in 1943, the club Bernabéu had played and worked for in various capacities throughout most of his life. Franco sought through soccer to crush the provincial challenge of the Catalans and the Basques, whose clubs had until then dominated Spanish soccer.

Under Bernabéu Réal pushed its rivals into the background, a success that began when Bernabéu secured the services of Alfredo Di Stéfano in 1953. This followed the Argentine's contract dispute in which River Plate, his original club, and Los Millonarios of Colombia, which had poached him, both claimed rights over his signature. Barcelona was also interested in the South American, but some pressure from Franco helped Réal gain his services. He was followed by others who, if not quite in the genius class, were close to it: Francisco "Paco" Gento from the Spanish club Santander and Hector Rial, an Argentine of Spanish origins who had also gone to Colombia. Most important, Bernabéu secured the services of Ferenc Puskas. After the 1956 Soviet invasion of Hungary, Puskas, who was joined by his wife, refused to go back to Hungary and with others of the Honved team went on a money-raising tour of South America. Before signing for Réal Madrid, Puskas had to fulfill the FIFA regulation that he stay out of soccer for a year, and by then Réal had won two European championships. It was the partnership of the two aging geniuses that lent a special flavor to the next three championships, the last of which was the incomparable final at Hampden Park, Glasgow, where a balding Di Stéfano and a stocky Puskas, both over thirty, shared seven goals between them against an Eintracht Frankfurt team that scored three. So enraptured were the 127,000 spectators that they refused to leave their places for a quarter of an hour after the game had finished, calling on Réal to take a bow.

Réal's main rival was Barcelona, which went on to build a new stadium, the Nou Camp, that might not have surpassed the Bernabéu in elegance but easily did in size and atmosphere: today it is regularly filled to its capacity of over 100,000. Despite defeat in the civil war, and despite the pressures from Franco, the Basque and Catalan teams refused to give up their regional identity. Athletic Bilbao was forced to change its name to Atlético, and Sporting Gijon switched to Deportivo, while Barcelona became "Club de Fútbol" instead of "Fútbol Club." But changing the names did not change the loyalties. Réal Sociedad continued to play only Basque players, and although the capital's Basque team, Atlético Madrid, retained its Spanish name after the death of Franco in 1975, Bilbao changed back to its original name. Barcelona and Bilbao in particular were confirmed as the champions of regional separatism, and throughout Franco's regime their supporters used the anonymity of the crowd at soccer matches to flout Franco's laws: to speak their own language, fly their own colors, and insult the dictatorship in safety. In this way their aims for cultural autonomy were kept alive despite the bans. In more general terms, Franco made his oppression more benign by feeding the impoverished peasants and workers a diet of soccer to keep their minds off their misery, particularly on May Day, the worker's annual day of celebration, when the state-run television channels played soccer from South America nonstop.

In South America itself the use of soccer as an arm of domestic policy was widespread among the dictators who ruled that continent, such as the generals in Brazil and Onganía of Argentina in the late 1960s; Pinochet in Chile in the 1970s and Stroessner in Paraguay bailed out financially troubled teams or actively assisted the national team, while the military leaders who came to power in Uruguay after 1973 saw it as propitious to help financially troubled Peñarol and encourage the national team. When Brazil's star player, Garrincha, was ejected in a semifinal game against the home nation at the 1962 World Cup in Chile, Brazil's prime minister, Tancredo Neves, dispatched an urgent telegram to FIFA secretary Stanley Rous asking that his misdemeanor be overlooked. In those days expulsion was not followed by an automatic suspension. Garrincha played in the final, and Brazil's shaky democracy lasted another two years.

Franco's involvement in Spanish soccer was never as direct as that of his soulmates in South America. He got off to a bad start on the international scene when he refused entry to the Soviet team to play Spain in the 1960 European Nations' Cup. The Soviets trumpeted their derision at the cowardice of the Fascists, but Franco soon re-covered his political nous and sports instincts. He persuaded FIFA to have the finals of the next edition played in Spain, and as fate would have it, Spain met the USSR in the final on 21 June 1964. The poten-tial embarrassment of Franco having to give the trophy to the Soviet captain (it was bad enough when Barcelona won the Franco Cup, and he had to present it to the jeers of the Catalans) was too much for some of his assistants, who wanted to dope the opposition. Such as-sistance proved unnecessary, however; Spain won 2-1, and the Span-ish press compared the soccer triumph to the growing power of the state that had been born out of the defeat of communism and its fel-low travelers in the 1930s.

The success of the Spanish national team was not sustained, how-ever, and did not match that of the club teams in Europe. Part of this was because so many of its star players were foreigners (although some took out Spanish citizenship, as Di Stéfano and Puskas did). The Hungarian-born Czech Ladislao Kubala earned a cap for a third coun-try when he played for Spain. Portugal also used foreign imports to ensure success, but they came mainly from its colonies, and players like Mario Coluña and Eusébio da Silva Ferreira from Mozambique were eligible for the national team. Portugal also automatically al-lowed Brazilians to play for Portugal, but by the 1990s there were so many young Brazilians flocking to play in the Portuguese leagues that restrictions had to be introduced. The most serious hindrance to Spain's international success under Franco was the unwillingness of Catalans and Basques to associate themselves with what they saw as a Castilian national team. They were more likely to support the op-position, a feeling that has lingered through until today.

In the late 1950s the success of the new European club competi-tions gave new life to the previously considered idea of a European superleague. There have been "superleagues" in soccer since 1888, for this is what the Football League was. In Europe the first super-league was the Mitropa, or Central European, Cup, founded by Hugo Meisl in 1927. Like the Football League, it was the natural extension of the top teams' preference for playing one another across borders rather than with the weak teams in their own leagues. There were calls to extend the Mitropa to a genuine European cup or league in the 1930s, but not with much hope that the British associations would be willing to take part. The English journalist Capel Kirby looked forward to the days when floodlights would allow games to be played regardless of the time of day and planes would take teams to a match and back without the need for an overnight stop. He also foresaw the use of artificial turf and private boxes. Herbert Chapman supported a European league as a big advance on "the holiday tours that England and Scotland have undertaken in the past" and warned that if they did not fall in with such a scheme, they would be left behind in the game's development. In France the journalist and former player Gabriel Hanot raised the idea of a European knock-out cup competition as the precursor to a full-scale league; he was enthusiastically supported by the wealthy president of Racing-Club de Paris, Jean-Bernard Lévy, a commercially oriented progressive who was behind the introduction of professionalism in France.

In 1949 the Latin Cup was introduced, the competition including the top teams in France, Italy, Spain, and Portugal, but it was barely known outside these countries. Scottish and English club teams had acquitted themselves well on the Continent, but they were constantly criticized for not taking these games seriously. This changed drastically beginning in the mid-1950s, when the long-nourished hopes for serious European competitions took shape in three distinct forms: a knock-out competition for league champions, one for cup winners, and another for those who had a "near-miss." All these competitions were under the jurisdiction of the first European soccer federation, founded in 1954, the Union Européenne de Football Association (UEFA), and none of them owed much to the British.

Like the World Cup and FIFA, the European, or Champions, Cup was of French inspiration. Its main promoter was Gabriel Hanot, still active as a football journalist with *L'Equipe* and its offshoot, *France Football*. The French were stung into action when England's Wolverhampton Wanderers beat Honved 3-2 in the mud of Molineux on 13 December 1954 and the English tabloids declared the team to be the champion of the world. Hanot and *L'Equipe* called for a competition to give substance to such claims. At first UEFA showed little interest, but Hanot and *L'Equipe* went ahead and received the support of some of Europe's biggest teams. Unable to ignore the popularity of the idea, UEFA took on the organization of what was initially called the European Champion Clubs Cup, contested by sixteen clubs in the 1955–56 season.

The first competition was an invitational tournament, but thereafter it was played between the league champions of each of the nations belonging to UEFA on a knock-out system based on two matches home and away, except for the final, which was held at a predetermined venue. Until recently, and apart from the first year, it has scarcely varied: a premium on away goals was introduced in 1967, and penalty shoot-outs replaced the coin toss to decide tied matches from 1970. It is now a seeded league competition, getting ever closer to a straight European league. In the beginning the Football League, as stuffy as the FA and even more arrogant in regard to Europe, would not allow Chelsea to take part in the first competition, but the Scottish League did permit Hibernian to represent Scotland. Matt Busby told the directors of Manchester United to ignore the League when they were invited to take part in the second competition.

The first years of the competition were dominated by the Latins, Réal Madrid and Portugal's Benfica being followed by the Italian clubs AC Milan (1963) and Inter-Milan (1964, 1965) and then Réal Madrid in 1966. The following year, however, Glasgow Celtic outclassed the millionaires of Inter-Milan in Lisbon, the first British club to win; all its players were Scottish born, and only one of them cost the team more than a few thousand pounds. Manchester United won in 1968, and then came the Dutch and Germans with their "total" football. Rotterdam's Feyenoord beat Celtic in 1970, then Ajax of Amsterdam, playing under Johann Cruyff and with other stars close to his class, won the next three, a feat equaled by Bayern Munich under Franz Beckenbauer between 1974 and 1976. English clubs then dominated until they were banned after the Heysel disaster of 1985.

The European Cup-Winners' Cup, for the winners of the domestic cup competitions, received a lukewarm response when it was suggested in 1958, many Continental nations being less enamored of the vagaries of such competitions. The first occasion was in 1960, and soon it caught on, while the romance of the rabbits who had triumphed in some domestic competitions carried on into Europe, most notably the Welsh clubs Cardiff City and Bangor, which gave a few of the big boys a fright in the 1960s. In the third European competition, the UEFA Cup, the part-time amateurs of Trelleborg from Sweden eliminated Blackburn Rovers in 1994, at the same time as Skonto Riga from lowly Latvia beat Scotland's Aberdeen.

The UEFA Cup grew out of the Inter-City Fairs Cup, a competition not between clubs but between cities that regularly held industrial or trade fairs. From 1960 the competition was held annually, and club teams replaced teams representing cities. In 1971 UEFA took over and donated a new trophy known as the UEFA Cup. The games are played between the top teams from the various European leagues that were neither champions nor cup winners, each country being allowed places according to a calculation of the country's success in previous competitions; thus, some countries can supply four teams, some three, and others two or one. Teams proceed as in the other competitions, on the aggregate score of home and away games, until the final, which unlike the other competitions is also played on a two-leg home-and-away basis.

The European Football Championship, or Nations Cup, is a national competition played over two years following the World Cup. It was an early idea of UEFA, which named the trophy after Henri Delaunay, the first secretary of UEFA and a driving force behind the organization of French soccer since its inception. Begun in 1958 without the participation of some of the leading nations, it suffers from being played in the shadows not only of the World Cup but of the European Cup. It did not fire the imagination before the 1970s, and although this period was dominated by powerhouse soccer forces like West Germany and Italy, in the 1980s small nations like Denmark and Belgium won success with some brilliant soccer.

The ultimate logic of these competitions is a world competition for clubs, either as a league or a knock-out competition. Many of the technical problems in enacting such an idea have been overcome, but the unofficial World Club championship started in 1960 suggests that there are still other problems to solve. The idea of this competition was to have European champions play their South American equivalents, the winners of the Copa Libertadores, which was started that year. In South America the national competition begun in 1916 had enjoyed reasonable success, but attempts to establish a club competition on a continental basis had been plagued with a variety of problems. With the prospect of a game against the European champions, however, the Copa Libertadores soon established itself as a worthwhile competition. Unfortunately, the encounters between the European and South American champions have been marked by some dreadful displays of violence and poor sportsmanship. Celtic played Argentina's Racing in 1967, and its third game, played in Montevideo after home and away stalemates, ended in mayhem, but it was Estudiantes de la Plata that set new standards for foul play over the next three years, adopting the tactic of deliberately inciting the opposition to retaliate. Their performance against Milan in 1969 was so bad that the Argentine president, General Onganía, who was watching the game on television, ordered severe penalties against the team and its players. European teams found reasons not to travel to South America, and the competition was saved only when it was taken up by the Japanese firm Toyota. Since 1980 it has been played in Tokyo before sellout crowds.

# Britain and the Brash New World: Soccer in the Sixties

The 1960s were a good time to be English, as the Beatles, the Rolling Stones, and other pop groups swept the world with their music and long hair, penetrating even the American pop market, while Carnaby Street encapsulated the spirit of swinging London, which came to rival Paris as the European center of the youth culture. Whether you were young or old and liked pop music or did not, however, if you were English, you knew that the country was back in its proper place when Bobby Moore held aloft the World Cup at Wembley Stadium in 1966 before nearly 100,000 fans and the millions watching on television. Despite complaints about the favoritism that allowed England to play all its preliminary matches at Wembley, and the hotly disputed third goal, England deserved its 4-2 victory over Germany in the final. It dominated the extra-time period, which Germany had gained only by the good fortune of a late tying goal following a doubtful free kick. The success on the field reflected the winds of change that blew through that decade, including the dusty corridors of power in English soccer. The result was the adoption of practices that had long been standard in most countries on the Continent.

England's World Cup–winning team of 1966 was the first to be groomed under a manager who was given the time and authority to build a national eleven, with the cooperation of the league teams from which he had to choose his players and without the hindrance of the FA. The all-powerful manager had been a familiar figure on the Continent for a long time, but for the English this had to wait for the revolution that took English soccer out of its paternalistic Protestantism and delivered it to the cold blasts of newer and more open markets.

The revolution began in the late 1950s with a series of changes off the field when a new breed of younger men took over from the dinosaurs directing the Football League, and professional players finally revolted against the contracts that bound them like serfs to their employers. For the British clubs to catch up with their opponents on the field, there had to be changes off it, and so they entered the brash new world of Continental football.

Heading the new order at the Football League was Alan Hardaker from Hull in Yorkshire, the son of a Methodist mother and a Liberal, rugby-playing father. Hardaker took over as secretary of the League in 1957 after suffering six years of suffocating boredom under the antiquated authoritarianism of Fred Howarth. Hardaker immediately launched plans for modernization, assisted by the younger Joe Richards, who replaced Arthur Oakley as president. The new order was coming, and although its resistance to players' demands showed an unbroken attachment to the past, in the coming world of easy money it was prepared to profit from sources that its predecessors had deemed tainted. As Hardaker himself said, "whenever I smelt money for the League I usually jumped straight in and let everybody know about it later."

The Football League, formed out of professionalism and never quite at home with the southern amateurs of the Football Association, nevertheless shared with the older body the essentially Protestant belief that soccer has a higher good than making money. Gambling was abhorrent, and sabbatarianism was accepted without question. The big teams were there to help the small, without whom they could not compete, and this was enshrined in the power structure of the League, where the lower clubs had inordinate power against those in the first division. Similarly, just as the best teams had their power curtailed, so star players were treated the same as their more pedestrian colleagues. This meant that teams regularly drawing large gates had to share power and some of their income with clubs struggling along in the lower divisions, and stars who regularly attracted thousands through the gate had to accept the same salary as their teammates. Clubs that paid above the stipulated limits were severely punished if found out, and indeed, this was the most frequent source of "corruption" to be found in British soccer.

When Hardaker came to power, he was determined to get the League out of its constantly parlous financial state, and to do so he set out to garner a full harvest of golden eggs from the pools, which in the 1950s had become the country's seventh-largest industry, employing 100,000 people. He initiated a successful court action, and on 13 May 1959 the pools companies were ordered to pay 0.5 percent of gross income to the English and Scottish leagues, with a minimum of £245,000 per annum. There was never any need to apply the minimum, for League income from this source burgeoned from year to year, not least when over the next two years it was discovered that countries throughout the world had been using the League's schedules.

Whereas some countries had pirated the British schedules, other countries used their own pools systems to earn income for the sole use of sports, most notably in the communist-bloc countries, where the entire income was in the hands of the state. The success of the all-conquering Magyars of the early 1950s was in part based on the return from the pools in Hungary, where 6,000 sports stadiums had been built since 1946 and all citizens were provided with free training, equipment, and health care. In Sweden, where the pools were based on British games, income had been used in the 1930s to start ambitious and successful welfare programs.

The willingness to accept "tainted" money was the beginning of an ideological watershed in British soccer, and it was not unrelated to events on the Continent. The League found itself with a windfall income from the pools and so embarked on some much needed expenditure on itself, not least a new headquarters, the need for which was driven home to Hardaker and Richards when they visited the luxurious and well-appointed Italian League headquarters in Milan in 1958. *The Times* suggested that the League set up its new quarters in Dover to be as near as possible to the Continent, "where most progressive ideas are to be found." In fact the League chose Lytham St. Annes, even further away than Preston. This maintained the traditional distance between the League and the FA—and left Hardaker with a convenient trip from home to work. Whatever the administrative distance between the two bodies, however, they were still morally bound in their opposition to soccer players rising above their station: this attitude entered a critical phase in 1960 when top professional players threatened to go on strike if their demands were not met.

Hardaker may have been prepared to jump in when he saw ways of making money for the League, but he was less than amused when players adopted the same attitude. In this regard he quickly fell back into the spiritual company of his predecessors and the men of the FA. From the earliest days some players had objected to their treatment as social inferiors, but usually to no avail. In 1921 Charles Buchan, while a member of the England team, refused to budge when asked by one of the FA officials to get out of what he saw as his own armchair at the hotel where they were staying. Another doughty fighter for players' rights, Jimmy Guthrie of Portsmouth, was equally incensed about discrimination against players. On one occasion, as he was on the way back across London to catch the train to Portsmouth after a game in the north, he saw two Portsmouth directors lined up for a cab; consequently, he ignored orders about taking the subway and took the players to Waterloo Station in taxis. Such social protest was not confined to England. In South America, as Tony Mason tells us, Argentine players who had just won the South American championships in Ecuador in late 1947 were expected to watch the bosses return earlier to enjoy the New Year holiday with their families. The players thought otherwise, and after an indignant protest players and bosses boarded the same plane.

---

Before pools money and television sponsorship, players were paid from the sixpences and shillings of those who passed through the gate or turnstile. There was a small amount of money to be made in advertising, and players could endorse commercial products, but before television this was not very lucrative. The alternative of players seeking a better future abroad was given wide publicity in 1950 with the threatened exodus to join the rebel league in Bogotá, but this promise turned out to be illusory, and in 1954 Colombia itself returned to the FIFA fold. Australia was banned in 1960 for playing rebel European professionals, but even that far outpost of third-world soccer could not live without FIFA contacts and ultimately made amends by repaying some of the outstanding transfer fees and returning to FIFA in 1963. For financially disgruntled players Italy offered the most lucrative contracts, and from the mid-1950s a few British soccer players looked seriously in that direction. Few, however, were prepared to put up with life in a foreign culture, and most failed to settle down.

British players' complaints about the restraints on their earning are as old as professionalism, but it was not until their eyes were opened to what was happening on the Continent that agitation for change gathered strength. Officials crushed threatened strikes or legal action before World War II, although there was further talk of a strike after it. On the eve of World War II there were rumblings of discontent and threats of "drastic action" that were put on hold during the war, only to reemerge as soon as it was over. Even during the war, when they were paid a pittance, players resented the way they were expected to forgo their rights while the clubs maintained a grip as tight as when they were providing full employment and full wages.

Despite the mammoth crowds of the postwar period, the League was usually successful in fobbing off the players' union, and by 1953 the only gain the players had made was a raise in the maximum and minimum wage, to £15 and £12 a week, respectively (£12 and £7.50 close season—the summer break, when no competitive games are played). By the late 1950s Britons were being told that they had never had it so good, and in material terms this was probably so. But some Continental countries were having it even better. By then ordinary workers in Britain were enjoying near full employment and earning more money than ever before, while in the entertainment industry stars were earning even bigger fortunes than usual. For the entertainers on the soccer field, however, the share of this expanding cake was getting smaller, and the average player was earning less in comparison not just with other entertainers but with ordinary workers. In some countries on the Continent, on the other hand, star soccer players received wages and treatment akin to those of pop stars.

Three individuals can be seen as metaphors for these changing times: Jimmy Guthrie, who carried out much of the spade work on behalf of the players but whose attitudes were rooted in the past; the demigod of football, Stanley Matthews, whose hand raised in favor of a strike if the players' demands were not met represented a crucial change in attitude; and Jimmy Hill, who brought most of the new demands to fruition and set himself on the proverbial path to fame and fortune.

Guthrie was one of the innumerable Scots playing in England in the 1930s, captain of the cup-winning Portsmouth team of 1939 and as hard on the field as he could be abrasive off it: he claimed that Matthews could easily be contained by what amounted to an early clogging (being kicked), and subtlety was never one of his virtues. As chairman of the players' union from 1947 to 1957, he antagonized those who paid his wages by refusing to abide by their resolutions, and his attempts to work through the press often rebounded on him, for public relations was not one of his strong points. As chairman of the players' union he was treated as a troublemaker by the directors and the officials, banned from their grounds, and branded as a communist because he spoke of "justice." He was very much at home in the immediate postwar climate, but when the Conservative party replaced the Labour party in 1951 and the increasing chills of the cold war were felt, his confrontationist approach and his talk of a "closed shop" in line with industrial unions did not go down well with soccer players who saw themselves as "upwardly mobile." At the annual general meeting of the players' union (shortly to be called the Professional Footballers' Association, or PFA) in 1958, he was expelled on the technicality that he was not a member of the Football Players' and Trainers' Union. That was the end of Guthrie and the beginning of a new career for Jimmy Hill, until then a staunch supporter of Guthrie.

Hill was as much at home in the changing circumstances of the late 1950s as Guthrie was out of his depth. Behind him lay a career as a professional with Brentford and Fulham; ahead lay an even brighter career as an innovative manager with Coventry City, a television presenter, and a sports promoter. A forceful and opinionated speaker who firmly believed in players' rights and had a gift for public relations, he was the ideal man to put the players' case before the media, which now included television. Of a middle-class background, he was somewhat contemptuous of soccer fans, whose ignorance of the game he deprecated, and he found their unwillingness to pay higher admission charges to help the players rather bad form. He was equally snobbish in his attitude to players, whose social graces he hoped to improve. Nevertheless, he did not flinch when faced by the League's intransigence and made it clear that professional soccer would come to a standstill if the maximum wage was not abolished and the transfer system not changed.

After Guthrie coined the term "soccer slave" back in the 1940s, several star players had mocked the term, usually in books whose ghostwriters had urged caution as regards the proper ideas that should be put before young readers. Some great players, such as Tommy Lawton (*Football Is My Business* [1946]), Peter Docherty (*Spotlight on Football* [1947]), and Charles Buchan (*A Lifetime in Football* [1955]), made no bones about most clubs' shabby treatment of players, but others, such as Billy Wright (*The World's My Football Pitch* [1953]), captain of the England team and one of the most popular players of the 1950s, claimed that players were lucky to get paid at all. His mawkish appeal that players be prepared to ask what they could do for the game rather than what the game could give them would later find an echo in somewhat more exalted political circumstances. Nat Lofthouse ridiculed the notion of soccer slaves in 1954 (*Goals Galore*), although his later biography (*"The Lion of Vienna"* [1989]) showed how poorly treated he was in the 1950s. Ronnie Clayton, another England captain, dismissed the talk of "serfs" in his book that came out in 1960, pointedly called *A Slave—to Soccer*. Unlike these star players, self-styled rebel Trevor Ford was no friend of the authorities, but the fiery Welshman was also a virulent anticommunist, out for himself and with no time for the union (*I Lead the Attack* [1957]). For such players the thought of a strike was anathema. It was in such circumstances that the appearance of Stanley Matthews (and Billy Wright) at a PFA meeting in Manchester in November 1960 to support strike action showed that discontent was at a dangerous level even among the most conservative and self-interested players.

The most famous name in football at this time, an age that boasted Di Stéfano, Puskas, and John Charles, was Stanley Matthews. By rights his career should have been over by the mid-1950s, for he was well into his thirties by then, but an inspired burst of brilliance in the closing minutes of the 1953 Challenge Cup final that turned what could have been Blackpool's 2-3 defeat by Bolton into a 4-3 victory, as well as some outstanding performances against Continental opposition after England's humiliations of 1953 and 1954, resuscitated a career that had begun in 1932 at the club level, when Matthews had just turned seventeen; two years later he played for England. It was no mere stroke of good fortune that the Maestro, a nonsmoker and nondrinker committed to a punishing physical fitness regime, could still turn out in professional competition after his fiftieth birthday. Matthews's commitment to his professional life was matched by a commitment to establishing his own security outside it, and it was to take up managership of a hotel he had bought in Blackpool that he left his native Stoke in 1947.

In 1938, when Matthews first asked for a transfer following a dispute over the payment of his benefit (a discretionary sum paid to some players for exceptional services), the whole of the Midlands district where he lived, known as the Potteries after its major industry, seemed to be engulfed in its greatest controversy since the abdication of the king two years previously. The bosses were on the same side as the workers on the issue, for production had been suffering, and a settlement was soon found. Its exact nature remains a secret, but it can easily be guessed, and the young star stayed in his hometown. When Matthews left Stoke for Blackpool in 1947, however, it was with the best wishes of the supporters, while the club consoled itself with the transfer fee and the knowledge that at the age of thirty-two Matthews was entering the veteran class. Moreover, the previous year a special appeal had resulted in 5,500 people donating £1,160 to Matthews—a long way short of the anticipated 20,000 people who were expected to give £5,000, but a vast sum of money nevertheless in a country that had just come out of a war in which many young men sacrificed more than six years of professional soccer. This in no way diminishes the reputation of a man whose sports mystique can be compared only to Don Bradman in cricket and perhaps Babe Ruth in baseball.

Matthews's entire career was spent with two clubs, Blackpool and Stoke. He ended his playing career where it began, with Stoke, repaying his transfer fee in the increased attendance at the first game on his return to his old club in 1961. He then repeated what he had done at the beginning of his career when he helped to take Stoke from the second division to the first. Despite all this Matthews was paid the same wages and incentives as other top players, although avenues to extra income were more open to him than to others: guest appearances, ghost-written books and articles, endorsements, and advertisements—the legitimate reward for a player of outstanding ability passing on his knowledge and inviting fans to share some of his experiences. Matthews was also prepared to give his name to a product that not only had nothing to do with sport but went against all that he stood for: cigarettes. He also advertised the advantages of the free enterprise system at the same time as he was bound to a contract that was its complete negation.

Although star players like Matthews and Billy Wright openly showed their support for the players, most of the rich clubs tacitly supported a big raise in the maximum wage—some even supported its abolition. Also behind the players were some well-known entertainers, and so too was the Labour party, although it found itself in something of a bind, anxious to support wage justice but aware that those freed from the existing regime were liable to fly straight into the ranks of the class enemy. In any event, the bosses' main problem was not the maximum wage but rather the retain and transfer system: workers who earn a fortune are one thing, but workers who can tell the bosses what to do with themselves and their job are another.

Despite the forces being arrayed against it, the League held out. So did Hill and the PFA, refusing to be bought off by the League's tempting concessions. The strike date was set for 21 January 1961, following a series of meetings in which unprecedented numbers of soccer players turned up to urge such action. Hill was also backed up by the Trades Union Council, which advised its members to support their brothers in the strike and to take appropriate action against any blacklegs (scabs).

Faced by this united front, the League backed down, the strike was called off two days before it was to begin, and the maximum wage was abolished. The bosses gave in only grudgingly, and various chairmen were called to a special meeting, in violation of their commitment to the League, to come to a "gentleman's" agreement not to pay any player more than £50 per week. In fact, many players would have been happier with an increased maximum of about £25 and larger bonuses, for only a few players would benefit from the end of ceilings, and as many soon found out, they lost their jobs as managements cut back on playing staff to pay the higher wages at the top.

In what Jimmy Hill called "The Great Betrayal," management then tried to renege on the deal it had made in regard to the retain and transfer system, so the battle over player contracts dragged on for another couple of years before the system was overturned in the Eastham case. Stars of such superlative ability as Alex James in the 1930s and Wilf Mannion in the 1940s had tried to beat this system by refusing to play, but with no success, and Frank Brennan of Newcastle United retired early from the game in 1954 when he was similarly unsuccessful, later taking up coaching. The power of the FA and League was in their success in keeping players out of the courts. As Alan Hardaker had openly recognized, however, there was no way the retain and transfer system could stand up before a court of law, and so it proved to be. Fresh from its success in the agitation leading up to the abolition of the maximum wage, the PFA urged George Eastham to go to court over his dispute with Newcastle United. After a drawn-out battle, the judge ruled that Eastham's contract with Newcastle United Football Club had not been binding because it was an unreasonable restraint of trade.

England's best players were still not able to command the salaries of their equivalents in Italy and Spain, but they were among the best paid in Europe. West German teams did not become professional until 1963, and before this their players had to hold another job and were on a maximum salary of $100 per month, plus bonuses for reaching the later stages of the regional play-offs leading to the German Cup final. Belgium was only turning professional in 1961, and its players could expect to earn $20 to $35 a week. In the Netherlands player payments were tied to international appearances, so that a player with ten or more "caps" could receive a maximum of $2,500 a year. Prior to the new deal, internationals were paid $70 for a win, but this was now increased by $210, which was placed in escrow until the player reached thirty years of age—unless he transferred abroad, in which case the money went to the Dutch football association. (German players were given nothing for international appearances.) In Portugal married players were paid more than single players. Because Swedish teams were still nominally amateur, its top players could make a fortune only by transferring to one of the big Italian or Spanish clubs.

In these countries player payments were a matter of a contract between player and club and as such were not public knowledge. Alfredo Di Stéfano, however, earned enough to buy a mansion in a
Madrid suburb where he could count the royal family among his close
neighbors.

Another barrier between Britain and the Continent fell with the
gradual adoption of Sunday soccer. This had been specifically banned
by the FA in 1949, when it had to discipline 200 players for playing
in the Sunday leagues, which were not under its jurisdiction. At that
time there were an estimated 2,547 clubs playing in seventy-three
leagues throughout the country. Seven of these teams were "public
house teams," and five were Jewish. Ten years later, however, the FA
was trying to integrate the Sunday football leagues into its own organization. When some of the Sunday leagues resisted this threat to
their autonomy, the FA countered by claiming that they were badly
organized and that their referees were usually poorly qualified, resulting in frequent "fights and bad language," as well as several serious
attacks on referees.

Sunday football had been tolerated during the war, but the dispen-
sation was revoked as soon as hostilities ceased. It had always been
accepted that teams visiting the Continent might have to play games
on a Sunday, but there were still a few anxious protests made in this
regard with the advent of regular European competition in the 1950s.
The first semiprofessional match to be played in England on a Sunday was in 1967. The breach was made, and it widened during the
energy crisis of 1973–74 when League and FA Cup games were played
on a Sunday, albeit under special condition: because an entry fee could
not be charged, admission had to be by programs that were printed
to suit the occasion and today are collector's pieces. It was only in
the 1980s, however, that Sunday was set aside for the "match of the
day," by which time the "Continental abomination" had become as
normal as sleeping late on Sunday.

------

Coaching had long been considered a Continental eccentricity, an
attitude that went as far back as the sixteenth century, when Richard Mulcaster vainly pleaded for the appointment of a "traiyning
maister" to improve football, as was the practice in Italy. It was an
aristocratic attitude opposed to that of the artisan, and in the early
days of professionalism the amateurs were scandalized when teams
from the north took time out to prepare for games. This changed
dramatically in the 1960s, when managers and coaches came to earn

more esteem than star players. The adherents of scientific coaching had their efforts justified with Alf Ramsey's triumph in taking England to World Cup victory at Wembley in 1966. Ramsey's "wingless wonders" did nothing to lighten the burden of the defensive tactics stifling the game in the 1960s, but Ramsey was never as negative as Helenio Herrera, whose entire tactics were to defend in depth with players drilled as automatons and with only one or two players up front hoping to score on the break. In this way he took Inter-Milan to joyless European success in the early 1960s. Ramsey claimed that his tactics were forced on him by the lack of competent wingers, but however that may be, the English triumph of 1966 was not a triumph of spectacular soccer. It was other managers who captured the public imagination, men whose drive came from an obvious love of the game and not just of winning: immortals like Matt Busby at Manchester United, Bill Shankly at Liverpool, and Jock Stein of Glasgow Celtic. Busby and Shankly had been Scottish internationals, but Stein was never more than a moderately good league player. These men did not allow tactics to dictate plans but adjusted tactics to the talents available.

The conversion to the virtues of coaching came after a plethora of articles in the 1950s debating the state of British soccer and the need for change to face the Continental challenge. Most player biographies of this time devote a chapter to the merits or otherwise of Continental soccer and the need for coaching. A foremost critic in this regard was Willi Meisl, Hugo's youngest brother, who came to Britain in 1934, took out citizenship, and continued his career as a journalist in his second language. In articles in *World Sports* and in his book *The Soccer Revolution,* he somewhat tediously pointed to the dreariness of British soccer and the need to brighten it up, but he also anticipated the "total football" of the Dutch and Germans of the 1970s in his description of "the whirl," a system in which every player plays every position and is involved in the game from start to finish. He was not alone in his campaign to substitute skill and brain for bash and brawn, which, despite a host of individual players of consummate artistry, were still seen to be the hallmarks of British soccer.

The old attitudes to coaching took a long time dying, and the process was not helped by star players like Stanley Matthews and other old-timers who thought (quite rightly in some particular cases) that they knew more than coaches could tell them. Jimmy Hogan was perhaps the most gifted coach to be sacked by English clubs, but he was not alone. George Raynor was in his prime when he offered his services to Coventry City in 1955 after his brilliant successes in Sweden, but he barely lasted the season. Like Hogan and John Madden he was revered abroad and treated with disdain at home. After the 1958 World Cup England began to adopt a more modern, or Continental, approach to the game, but it took time to change the prejudices exhibited by the director of a major English team who boasted that he would rather see his team win the League than England win the World Cup. In Scotland, where progressive ideas on coaching were equally hard to find, changes came even more slowly. One of the Scotland manager's complaints at the 1954 World Cup was that he had almost no control over the team. This was a common attitude in Britain at this time, with directors who thought that because they owned the club they had a right to run it. The passing of power to the managers, the professionals whom the directors appointed to do the job, marked one of the major changes in British soccer in the 1960s. Matt Busby had to fight the interference of directors before his obvious abilities won him the right to sole control, and Stein's success with Celtic came when he made it clear to chairman Bob Kelly that he would be picking the team in the future. This was the mid-1960s, and by then most teams were being run by managers with an intimate knowledge of the game. Directors were left merely with the right to hire and fire.

———

Stein with Celtic, Busby with Manchester United, and Ramsey with England showed that British teams had returned to world class, as good as the great Latin teams before them and the Dutch and German teams to come. But there was no doubt in anyone's mind that the two best teams of the 1960s came from South America: Santos, the club team from the Brazilian São Paulo league, and the Brazil national team. What both teams had in common was the blossoming talents of Pelé, in most people's mind the greatest player ever to grace the soccer stage. After its success in Sweden in 1958, Brazil went on in 1962 to win a second World Cup in Chile and took permanent possession of it in Mexico in 1970 by winning it for the third time. Brazil's World Cup team of 1958 had more individual stars, but that of 1970, with no shortage of stars, was a better team. Brazil's hopes of winning the World Cup in 1966 were weakened by administrative blunders and widespread discord among the players over preparation and then destroyed by the vicious tactics of defenders following the cynical maxim made popular about this time that "winning is the only thing." In this spirit the Bulgarians brutally manhandled Pelé and then the Portuguese literally kicked him out of the tournament. As a result, Brazil failed to make the quarterfinals. Brazil had won in 1962 despite an injured Pelé, with Garrincha at his startling best, and it has never been short of players of outstanding ability, from Arthur Friedenreich in the early days through Leônidas da Silva in the 1930s and a whole galaxy of stars after the 1940s, but outshining all of these was Edson Arantes do Nascimento, known the world over as Pelé.

Pelé was born in Três Corações, Minas Gerais, in 1940, the son of a semiprofessional soccer player. At barely sixteen years of age he was earning $20 a month, nearly twice as much as his father and enough to help build a house for his family. His father taught him how to head the ball and kick with both feet—he is unquestionably the most complete soccer player of all time—and in Bauru, where he was brought up, he had to play with others much older than himself until his obvious genius brought him to the professional ranks, to Santos, the team of the port city of São Paulo. At sixteen he starred for Brazil in the Rio Branco Cup, and at seventeen he did the same in the World Cup. Pelé then went on to become the most famous Brazilian in his country's history. In 1960 offers from Italy of over a million dollars led to him being declared a "nonexportable national treasure," with private sponsors such as the Brazilian Coffee Institute making up for the money he could not accept. With his relaxed temperament and gracious smile, refusing to advertise alcohol or cigarettes, he was a perfect role model for youngsters all over the world. There was little he could do about the poverty that existed in what is one of the richest countries in the world, and none of the poor grudged him the mansion he built far from the favelas from which he had come. In 1964 a new military regime was installed in Brazil, helped by the CIA, and the socialist ideas that Pelé was later to proclaim had to be put on hold. Instead, he was used to justify the continued failure of the authorities to spend money on much-needed public facilities such as health and education—after all, Pelé had got by without such state interference. The state did interfere in soccer, however, and seemed to spend more time and money on soccer than it did on education: many stadiums were erected around the country, some of them among the biggest in the world (one, in Erechim, held only 35,000 spectators, but then only 25,000 people lived there). Pelé's marriage to a white women was cited as proof that the country had overcome the racism that Pelé himself had been forced to fight on his rise to stardom, but the paternalism at the top of the Brazilian Sports Federation is as bad today as it was then: João Havelange was president of that body in the 1960s, and three decades later, as president of FIFA, he still saw soccer players as children with no right to query the injustices as rife in Brazilian soccer as they are in Brazilian society.

Brazil's new military regime in 1964 immediately acknowledged its debt to the United States by canceling an invitation to a Soviet soccer team to visit the country, but the regime's major success came with Brazil's triumphal march to its third World Cup victory in Mexico in 1970. Brazil's players provided a feast of fast, entertaining soccer and spectacular goals. Winning its group, including a classic match against England, Brazil went on in the knock-out rounds to sweep aside Peru (4-2) and Uruguay (3-1) before crushing Italy 4-1 in a devastating display of passing, individual flair, and clinical finishing. The dictatorship identified the victory with the fight for national development and the players' commitment to the "collective good" and granted the players a tax-free bonus of $18,000. They were flown directly to the president's palace in Brasília for an official reception, to allow the president to be shown sharing their joy. For the rest of the nation the government declared a day's holiday, in the celebration of which dozens were killed and hundreds injured.

The military had interfered in the national team selection just before the 1970 finals, exerting pressure to have leftist-leaning João Saldanho removed in favor of Mario Zagalo, but it was too late to upset the team's rhythm. The military then had four years to upset the team for the World Cup in West Germany and wasted no time in forcing the players to assume nationalistic postures, adopted the song written for the 1970 World Cup as its own, and commissioned other songs in which the government and soccer were merged. Pelé was forced to say nice things about the regime. The generals even tried to dictate how the team should be run, with the result that the free-flowing Brazilian game was clogged by "European discipline," and the team came back from Germany having failed to make the top three: in the play-off for third place it was beaten 0-1 by Poland. Pelé was bitterly disappointed that he was not selected for the 1974 national team, particularly as it would have made him one of only two players, along with Antonio Carbajal of Mexico (1950–66), to have taken part in five World Cups. He was then thirty-four, but as he was shortly to show in the United States, he was far from finished.

As a club player with Santos, Pelé embarked on many world tours for fees much bigger than Santos could command in Brazil, where government control reduced revenue by limiting the price of the standing areas of all grounds to allow the poor to attend. When Santos and Pelé played in Europe and other continents, it was invariably before sellout crowds. Pelé claimed that in one year he played in 121 games and had only three weeks' rest, and it was nothing for him to travel over 20,000 miles through several countries to play a dozen friendlies in a month. In the course of these tours Pelé was besieged with offers from other countries, but with the money guaranteed him in Brazil, he was never snared. In games for Santos and the national team Pelé amassed a total of 1,282 goals in 1,364 games: 1,088 in 1,114 for Santos, and 65 in 108 for Brazil, surpassing the 1,032 goals scored by Austria's Bimbo Binder, but less than the 1,329 attributed to Pelé's Brazilian predecessor, Arthur Friedenreich (Friedenreich, however, scored when goals were much more easily come by). Pelé managed an even more amazing feat in 1969, when the warring factions in the ghastly Nigerian civil war agreed to set aside hostilities during Santos's visit to the country. Another near minor miracle awaited Pelé when, playing in the United States in the late 1970s, he helped attract to soccer crowds that rivaled major baseball attendances. This was in his appearances for Cosmos, the only club team other than Santos for which he played.

---

The United States' defeat of England in 1950 created barely a ripple in the U.S. sports world, and throughout the 1950s soccer in the United States was restricted more than ever to those neighborhoods with strong ethnic communities, played by teams that adopted names emphasizing their ethnic affiliation. Even Marilyn Monroe's appearance to kick off a game in 1957 at Brooklyn's Ebbets Field between an American select and Hapoel from Israel provoked little more than passing interest—and she was there mainly to support the efforts of her husband, Arthur Miller, to raise funds for Israel. Visiting European teams, above all Italian, could always attract a large crowd to soccer, especially in the New York–New Jersey–Connecticut triangle, but the local German-American Soccer League struggled along. So it was that when Bill Cox, sports promoter and former owner of the defunct Brooklyn Dodgers professional football team, founded his International Soccer League in 1960, he relied on eleven European and South American teams, along with an American all-star team. The competition was restricted to the European off-season, which meant that games were played in the heat of the American summer, but the league did little more than give the visitors some extra pocket money.

The United States Soccer Football Association (USSFA; "Soccer" was added to the name in 1945) was never happy with Cox's importation of foreign professionals and finally canceled his league in 1965, prompting Cox to take legal action against the USSFA. By then the interest surrounding the World Cup in England, the first to be shown on television across the Atlantic, opened the eyes of some of America's sports entrepreneurs to soccer's commercial possibilities. Suddenly the USSFA (along with the Canadian FA) found itself courted by three groups anxious to secure the franchises that the USSFA alone could bestow. It chose the group led by Jack Kent Cooke, owner of the Los Angeles Lakers, and later called the United Soccer Association (USA). The other two groups, one led by Cox, then merged to found a pirate league called the National Professional Soccer League (NPSL). Operating outside FIFA, and so deprived of international competition, the outlaw NPSL comforted itself with a CBS television network contract to broadcast one game per week.

In its rush to get a return on its franchises, Cooke's USA invited eleven European and Latin American professional teams to form a league to begin in 1967. Each of the teams was allocated to an American city and given a name that the promoters hoped would appeal to Americans: the Wolverhampton Wanderers, which was newly promoted from the English second division and would win the league, was sent to Los Angeles and called the L.A. Wolves; Aberdeen from Scotland, which lost 5-6 to the Wolves in the thrilling final, was placed in Washington as the Whips; the Irish team Shamrock Rovers went to Boston; and America's Italians had to make do with Cagliari from Sardinia, which was placed in Chicago as the Chicago Mustangs. Canada provided two locations, Toronto for Hibernian from Scotland and Vancouver for Sunderland, which played as the Vancouver Royal Canadians.

Neither the USA league nor NPSL did much to bridge the chasm between the sports cultures of the two continents. Visiting journalists and radio commentators criticized the standard of play and could scarcely believe it when they saw televised games being interrupted so that commercials could be run. Goals were scarce in the USA games, and this and some riots, notably on the part of the Italians (although the Irish and the Brazilians made their contributions), helped to confirm the few things most Americans knew about soccer—that it is a game with no scoring played by foreigners and ending in violence.

The competition of the two leagues resulted in large losses for the investors, and in 1968 they came together in the North American Soccer League (NASL). Over the next few years fortunes continued to be lost, which at least prevented them from breaching FIFA's rule against private profit making. In the early 1970s, however, there was a steady rise in interest in the game, which suddenly soared to previously unheard of heights when Cosmos enticed Pelé out of retirement with a contract of more than $4 million. Pelé had come to enjoy life in the United States, and this—as well as some debts that had to be paid, encouragement from Henry Kissinger at the state level, and concessions made to placate the Brazilians who thought that he was betraying them—encouraged Pelé to accept the deal. The agreement stipulated that, in exchange for Pelé's bringing his soccer skill to the United States, American experts in several sports be sent to Brazil, while Warner Communications, the owner of Cosmos, promised to set up soccer schools in Santos and to provide some money for the pupils' education.

Pelé, joined by Giorgio Chinaglio in 1976 and then by Franz Beckenbauer and Carlos Alberto in 1977, attracted crowds to soccer that continued to break U.S. records, culminating in the 77,691 people who came to Giants Stadium to see Cosmos beat Fort Lauderdale in the divisional championship play-offs in 1977. When Pelé made his emotional retirement in 1978, it was in a game between Cosmos and his old club, Santos, in which he played one half for each side. Cosmos continued to play before big crowds, averaging 47,856 in 1978, 46,689 in 1979, and 42,804 in 1980, but after that it was all downhill, and the big bust was not too far away.

———————

The 1966 World Cup is credited with starting what led to the boom in soccer in the United States. It has also been blamed for bringing to British soccer a focus on its more unruly fans leading to a spiral of violence that continued to escalate over the next two decades, making the British, especially English, soccer fan synonymous with hooliganism. Before the 1960s hooliganism was seen as a Continental failing, and Britons disparagingly dismissed the fences, moats, and police protection that were needed to allow games to be played in most European and Latin American grounds. By 1970 spectator fences had been erected in soccer grounds in England and to a lesser degree in Scotland. None of this was "caused" by the World Cup, which at most set in focus and helped amplify a problem that had been appearing over the previous years, alternately to be denounced or dismissed as a temporary aberration. With the eyes of the world about to turn on England during the televising of the World Cup, attempts to identify and deal with the problem gave it additional publicity, and for hooligans hoping to achieve a few minutes of fame, a riot at the soccer match might give them a chance to seen on national television. It was not television that created the problem, however, any more than it caused the other social disturbances of the 1960s that were sparked by the conscience of a younger generation no longer willing to accept the prejudices of its elders. The soccer hooligans were hardly out to create a better world; rather, they represented the darker side of the 1960s, the greed that unprecedented wealth in the Western world encouraged, promoted in television advertisements and flaunted in the lifestyles of the newly rich and famous. The equivalent in sport was the ugly "winner" mentality. For the vast majority who could never be winners, some found an outlet for their frustration in an exaggerated devotion to the local soccer team.

In Italy and Spain, as in Latin America, soccer players had always been accorded star status and were paid and acted accordingly. They were made into heroes by a press that devoted pages to their every exploit and gave the minutest details of the moves leading up to goals, while radio commentators would rush onto the field or ambush players coming off it to get their impressions of their moment of glory or despair. The downside was the reaction when players failed and teams lost and an Italian gutter press that lived off the players' indiscretions. When John Charles returned to British soccer after his five-year spell in Italy, he cited the fans and the press as two factors that set Italian soccer apart from British. He learned to live with the abuse directed at players who made the slightest mistake and enjoyed fevered acclaim following a brilliant performance or a winning goal, with fans clubbing together to collect large sums of money to add to the player's bonus. George Raynor, who was less impressed than Charles by the big-business aspects of Italian soccer and the corruption that was accepted as a way of life, was also less impressed by the fans' volatility and pointed out that although he could get free meat deliveries and other gifts when his team was doing well, this ceased when things went otherwise. Adoring fans could turn into wild men who scratched his car and slashed its tires. This side of the Italian sports fanaticism could be turned on the players: when Italy lost to England in Turin in 1948, there were demonstrations calling for Pozzo's death, and when Italy returned from England in 1966 after a humiliating exit from the World Cup at the hands of North Korea, fans met them at the airport with rotten fruit and vegetables.

More than two decades later Italian fans still took their duty as supporters seriously. During the 1994–95 season Fiorentina devotees burned some players' cars after a poor performance, Brescia fans issued death threats to one of their own defenders who played badly, and Lazio supporters turned up at a coaching session to encourage

the team with abuse and rotten tomatoes after a UEFA cup defeat—
later they showed more positive militancy when they besieged the
club's offices after hearing that star player Giuseppe Signori was about
to be sold, prompting the club owner, Sergio Cragnotti, to say he
would sell his stake in the club. It appears that there was still a wide
gap between the fan culture in Britain and that on the Continent. After
a varied career with several European clubs, Jürgen Klinsmann transferred to Tottenham Hotspur for a remarkably successful season in
1994–95; he was at first astonished but soon came to enjoy having
spectators close to the field without fences, nets, or ditches separat-
ing them from the players. When Brian Laudrop went to Glasgow
Rangers from Fiorentina in Italy in that same season, he found the
Glasgow fans—far from the meekest in the British Isles—much friend-
lier, a far cry from the 500 Fiorentina fans he claimed stoned the bus
carrying the team home from a bad loss against Udinese.

British fans almost never attacked their own players, but they
adopted many of the antics of their Latin colleagues and then went
on to invent a few of their own. Much of this came from a misplaced
loyalty to the team and a desire to enjoy a closer rapport with it, but
some of it was a perverse reflection of the more extroverted behavior of the players on the field. The improved rewards for players discouraged club loyalty, as the stars set out in search of richer pastures
and players from working-class origins seemed intent only on making enough money to distance themselves from their pasts. Young
people who did not have these choices found in rebellion and rock-
and-roll music a means of expressing their contempt for authority. In
British soccer spontaneous chants and roars became rituals of singing and abuse, and good-natured banter gave way to expressions of
vocal hatred. Fans took first to rushing the field to celebrate goals and
then to crowing over the opposition and occasionally to stopping the
game when their team was losing.

The media recorded all this, with the press trying to compete with
television in short snatches and sensational scoops that often concerned the players' private lives rather than their actions on the field.
The British press slipped steadily into the gutter as checkbook jour-
nalism encouraged lurid stories by paying large sums of money for
them and players employed agents to ensure that they got every penny available. The visual images and immediacy provided by the television sets that were now in virtually every home in the Western world
forced newspapers to reappraise their coverage. Some went for "in-
depth" analysis, but more went for crude snatches, as the gulf between

the quality press and the tabloids widened to mirror that between the increasingly wealthy rich and the increasingly desperate poor. In the late 1960s television coverage of soccer changed its focus to specially packaged highlights with more emphasis on off-the-field activities. Either way, players were being courted as never before, and as "personalities" in the new "package" they expected to be paid an appropriate fee. The spectators, who provided the atmosphere without which televised sport can barely survive, developed their own interpretation of the new ethos in outbursts of triumphalism that owed less to greed than to a twisted sense of loyalty to the local team.

Prior to the 1966 World Cup established soccer powers in Europe and South America displayed an attitude to the game in Asia and Africa similar to that of the British to the Continentals before the 1950s. These attitudes received a severe jolt with the performances of the North Koreans, who were the sensation of the tournament. They won the hearts of English supporters as they disposed of Italy (1-0) and drew with Chile to go on to the elimination rounds. There they took an early 3-0 lead against Portugal in the quarterfinals, only to meet the star of the tournament in scintillating form, as Eusébio, the "Black Panther" from Mozambique, inspired the Portuguese in a revival that saw them emerge the winners by 5-3.

North Korea's passage to the finals had been won rather cheaply, for it had to play only one game, against Australia. The reason for this reduced schedule was that the Asian and African nations had staged a boycott to protest being allowed only one place in the finals. None of the major soccer powers took this boycott too seriously, however, and they ascribed the Koreans' success to the single-minded purpose with which the North Korean regime had pampered and drilled the team for international success, much as the Hungarian government had done for the Hungarian team of the early 1950s. Moreover, no other Asian team seemed to be anywhere near its class. Japan, inspired by Kunishege Kamamoto, had done well on home ground at the 1964 Olympics, and at Mexico in 1968 it became the first team from Asia or Africa to win a medal in soccer. To get to Mexico, Japan had to beat South Korea, Lebanon, South Vietnam, Taiwan, and the Philippines. Burma, India, Iran, and North Korea all withdrew rather than play Israel, leaving Japan and Thailand to represent Asia. In the group matches in Mexico, Japan beat Nigeria and drew with Spain and Brazil to advance to the elimination rounds.

There it beat France 3-1 but lost its semifinal against the Hungarian amateurs (0-5). In the play-off for the bronze medal it beat Mexico 2-0 before 120,000 delirious but disappointed home fans.

Despite the success of Japan and North Korea, it was Africa that excited the hopes of those whose soccer vision went beyond Europe and South America, and no less a commentator than Eric Batty in *World Soccer* frequently discussed the potential of the emerging African teams. He even predicted in November 1963 that the World Cup final of 1978 would be contested by Ghana and Egypt. He was not the only expert to make such predictions at this time, but it was in the corridors of power rather than on the field of play that the emerging nations first made their presence felt. Their voting power in FIFA was a much more powerful weapon than the boycott to bring about what they thought was a proper recognition of their place in the soccer world.

# Contracting World, Expanding Markets

The World Cup final of 1974 was played in Munich, between the Netherlands and West Germany, the host nation. The Germans won 2-1 in a close game between two teams whose "total football," involving every player on the field being able to play in every position, had wrested supremacy from the Latin countries. It was a remarkable rise to prominence for two countries that had only recently entered the full-time professional ranks: the Netherlands took up part-time professionalism in 1954 and full professionalism in 1967; West Germany became fully professional with the introduction of the Bundesliga in 1963. The referee at the final was an Englishman, and since Poland beat Brazil for third place, all the final honors went to Europe. It is ironic then, that at this moment of (northern) European supremacy, control of the game was passing into the hands of non-Europeans, backed by the voting power of the Third-World nations that had been admitted to FIFA over the previous decade. The major soccer event of 1974, in fact, was not so much the World Cup played that year but the annual meeting of FIFA held just a few weeks before the finals took place.

At this meeting multimillionaire João Havelange replaced former schoolteacher Stanley Rous as president of FIFA. The consequences were revolutionary, not just because one was English and the other Brazilian, although that was important, but because the two men represented two different historical forces; Havelange was a man more tuned to the realities of Third-World economies, having amassed a fortune in the midst of dire poverty, whereas Rous was anchored in a past where decency prevailed as long as subordinates did what they were told and did not rise above their station. The nature of the election was as significant as the result, with Asian and African representatives being assiduously courted by both candidates. Havelange was expected to win the election, thanks to a wide range of promises with both immediate and long-term rewards, but the lobbying for Rous by Adidas's Horst Dassler made it a close-run event. Havelange immediately brought Dassler over to his side and with his assistance set about fulfilling his election promises for the development of soccer in Third-World countries.

When the Asian and African countries boycotted the 1966 World Cup, few people paid much attention, but in 1974 they could not be ignored. In the mid-1950s there were only eighteen Asian and five African nations among FIFA's eighty affiliated members; two decades later they comprised just over half of FIFA's membership of 141: thirty-nine countries from Africa (including suspended members South Africa and Rhodesia) and thirty-three from Asia. FIFA was then presiding over six regional confederations that spanned the entire globe: CONMEBOL, which had been founded in 1916, controlled South America; UEFA, formed in 1954, controlled Europe; the Asian Football Confederation (AFC), also formed in 1954, governed the Asian game; the Confédération Africaine de Football (CAF), the controlling body for African soccer, was founded in 1957; CONCACAF, which was finally forged in 1961, comprised the North and Central American powers; and lastly the Oceania Football Confederation brought the island nations of that region into the international family in 1965.

By far the biggest of these confederations is the AFC, which according to FIFA had nearly 54 million registered players in 1990. There had been several regional competitions in Asia before the founding of the AFC, and in 1951 soccer was included in the first Asian Games, but the first all-Asia soccer competition—the Asian Cup—was held in 1956. It took place in Hong Kong and was won by South Korea. Since then it has been played every four years, with a regional group deciding which countries (at first four and later eight) should proceed to the finals. An Asian club championship, the Asian Champions' Cup, got under way in 1966, although it was beset by problems from the outset. More successful was the Asian Youth Cup, which was held as an annual event from 1959 to 1980, when it became biennial. At the regional level there have been some excellent competitions, in Seoul, Bangkok, and Kuala Lumpur in particular. In the Middle East, which for FIFA purposes is included in the Asian confederation, soccer took off in the 1970s with the bonanza in oil prices. There is now a host of Gulf, Arab, and other club and national competitions. Most recently

Saudi Arabia has staked a claim to be the venue for a regular intercontinental nations cup for the champion nations of each confederation, but Europe and South America have yet to take it seriously.

The organization of African soccer has had to face problems similar to those in Asia, distance on the one hand and politics on the other, but under its powerful controlling body, CAF, a series of continent-wide competitions for clubs and nations, as well as many regional competitions, has reflected the passion for the game throughout the continent, be it in the Muslim countries north of the Sahara, the various sub-Saharan nations, or South Africa. By contrast, the Oceania Football Confederation is dominated by Australia and New Zealand; in neither of these countries is soccer the major football code, but their teams are still usually too powerful for the small island nations scattered throughout the Pacific Ocean that make up the rest of the confederation.

Havelange has been criticized for overcommercializing soccer, but under his presidency many of the weaker soccer countries have benefited from the provision of coaches and equipment and, perhaps above all, by the institution of youth competitions weighted in favor of the weaker confederations. The most successful of these is the World Youth Cup, which is restricted to players under twenty. Sponsored by Coca-Cola, it was first held in Tunisia in 1977 and has taken place in a different country every two years thereafter. In Australia in 1981 it became an official championship, the FIFA/Coca-Cola World Youth Championship, and since then it has gone from strength to strength—in Portugal in 1990 the crowd of 127,000 fans who saw the home nation lose to Brazil on penalties was the biggest crowd at a FIFA competition since Brazil hosted the World Cup in 1950. The FIFA Under-Seventeen World Championship began as a schoolboys competition, first played in China in 1985 and won by Nigeria; it has been played every two years since and in 1991 became an official championship. None of these competitions would be complete today without the agents of the big professional clubs on the lookout for the stars of tomorrow.

In the eternal disputes at the Olympics over what constitutes amateurism and how to equalize the chances between countries that are heavily professional and those that are not, FIFA finally solved the problem in 1992 by limiting the soccer competition to players under twenty-three years of age. From 1952 the communist nations and rigorously amateur countries like Denmark had participated fully in the soccer tournament of the Olympic Games. By the 1970s the amateur ideal had become as farcical as it had always been hypocritical, and some nations' soccer teams included obviously professional players. More to help the weaker soccer nations than out of respect for the Olympic ideal, FIFA decreed in 1978 that any European or South American soccer player who had already played for his country would be banned from the Olympics. The countries of the state amateurs, whose players floated freely between Olympic and World Cup teams, were the most affected and the most indignant. The issue was finally resolved by making soccer at the Olympic Games a youth tournament, much to the annoyance of the new keepers of the Olympic flame, who want to see all sports geared to their highest commercial potential. One welcome addition to Atlanta in 1996, however, will be women's soccer.

------------

In the 1960s, when many predictions were being made about the future of African soccer, few such forecasts were made about the future of the game in Asia, despite the success of North Korea in 1966 and Japan in 1968. Soccer's popularity in Asia has been masked by the success of Asians in elite sports such as cricket, squash, hockey, badminton, and volleyball, as well as swimming and track and field in Japan and China. Soccer players seldom win the Asian sports personality of the year award, but this is most likely a reflection of the social snobbery that has been associated with soccer from its early days, for although soccer is an essentially middle-class game in most of Asia, it is still not high on the register of sports fashions. When China hosted the eleventh Asian Games in 1990, it headed the medals table but failed to win a medal in soccer, being eliminated by Thailand in the quarterfinals. As a result, riot police had to be called out to quiet angry crowds yelling that they would sooner trade the 100 medals won in other sports for a single medal in soccer. The people's game has reached into every part of Asia, and in some countries and regions it has a powerful hold, drawing crowds of well over 100,000 in India and as many as 150,000 in Korea and Indonesia. Games in Thailand and Malaysia are played before sellout crowds, and one of the worst disasters in Asian sports history was when a reported ninety-three spectators were crushed to death at a packed soccer stadium in Nepal in 1988.

The British, and to a lesser degree the French, brought soccer to Asia, but it was only after 1945 and the postcolonial period that the game started to boom there. The AFC comprised thirty-three nations in 1992, the Middle East countries included, with Bhutan and Mongolia waiting for admission and Guam an associate member. Beginning in the late 1950s many regional competitions were introduced, the most successful of which was the Merdeka ("independence") tournament started in Malaysia in 1957 to celebrate that country's freedom from colonial rule. Various other competitions followed, the most notable of which are the King's Cup in Bangkok (founded in 1968), the President's Cup in South Korea (1971), the Kirin Cup, which began as the Japan Cup in 1978, and the Nehru Gold Cup in India, founded in 1982 in honor of the most revered name in Indian nationalist history. Pakistan, Bangladesh, and China also have their tournaments.

Most of these various tournaments are invitational competitions, where teams from all around the world are invited, but the professionals of Europe and South America are more likely to send youth or B squads rather than their first team—which does not prevent the locals from billing them as Argentina, Brazil, Germany, or whatever country they come from. In contrast to the situation in most of Europe outside the former communist bloc, national teams in Asia usually take precedence over club teams, national glory being prized above private interest. Sometimes an Olympic or national all-star team is included in the domestic league to give them regular practice. Professionalism has had a checkered career in the region: Hong Kong inaugurated a professional league in 1969, a minuscule version of the North American Soccer League with all its faults and none of its star attractions—its major imports were usually Europeans past their prime or young hopefuls on the way up. Professionalism was introduced in Malaysia in 1990, and more recently it has been permitted in restricted form in Indonesia and Bangladesh.

One of the reasons for the introduction of professionalism in Malaysia was to help control the craze for gambling that runs like a fever throughout the region. In late 1994 the bribery and corruption that made a farce of the Malaysian league and that tainted those in Indonesia and Thailand, with some players disgusted at colleagues who merely went through the motions to achieve a fixed result, were alleged to have spread to the fixing of Premier League games in England. Some star players in England were accused of complicity in match fixing, and in Malaysia itself the initial investigations resulted in over 100 arrests and many players suspended or sentenced to internal exile. Whatever the final result of this investigation, it already promises to be the most scandalous incidence of corruption in soccer's history.

Nor is violence a stranger to the game in Asia. In India riots are as common in soccer as they are in cricket, and referees have gone on strike to protest their lack of protection; North Korea was banned for two years after its players attacked a referee at an Asian Games semifinal in India in 1982.

Administration is often of a low standard, and the popular enthusiasm for soccer in Asia has still to be converted into international success. Indonesians have won world acclaim in badminton, which has become virtually the "national" game there, but soccer is even more avidly followed, being played before crowds of well over 100,000 in Djakarta, and 150,000 fans are said to have been packed into the Stadion Utama Senayan Pintu VII for the big games—a stadium restricted for safety reasons to well below that figure. More recently restrictions have been lifted on playing imported players, but it remains to be seen how this will profit the national team. In India, Calcutta has been a veritable caldron of soccer fever for most of this century, with crowds of over 100,000 fans watching the local derbies between the big three, Mohan Bagan, Mohammedan Sporting, and East Bengal. Teams from Kerala, Bombay, and Goa have at times challenged the Bengal supremacy, but India has still to produce a strong national team.

A new source of Asian talent could come from the breakup of the Soviet Union. In 1991 Novbakhov of Uzbekistan played before average crowds of over 35,000, the best in the quickly disintegrating empire. In 1994 the then-independent republic of Uzbekistan won the Asian Games tournament held in Hiroshima, with victories over a weakened Saudi Arabia (4-1), South Korea (1-0), and China (4-2) in the final. Turkmenistan also did well in that tournament, but it was the Uzbekis who caught the eye. With Kazhakstan, Tajikstan, and Kirghistan still to join international competition, the possibility of a new soccer power in central Asia to challenge South Korea and the ever-improving Japan looks promising. In the meantime agents from other nations are casting their eyes in the direction of what they hope might be a new talent pool.

A major dilemma in Asia, as in all emerging soccer nations, is the influence of the more highly sophisticated European game. Top European and South American professionals have toured Asia for decades, but with television the world game has been brought to tens of millions of Asians, encouraging a new interest but also showing the local product in a poor light: South Korea refused to show overseas soccer on television, but other Asian nations have shown highlights from the best leagues in the world, most notably Italy's Serie A. In China soccer has come to dominate the sport programs that are becoming increasingly popular, and despite the high charges to cover the costs, visits from overseas teams can be guaranteed a sell-out crowd—even a small wealthy elite represents a lot of people in this populous nation. In the meantime the domestic game struggles along, although it is improving.

The balance to be reached between overseas example and imported players against the local product is a constant problem. Attempts to limit foreigners or ban the playing of expatriates in the national team have met with mixed results. When the Hong Kong league introduced a three-foreigner limit in 1984, Bulova, runners-up in the 1983–84 season, withdrew in protest. South China, the most successful team in the Hong Kong league, played only Chinese athletes and remained amateur even when the league went professional. Eleven years later it adopted professionalism, employed a German coach, and in the 1981 season signed non-Chinese players. Players are not allowed to leave China before they are twenty-eight years old.

South Korea founded a professional league in 1983 made up of only eight teams; today there are seven, but the players are paid up to £120,000 a year by the big industrial concerns that run them. Professionalism was introduced into a China that still called itself communist in 1994, and an average of 16,600 spectators watched the 132 league games in that first season. The best player in the world's most populous country, Xu Hong of Dalian, was estimated to earn about £100,000 (nearly $170,000), ten times more than the best players in India. In Singapore players are paid anything up to ten times what their counterparts receive in the much larger Malaysian competition—a factor said to make it easier to bribe Malaysian players. It is in Japan, however, that a league to rival those of Europe appears to have come into existence: the professional J-League, inaugurated in May 1993 and growing in strength. Teams are restricted in the number of overseas players they can play, all of whom are on lucrative contracts in what some have called "the land of the rising salary." Even the local players are well rewarded, and to the material reward has been added the adulation of young Japanese, who are forsaking baseball in favor of "Sokka."

Soccer in Asia, however, is still a long way short of world standards, and this is reflected in the few Asian players who have made the grade in the top teams in the European leagues. Their success has only underlined Asia's failure to produce world-class soccer players. Among the best was Kunishege Kamamoto, star of the Japanese national teams of the 1960s, who attracted unprecedented crowds to see him play. Jarnail Singh was another star of this epoch, a Punjabi who played his best years with Mohan Bagan in Calcutta. Rong Zhihang of China was praised by Pelé as a "superstar" after a game between Cosmos and China in 1978. Inder Singh, another Punjabi of great skill, refused offers from Bengali clubs, the Malaysian government, and Khalso Sporting Club of Vancouver, preferring to stay in his native Punjab. Another gifted player who stayed in his native land despite overseas offers was "Supermok" Mokhtar Dahari, star striker for Malaysia in the 1970s and 1980s. He declined an offer from Réal Madrid, but the government amply compensated him for his patriotism with the offer of a well-paid and not very strenuous job in a government department.

Of those who tried their luck in Europe, Cheung Che Doy, who was born in mainland China in 1942 and was a star of the Hong Kong league and a regular for the Taiwan national team, had little success. Singapore's Fandi Ahmad became Asia's first soccer millionaire, mainly through sponsorship deals with MasterCard, Coca-Cola, and local firms, but his success in Europe was limited. He starred in several games for the Dutch first-division team Groningen in the 1983–84 season, but he disappointed in the next. In 1994 Groningen tried to woo him back, but at thirty-two he thought he was too old to make the change. The greatest of the Asians to play abroad was Cha Boom Kun of South Korea, who starred in the German Bundesliga from the late 1970s. Another Asian success in Germany was the Japanese player Yashuhiko Okudera. Most of those from Thailand, China, South Korea, and Singapore who have played in Europe since then have failed to raise much excitement. It remains to be seen whether some of the more recent stars who went on show in the United States in 1994 will be attracted to wealth and fame in Europe. One who did not make it to USA 1994 was Japanese sensation Kazuyoshi Miura. Miura went to try his luck in Brazil when he was only fifteen and earned a place in the Santos team. He returned to Japan four years later, in July 1990, to take his place in Japan's bid for USA 1994 and was one of the highest-paid players in the professional J-League. Indeed, when Miura signed for Italy's Padua after Japan's failure to qualify for USA 1994, he reportedly took a drop in salary, from over $2 million to $500,000.

---

Miura is something of an exception, and it is an irony that the relative prosperity and perks in Asia can act as a restraint on ambition. Princely rewards have been offered to Asians from governments anxious to improve the domestic leagues, and there are some multimillionaires who run soccer clubs as a hobby, but unless Asians engage more in the tougher, more competitive climate of Europe or even Latin America, the Asian game is liable to stagnate. Africa, on the other hand, offers neither the perks nor the stability to keep talented soccer players in the domestic game. As a result, they have flocked to Europe and now star in nearly every team in the best European leagues. They have taken much of this expertise with them when they have returned to play for their national teams, with the result that African players and African soccer have recently distinguished themselves at the highest level.

Organized soccer came to Africa with emissaries in the familiar forms of traders, settlers, and missionaries and then with the military in two world wars. The British played their usual role here, but it was the French who developed soccer in North, West, and Central Africa. Nevertheless, it was only after 1960, when most countries in Africa had gained their freedom, that the game flourished throughout the continent. The African Football Confederation, known by the acronym of its French name, Confédération Africaine de Football (CAF)—just as the Nations', Champion Clubs', and Cup-Winners' Cups are officially known by their French titles—was founded by African nationalists whose aims were grander than merely sharing the joys of sports; they sought also to secure African unity, combining love of soccer with hatred of colonialism and apartheid. The idealists have found it much easier to condemn these evils than to overcome the problems of self-interest that sports have not always discouraged. Even an idealist like Ydnekatchew Tessema, long-serving member and vice president of CAF and president from 1974 until his death in 1987, who added alcohol, nicotine, and professionalism to the political evils of colonialism and apartheid, had to battle against the problems of personal ambitions and national pretensions, exacerbated by the religious and linguistic differences that divide the continent. Now that apartheid is gone, the perennial problems remain, but the miracle of African soccer is not so much that it took so long to fulfill some of the promise of the early 1960s but that it has managed to do so despite the rise and fall of governments and personal dictators, some of whose interests seldom extend beyond their extended family, let alone to the nation.

Sudan, Egypt, Ethiopia, and South Africa were the four nations with representatives present at the birth of CAF. They met in Khartoum, the capital of Sudan, on 8 February 1957 to create a controlling body for soccer in Africa and to initiate a regular international tournament. Egypt could not hold the meeting because of the Suez war that broke out the previous year—it withdrew its soccer team from the Melbourne Olympics, its grounds were used as ambulance facilities, and top teams like Zamalek and National played games only to raise funds for the war effort. Despite such problems, the new body, CAF, became the supreme authority over the many regional bodies in Africa; from 1963 it ruled through an executive committee made up of two delegates from each of six geographical regions, but its most immediate task in 1957 was to organize an international tournament that it named the African Nations' Cup.

Sudan, to commemorate its independence from Anglo-French control the previous year, was appointed to host the first tournament, from which South Africa was expelled for refusing to allow its whites to play in the same team as nonwhites. Ethiopia was due to play South Africa and went straight into the final when its opponents withdrew, refusing to agree to a rearranged triangular tournament. The games were played in a stadium specially built for the occasion by Sudan's new dictators, and 30,000 spectators crowded in to see Egypt win both its games against Sudan and Ethiopia. As a result, Egypt became the first holders of the cup presented by CAF's first president, Abdelaziz Abdallah Salem from Egypt. The second cup competition was held in Egypt in 1959, by the same three national teams, in the massive Al-Ahly Stadium, the first on the continent to hold 100,000 spectators. Ghana, Nigeria, and Uganda had gained their independence by this time and were members of CAF, but they declined to enter. Egypt won again.

The African Nations' Cup due to be held in 1961 was delayed because of widespread political instability in the wake of new nations gaining their independence and was held in 1962 instead. This time Ethiopia was the host nation, and the games were held in Addis Ababa, at the remodeled stadium named after Haile Selassie, the venerable Christian "emperor," dictator, and soccer fanatic whose rule had been brutally interrupted by the Italian Fascists in 1935. He was there in person to see his nation win the final against Egypt, 4-2, in extra-time. Absent in 1962 for internal political reasons was Sudan, but present were Tunisia, which placed third, and Uganda, which placed last in the four-team tournament. To restore the games to their original biennial schedule, they were next played in 1963, with Ghana as the host. The increased entries meant that games had to be played in two sections, one in Accra and the other in Kumasi. Sudan returned to the competition, and Nigeria made its first appearance. Ghana and Sudan won their sections, and Ghana went on to beat Sudan in the final. It was at Tunisia in 1965 that the sub-

Saharan nations came into their own. In its first appearance Senegal placed second in its group, which Tunisia won, while Ethiopia placed last; the other group was made up of three teams: Ghana and newcomers Congo-Léopoldville (later Zaire) and Ivory Coast. Egypt and Sudan were missing from the fifth cup competition in 1965, Egypt because of a dispute with Tunisia, the hosts, over what seemed to be their too friendly attitude to Israel, and although such political problems would continue to plague the games, from this time on they never looked back. In 1978 Ghana won the Nations' Cup for the third time and so won the right to retain it. From 1980 it became known as the Cup of African Unity.

By then the All-Africa Games had been set up, but this was essentially an amateur athletic competition, used to prepare for the Olympics, and its soccer tournament was of secondary interest, especially to the major soccer nations. For them, the Nations' Cup, the Champions' Cup, and soon the Cup-Winners' Cup were the true all-African games, with soccer the one game that was played throughout the vast continent.

The continent-wide competition for champion clubs, the Coupe d'Afrique des Clubs Champions, was introduced in 1964. It is played by the league champions of each CAF member nation on a home-and-away basis, including the final, for the Kwame Nkrumah Cup. The Cup-Winners' Cup, the Coupe d'Afrique des Vainqueurs de Coupe, began in 1975 and was renamed the Nelson Mandela Trophy in 1986. In 1978 an African youth championship was founded and named after another hero of African nationalism, CAF president Tessema. The senior competitions were dominated by sub-Saharan nations in the early years, in part because the nations north of the Sahara were put off by the distances involved and by their closer affinities with other Arab nations of the Middle East. The North African nations were part of CAF, however, and any reservations they had about the quality of soccer played by their southern neighbors was soon overcome.

West Africa has produced some of the strongest soccer teams on the continent: apart from Ghana and Nigeria, most were former French colonies. Ivory Coast and Guinea, rivals in soccer and politics, were contenders for the top honors in international competition in the early days. Guinea, under the guidance of their Marxist soccer fan and president, Sekou Touré, opted to cut off diplomatic relations with France after independence but retained full sports contacts. The Ivory Coast, under the one-party rule of Houphouët-Boigny, enjoyed one of Africa's most buoyant economies. Its capital, Abidjan, boasted three powerful teams: Stella, ASEC, and Stade d'Abidjan, which was the African champion in 1966. In central Africa the former Belgian Congo became Zaire, and under its dynamic and soccer-loving president, Mobuto Sese Seko, its team won the African Nations' Cup twice, in 1968 and 1974; its club teams Vita of Kinshasa in 1973 and Englebert Lubumbashi in 1967 and 1968 did well in the African Champions' Cup. Zaire represented Africa in the World Cup in West Germany in 1974, and the grateful government promised the players glittering prizes for qualifying, but they came home in disgrace, outclassed by Brazil (0-3), Scotland (0-2), and Yugoslavia (0-9).

Ghana was the first sub-Saharan nation to form its own football association, which it did in 1957, and the first to join FIFA, in 1958. Its team won the African Nations' Cup in 1963, and the following year it was the first from the region to qualify for the final rounds of the Olympic Games. It advanced to the finals on other occasions, refusing for political reasons and in solidarity with other African nations to go to the Montréal Olympics in 1976. Nigeria, the most highly populated of the sub-Saharan nations, also has the largest number of registered players. It has also been the greatest supplier of players to the professional leagues of Europe. Until recently its national and club teams seemed to make a specialty of placing second in major tournaments, a failure due at least in part to disputes about whether to recall expatriate stars. It was not until 1993 that it qualified for the finals of the World Cup, although it was only the toss of a coin that saw Morocco and not Nigeria make it to Mexico in 1970. It went to USA 1994 as the African champion, having defeated Zambia in the final of the 1994 African Nations' Cup after outclassing all its opponents on the way to the final. In the United States it played some exciting soccer but surrendered a single-goal lead in the dying minutes of its quarterfinal game against Italy and lost in extra-time.

Of the other sub-Saharan teams, Zambia distinguished itself at the Seoul Olympics in 1988 and in its march to the finals of the 1994 African Nations' Cup, despite its tragic losses in an air crash the previous year, but it is South Africa, with its more stable infrastructure, that appears to be the African nation most likely to succeed in world competition. Since the lifting of the antiapartheid boycott, its teams' early encounters with the wider world of sports at club and national levels have been disappointing, but now that they are free to play with the best teams of the continent and the world at large, the promise shown for years in its domestic league must soon be realized. In Kaizer Chiefs, a team from Soweto that has always played white stars, South

Africa has a team that enjoys a nationwide loyalty similar to that of some of the big European and South American teams.

The problems facing soccer in Africa have been regularly aired in CAF bulletins and official histories. At the twelfth meeting of the CAF general assembly in 1976 some specifically African problems were raised, described as "evils" that "take the form of tribalism, ju-ju and other primitive magic which have always been encouraged in our countries and among our people by colonialism in the hope of obliterating the African personality and controlling our people." To combat the problem CAF has imposed heavy fines and suspensions: for teams not turning up because their shaman said too many players would be injured and for riots started when players were believed to wear magic armbands or were seen to bury magic charms near the goal. On one occasion four players from Zimbabwe's first-division team Tongogara were suspended for indecent exposure when they urinated along the field to remove a spell after their team went a goal down. On another occasion a team entered the field on bicycles to overcome spells laid around the touchline.

Africa's problems are essentially variations of those that have plagued most countries at some time or another, although the prospect of overcoming them seems to be getting dimmer rather than brighter. Among these are the perennial ones of a biased and sensationalist press or the frequent firing of coaches, as well as players and spectators who are ignorant of the rules. Worst, however, are the violence and corruption, with the police sometimes supporting players' and fans' attacks on referees. These attacks perplexed CAF president Tessema, who was driven to wish that some British law and order might come to pass. In the official history of CAF Tessema castigated the tribal, religious, and political bases of some teams and the inability of some people to accept a defeat against what they saw as "their tribes' dignity or their religious virtues." Despite Tessema's depressing account of the game in the mid-1980s, his successor, Issa Hayatou, claimed that the situation had deteriorated even further, blaming the declining standards of refereeing. In view of the violence to which referees so often seem to be victim, one has to wonder where the problem begins.

To date Africa has been denied a chance to host the World Cup, and in 1995 Nigeria was due to hold the World Youth Under-20 Championship, but FIFA withdrew the privilege at the last moment. A health scare was one excuse, but fears were also expressed for the safety of the players because of the political situation. When Qatar was awarded the venue, despite Nigeria spending $100 million to bring its stadiums up to FIFA's standards, Nigeria unsuccessfully tried to instigate a boycott of the competition. As a result it was expelled from the tournament, allowing Qatar to take its place.

It is only in fairly recent times that Western rulers have associated themselves with sports, and today they are anxious to have themselves photographed alongside a successful and popular team. In Africa many leaders have no such political motivation; they simply love the game: Zambia's national team was known as the Kenneth Kaunda XI (KKXI) for the deep personal interest their president took in the game. Government support for soccer, however, has often been capricious. Soccer stadiums built with copper wealth in Zambia and oil wealth in Nigeria in the 1960s have fallen into disrepair with shifts in the world's economy, but in the case of the Cameroon government, show-piece stadiums came to be used as parking and storage areas for tanks and other military equipment. The government of Ghana promised large bonuses and houses to the players of its national team for winning the African Nations' Cup in 1978, but the players were not paid and threatened to boycott the 1980 finals in Nigeria as a consequence. Nigeria won that competition and was lavishly rewarded by President Shagari and millionaire tribal chief Abiola, one of the great patrons of the game and owner of the highly regarded Abiola Babes.

In the early 1980s the governments of Zambia, Zaire, Ghana, and Nigeria all actively interfered with their soccer administrations. On other occasions soccer interfered with parliament: in Ghana in 1993 parliamentary sessions were disrupted so that members could telephone Abédi Pelé to persuade him to come out of retirement and play for the national team. In March 1994 an attempt to end a three-year stalemate in the Zaire government between Mobuto and a broad opposition movement foundered on the lack of a quorum because too many members were watching the African Nations' Cup on television.

African countries with poor roads, the barest of domestic amenities, and barely developed health or education systems have more pressing problems than the success of the national soccer team, but soccer is a cheap pleasure, and since some of the other necessities seem as far off as ever, there is little reason why the poor should be deprived of the pleasures they have. As in Brazil and other Latin American countries facing the same problems, the poor in Africa seem to hold no grudges against those who make it out of the slums and shanty towns.

For the vast majority of young Africans who practice in the streets from dawn to dusk with makeshift balls, the chances of making a decent living from the game at home are slim. There may be the occasional bonanza of a grateful government or the odd millionaire, but these cannot stem the steady exodus of players to richer pastures. In Africa itself the richer countries, such as Ivory Coast before the 1980s and then Gabon, attracted the best players from their neighbors, but Europe is the soccer mecca, with the Middle East and more recently Japan opening up new prospects. France has profited from African stars since the 1930s, Portugal has done so since the 1950s, and today there are too many African stars in Europe to list. These players have often returned to play for their national teams with the benefit of their European experience. Stars of an earlier period did not always have that option: Larbi Ben Barek came from Morocco in 1938 to play for Marseille and France, and Mario Coluña and Eusébio left Mozambique to play for Portugal in the 1950s and 1960s. France still has several black stars in its national colors, sons of Africans or individuals who arrived as infants: among these are Basile Boli, the son of a bodyguard to General de Gaulle but born in Ivory Coast, and Marcel Desailly, born in Accra of unknown parents and adopted by the French consul-general who brought him to Nantes when he was four. Both men have figured prominently in recent European Cup finals, Boli scoring the winner for Marseille against Milan in 1993, and Desailly, who was a member of the winning Marseille team in 1993, going on to score a goal in AC Milan's 4-0 victory over Barcelona the following year. The most scandalous aspect of the African soccer drain, however, and one that has been denounced by the African player of the year on more than one occasion, Abédi Pelé, is the practice of selling young teenage players to European teams for a pittance, with no benefits to the game in Africa.

---

The French encouraged soccer in their North African colonies, but it was Egypt that first represented Africa in world competition. It entered the Olympic Games soccer tournament in 1920 and the World Cup in the 1930s. In the meantime the French colonies of Algeria, Morocco, and Tunisia boasted strong league and cup competitions, helped by the French football federation, which frequently sent teams to play there. When freed from colonialism these countries' football associations entered FIFA, and their teams were the first from African nations to do well in the World Cup. Morocco represented Africa in Mexico in 1970 and tied with Bulgaria; Tunisia went to Argentina in 1978, where it beat Mexico (3-1) and tied with West Germany (0-0), only narrowly failing to reach the quarterfinals. Algeria was an even more fanatical soccer power than its two neighbors to the east and west, but its passage to independence was bloody. The war of liberation that was launched in 1954 was planned under the cover of the World Cup in Switzerland in that year, and from 1958 the National Liberation Front (Front de Libération Nationale [FLN]) entered a soccer team in the struggle. The FLN "revolutionary XI" played out of Tunisia and toured countries sympathetic to the Algerian cause. Algerian soccer players living in France returned to join the team, including stars like Rachid Mekhloufi and Moustapha Zitouni, who could have played for France in the World Cup in Sweden that year. The French government launched its counteroffensive in soccer, playing some key domestic games in Algeria and arranging internationals to be played there.

After Algeria obtained independence in 1962, soccer there continued as an arm of Algerian domestic policy and along with oil discoveries helped to keep the people's minds off the fact that they were still living under a dictatorship. The petrodollars fueled the good years, which lasted until 1982, and one of the country's leading historians, Benjamin Stora, made a parallel between social and economic success and that in soccer, claiming that "these were Algeria's great years, culminating in the victory over Germany in the World Cup in Football" (*Le Nouvel Observateur*, 4 May 1994). The military refused to give up its grip on power, however, the militancy of the Muslim extremists intensified, and in 1988 the revolt of young people who had not known the years of struggle against French imperialism was crushed with about 500 deaths. Prior to this the young dissidents had used the safer havens of the soccer stadiums as a theater for their protests, and this continued as a major outlet for Islamic Salvationist Front (FIS) and Berber discontents. Many in the middle protested the secular regime by voting for FIS in the elections of 1993, which were overturned by the government. Currently the entire country is in a state of self-imposed siege that soccer, although it continues to be played, can barely relieve.

———

Soccer in the Middle East took off in the 1970s and started to bear fruit on the international stage in the 1980s. The British first went there to protect their trade routes and oil interests and brought their soccer with them. Some of the more fanatical leaders of Islam saw soccer as a Western abomination and affront to their religion, but they were unable to convince their less-religious brethren of this and eventually had to go along with them. Iran was the most successful of the

Middle East countries in the first two decades of Asian competition, and the first to make it to the finals of the World Cup. It qualified for Argentina in 1978, where its best result was a 1-1 draw with Scotland. Soccer has a long history in Iran, where it enjoyed the support of the shahs back in the 1920s. The Amjadiyd Stadium was built in Teheran in 1939, but Persia, soon to change its name and nationalize the Anglo-Iranian Oil Company, did not send teams to serious international competition until 1950. In 1962 the shah introduced a "revolution from above" that involved a series of social reforms and the creation of the first national soccer league. European and Brazilian coaches were employed on lucrative contracts, and the players, technically amateurs, received rich rewards; in 1973 soccer became semiprofessional. Derbies between Persepolis FC and Taj FC in Tehran could now regularly pack 100,000 into the Aria Mehre Stadium. The game enjoyed a tremendous boost when the national team qualified for the World Cup in Argentina, but it received a setback the following year when the Ayatollah Khomeini came to power and tried to turn back the modernization programs of his predecessors. He could not ban soccer and so insisted on minor concessions: in team photographs a portrait of the ayatollah was prominently displayed, and when the war with Iraq began, star soccer players were shown in army uniform, defending the nation against the aggressor. Inside the sports stadiums, however, fans found one of the few areas where they could voice their discontent with the regime. Signs that the regime might be softening can be found in a decree of 1994 that allows women to attend soccer matches.

International soccer was banned in Iran and Iraq when the two countries went to war in 1979, and Kuwait established itself as one of the strongest soccer nations in the Persian Gulf. A country with a small population, Kuwait is oil-rich, like Iran, and used its wealth to import foreign coaches. Soccer was introduced to the schools in 1948, and the country's first football association was formed in 1952 but did not enter FIFA until 1962, the year after the British finally left. The ruling Al-Sabah family's vast expenditures on soccer, to reward players and discourage opponents, finally paid off when Kuwait qualified for the World Cup in Spain in 1982: its best result was a 1-1 draw with Czechoslovakia; its worst, a loss to France that was far from dishonorable but was made so by the appearance on the field of Sheik Fahd, apparently to give his support to his players' protests about a French goal. Kuwait's close rivals were Saudi Arabia, where soccer had been held back by the strength of Islam. The ruling house of Saudi Arabia gave its blessing to soccer only in 1959, when the King's Cup was introduced. In the 1970s it too adopted the fashion of importing foreign coaches but found success under a Saudi coach. And to ease any conscience troubled by soccer being played in the homeland of Mecca, Islam's holy city, matches begin and end with prayers.

If soccer had the pacifying mission that has often been attributed to it through the ages, then the Middle East would be one of the most peaceful regions on earth. But sports there have no more been free from the problems of the real world than they have been elsewhere. Iraq shared the region's fanaticism for soccer, the country being one of the most lavish in its gift-giving as well as the most ferocious in its attitude to defeat. Saddam Hussein and the ruling dictatorship frequently interfered in games, even while they were in progress. In March 1994 one of Saddam's friends ordered a change in referee at a game he was watching on television, because his team, Al-Zauraq, was losing. Al-Zauraq was down 0-2 at halftime, but the change in referee worked wonders, and Al-Zauraq won 3-2. The local fans in the crowd were not amused, but they found themselves fired on when they rioted. Iraq's Kurds have a first-division team in Arbil, near the border with Turkey, where the portrait of a soccer-playing hero who died in the fight for Kurdish independence from Iraq takes precedence over that of Saddam Hussein, whose portrait is used for shooting practice. With the increasing tensions between Kurdish claims and Saddam's dictatorship, games were banned in Arbil, leaving the Arbil fans with a seventy-mile trip for their home matches. Iraq's only serious attempt to win friends in the Arab world has been in its condemnation of Israel, the one issue on which all the Middle East countries—except Israel—can speak with one voice.

Soccer in Palestine was first played in Jerusalem's English College from 1904, but the first official teams were made up of youths from the Maccabi organization. In 1908 Maccabi Jaffa (now Tel Aviv) was founded, with a journal that came out in Hebrew. An organized league was founded in 1918 when British troops arrived as a result of the postwar settlement and the ambivalence of British promises to Arabs and Jews. Another league was set up that lasted from 1920 to 1925, followed by the Palestine Cup, which ended in 1927 when it was won outright by a Royal Air Force Team. By then the many Jews arriving from central Europe were beginning to transform the sports balance: by 1930 there were about forty clubs, and ten years later the Jewish population of about 500,000 supported thirty-eight teams in a league founded in 1932. In the 1930s the two leading Jewish teams had gained the edge on British teams such as the Palestine Police, the first winners of the league; these were Hapoel Tel Aviv, the workers' team, and Maccabi Tel Aviv, the Israeli nationalists' team. At this time the Arabs' only interest in soccer was occasionally to burn down a Jewish soccer stadium.

The troubles that were a normal way of life in Palestine before the creation of the state of Israel in 1948 continued thereafter, as Israel had to roam the world in search of a confederation that it could call its own. The power of the Arab nations of North Africa and the Middle East blocked Israel's entry into Africa and Asia, so it had to play many of its major internationals against teams from the Oceania zone, especially Australia. Finally, in 1992, Israel was accepted by UEFA and entered the European club and national competitions. Prior to this, Israel joined the AFC in 1956 and shared the major trophies in the region with Iran, but it was constantly faced by political opposition. Israel's first major success on the world soccer scene came at the 1968 Olympics, where it made it to the quarterfinals, only to be eliminated by Bulgaria on the toss of a coin. The Mexico experience paid off when Israel, having eliminated South Korea and Australia, qualified for the 1970 World Cup finals, where it lost only 0-2 to Uruguay and went on to hold Sweden and Italy to draws.

---

Taiwan was the other outcast of the Asia-Africa zone, and Havelange's election in 1974 did not bode well for it, for the new president made no secret of his wish to see China enter FIFA. Taiwan has never been a serious soccer power, in part because of the U.S. influence, and its national team has usually been made up of players from Hong Kong. Taiwan's problems stemmed from the power politics that had the United States backing the tiny island's claim to be China and thus denying the name to the mainland regime that turned communist in October 1949. The communists were able to call on strong anticolonial sentiments in the countries of Asia and Africa, and from 1974 they could call on Havelange.

Supporting Havelange was Hong Kong millionaire Henry Fok, who wanted to open up the mainland to soccer and trade and who won the backing of the Middle East countries by supporting them against Israel. As a result, FIFA turned a blind eye when the AFC expelled Taiwan in 1976 in order to admit the People's Republic of China. China finally joined the world body in 1980, and Taiwan was forced to play in Oceania. Havelange's support for China came in large measure because of the step toward making the game truly global its inclusion would constitute. Up through the 1960s India promised to be the giant of Asian soccer; in the late 1970s that mantle fell on the

People's Republic of China, but whatever the world body gained in statistics, there was little reward in quality, for although more than 20 million were added to the list of FIFA's registered players in the 1980s, China's performance in Asian and world competition has been mediocre, at least until recently, and the organization of the game has at times verged on the farcical.

China's role in soccer since 1949 contrasts to the one it had played before the communists took over. In the 1930s the Chinese won their independence against the Europeans, entering FIFA in 1931, but they were to find the Japanese a much more vicious enemy. From the Japanese invasion of Manchuria in 1931 to the full-scale war between Japan and China that broke out in 1937 and lasted until 1945, and the civil war against Chiang Kai-shek that lasted until 1949, China found its attentions centered on matters other than sports. China's peasants, most of whom lived in dire poverty, made up the vast bulk of the population and carried the brunt of the civil and foreign wars, and so soccer was played mainly by clerks and students for teams that were often owned by millionaire businesspeople. The players on the team that China sent to the 1936 Olympic Games were all in middle-class occupations. When Mao Zedong came to power in 1949, many of the mainland's best players fled to safer havens, but some stayed on, and as the great leader had written a treatise on the need for physical education early in his revolutionary career, the new regime set about creating the healthy bodies for politically healthy minds.

Under the communists soccer in China has fluctuated in rhythm to the politics of the day, with state interference retarding the vast population's progress toward reaching its potential. In the early years games were played against varied opposition, but these were usually teams from fellow communist regimes. After the big split between Beijing and Moscow, China severed relations with the Warsaw Pact countries in 1960. Then came the black hole of the Cultural Revolution, which began in 1966, with the fanatical anti-elitism of the leaders sending intellectuals to plow fields and sports stars to clean streets. Beginning in 1971 "ping-pong" diplomacy brought sports back into favor, and Henry Fok set about having China admitted into FIFA. Before this was realized, however, Chinese teams were allowed to play against those of FIFA member countries, although China was not itself a member nation. Many acute observers at this time were led to believe that China was a sleeping giant that would be a leading soccer power by the turn of the century. A scheme for professionalism was introduced in 1993, along with a new ten-year plan, but despite the success of this first season, the immense distances and poor travel facilities still present formidable obstacles to the domestic game.

---

At the same time as China was being tipped as a soccer power of the future, much the same was being said about that other "Third-World" soccer power, the United States, then going through its Pelé-inspired soccer boom. The crowds continued to come to the games after Pelé retired, and not just in New York: the Tampa Bay Rowdies and Golden Bay drew large crowds, and Seattle, with average crowds around 20,000 for several years, was a surprise packet. Even Minnesota averaged 30,926 in 1978, but a few years later the team no longer existed. In Canada Vancouver hosted the best crowds, averaging 15,736 in 1978 and rising as high as 29,130 in 1983, whereas in Toronto crowds increased from an average 7,336 in 1978 to 15,040 in 1980. There were some major sponsors, but most of the money went to the overseas players and administration. No amount of money can buy tradition or create a homegrown star: the game was as un-American in the early 1980s as it always had been. When Cosmos went bankrupt in 1984, it was merely a reflection and not a cause of the failure of professional soccer in the United States. In the meantime its popularity continued to grow among boys and girls, mainly white, who happily played the game until they went to college and began to play more important sports—or more lucrative: as Walter Bahr, one of the longest surviving members of the 1950 U.S. World Cup team, told Helmut Kuhn in regard to his sons, who were successful in both soccer and American football, "Their hearts beat for soccer, but their wallets belonged to football" (*Fussball in den USA,* 1994). And Tony Meola, despite his success as a goalkeeper in the United State's two recent World Cup ventures, opted to join the New York Jets as a placekicker.

---

While observers were predicting that China and the United States would have a rosy soccer future, Japan and Korea were modest participants on the world scene. Today they are prime candidates to lead Asia into the new century. North Korea faded from the picture after briefly stunning the soccer world in 1966, and although South Korea is one of the most successful soccer nations in Asia, baseball was a more popular spectator sport there in the 1970s. Part of South Korea's problems was its refusal to recognize professionalism, so that many of its best players sought careers elsewhere in Asia or even in

Europe. The South Korea football association finally tried to solve the problem, introducing first partial professionalism in 1980 and then a fully professional "superleague" in 1983. The top club, Hallelujah, was founded by evangelical Christians and the first to take advantage of the new regulations. It was joined by five other teams in the new league, with two amateur teams taking the numbers to eight. The influences were industrial and American, as could be seen in the names of the teams and the attempts to brighten up the game by eliminating draws and making awards for special players and coaches, but the interests of the state prevailed against those of the clubs, which lost players who were needed for World Cup preparation. The domestic league suffered as a result, but it was more important to the authorities that the national team do well, and so the ban on playing expatriate professionals was lifted. As a result, South Korea qualified for the next three World Cups: a spirited performance in 1986 was followed by a poor run in 1990, but at USA 1994 South Korea performed brilliantly at times, and with more consistent firepower up front it easily could have gone on to the quarterfinals. South Korea's success in holding the 1988 Olympic Games, its continued dominance of Asian competition, and the possibility of reunification make the country a front runner to host the 2002 World Cup. It is rumored that Korea has the support of Havelange, setting his sights on a Nobel Peace Prize by bringing the two Koreas together to host the event—a prize denied his Olympic colleague, Juan Antonio Samaranch, when Sydney beat out Beijing for the 2000 Olympic Games.

In the early 1980s Japan as a soccer power was best known for staging the Toyota Cup. Ten years later it was known throughout the soccer world not for anything it had achieved but for what it looked like it would achieve with the introduction of the fully professional J-League in May 1993. Sumo wrestling has always been Japan's national sport, and baseball the most popular spectator sport, but now, in its move to make soccer fully professional, Japan appears to be succeeding where the United States and Hong Kong have failed, with plans for several modern soccer stadiums and budgeted deficits for years to come. Japanese baseball teams have never reached a higher standard than that of the U.S. minor leagues, but the prospects of Japanese soccer players competing at world level are increasingly bright. Certainly, making a world-class soccer team is a more formidable task than producing a quality automobile or television set—Kamamotos do not come off the assembly line, and team tactics cannot be worked out on computers—but already soccer is proving to be more popular than baseball with young Japanese, who have found in the game's continuous flow, speed, and free expression a means to express their personalities, which are often lost in the wider society. Local players are proving to be more than a support caste for the three foreign professionals in most teams, and stars can earn huge fees for advertisements and appearances on television, where they have replaced baseball players as favorite subjects for interviews. Even its team's failure to qualify for USA 1994 has failed to shake the ambition of Japan to make it to the top ranks in soccer, and the average attendance for the season concluded in 1995 was nearly 20,000. Moreover, Japan seems to have escaped the hooliganism and financial scandals that plagued the European and other soccer leagues in the 1980s.

# New Faces, Old Problems

The 1990 World Cup was held in Italy, but the country that has produced some of soccer's finest teams and players could do nothing to bring alive a competition in which most games limped through to the worst final ever seen: West Germany, playing with precision but little flair, defeated an Argentine team that had struggled from round to round without a single redeeming grace, a shadow of the team that Diego Maradona had inspired in Mexico four years previously. The vast viewing audience, variously calculated to suit administrators and would-be sponsors, was nevertheless the largest ever to watch a single sports competition, a reflection of the global popularity of soccer but also a measure of the spread of television sets into the poorest Third-World countries. For those with interests beyond sports, television provided a market to be tapped as a commercial opportunity for entrepreneurs or as a publicity opportunity for politicians or others in search of power or fame. Television is the image maker of the modern—or should that be postmodern?—age, and although it had been an integral part of the lives of most people in the developed world in the 1960s, the technological advances and ideological fashions of the 1980s made it an inescapable part of daily life, along with fax machines, mobile telephones, portable computers, and video games. Although this has made remarkably little impact on soccer as a game, it has revolutionized its organization and transformed its effect on the public.

Through television the artistry of great players and the performances of great teams can now be brought into the homes of people who would previously have only read or heard of their exploits. It was also through television broadcasts, beamed into millions of homes throughout the world, that three of the world's worst sporting tragedies were brought live to viewers: the horror on 29 May 1985 at the Heysel Stadium in Brussels, when rampaging Liverpool fans charged Juventus supporters into a wall that collapsed, resulting in thirty-nine deaths before the start of the Liverpool versus Juventus European Cup final of that year; the inferno two weeks earlier that engulfed the stand at the Valley Parade Ground, Bradford, and took the lives of fifty-six people; and the even greater horror at Hillsborough Stadium, Sheffield, on 15 April 1989, when ninety-six spectators, mainly Liverpool supporters, were crushed to death against a spectator fence just before the start of an FA Cup semifinal between Liverpool and Nottingham Forest.

Television cannot be blamed either for the dull soccer at Italia 1990 or for the tragedies at European soccer grounds, and it played an only peripheral role in the spread of the hooliganism that reached its peak in the first part of the 1980s. Television was responsible at least in part for the sparse attendance that presented such a sorry sight at many soccer grounds throughout the world in the 1980s, and it was a major reason for the degeneration of some of the players' standards of dress and behavior on the field. Out of sight of the cameras, it was television that encouraged the unseemly scramble by players, directors, and entrepreneurs to help themselves to the rich pickings that television sponsorship offered. But the all-seeing eye of the television camera also helped to rid the game of the thugs and cheats behind the play who had prospered in earlier times. So far soccer has resisted the most blasphemous suggestions of those who would change its rules to encourage "brighter" play or to allow for the intrusion of commercial breaks. Some sports have been tampered with to suit television, but soccer has so far been spared this: the most significant changes have been minor ones such as the introduction of shoot-outs to avoid replays in cup games and the rearrangement of the sports calendar: Saturday (in Britain) and Sunday (in many Latin countries) are no longer the days set aside for soccer worship, and world championships have been played in the heat in one continent to suit prime-time viewers in another: in Mexico in 1970 and 1986 and above all in the suffocating conditions of USA 1994. The players, however, were well rewarded financially for their discomfort.

For better and for worse, television has become an indispensable part of the world game, spreading its finest moments to people who could never hope to see them live and magnifying its worst with visual images that black-and-white photographs and columns of the printed word can convey only partially. The magic of Maradona is a reality to millions throughout the world, whereas the tales of the characters from the pretelevision age are no more than the myths of an older generation. The riots at the Heysel and the faces of the dead crushed against the fence at Hillsborough will live in the memory of millions who were not at the game, whereas the 318 people killed in Peru in 1964 at the end of the 1964 Olympic qualifier between Peru and Argentina are merely something you read about.

Television was no more than a curiosity at the 1936 Olympic Games, and the few soccer matches shown on television in the years after World War II reached a very limited audience. The number of receivers increased slowly and the transmission range gradually expanded, however, so that in 1953 the whole of Great Britain was able to watch the "Matthews" Cup final between Bolton Wanderers and Blackpool, and the following year the World Cup games played in Switzerland could be seen throughout most of Europe. In 1966 the World Cup was beamed across the Atlantic, and in the 1970s television could show live matches taking place on the other side of the globe.

By this time the images put before the viewer had improved dramatically through several developments: slow-motion replays in the mid-1960s, quality color a few years later, and from the 1970s improvements in technology that allowed aerial panoramas to show packed grounds and close-ups to register the anguish or delight of the players or fans. By the 1980s split screens and the use of multiple cameras allowed goals and close shaves to be repeated from a variety of angles. Video had arrived by then, creating a new market, and there were by this time so many television cameras at games throughout the world that it was technically possible to present a fifty-minute (not sixty, for ten minutes had to be left for sales to commercial channels) package of the most exciting moments in soccer throughout the world that particular day or week or live coverage of the most attractive match from any country in the world. The attractions of armchair viewing meant that only the most committed fan braved the weather and spartan conditions of the terrace, regardless of whether there was a top-class match to be seen or a world-class star in action.

Football of any code, and soccer in particular, became the major sports attraction for television viewers in the 1960s. Before then dramas, comedies, news, and musicals were television's main fare, or sports like boxing, where the camera did not have to chase the action over a wide area. As reception improved, so that games did not have to be watched through intermittent snow storms, and cameras became more portable and covered wider angles, sports became increasingly popular. For football, as for music, sex, and violence, there was no language barrier, and so it easily translated across national boundaries. From the 1960s television producers had to conform to this changing demand, with schedules altered to allow for games going overtime, while politicians in democratic countries who had never before shown much interest in sports found it convenient to become associated with them.

———————

In Europe before the 1980s most television was in the control of a national broadcaster, with strict controls on the timing and nature of advertising on those channels, where it was permitted at all. As a result most soccer matches were presented free from interference. Many soccer authorities were still worried that televising games live would hurt attendance, and they restricted the number of games they allowed to be shown. The fee they received then was nominal. This changed when the competition of rival and privatized channels led to the soccer authorities being offered vastly increased sums for the rights to televise games live. Commercial entrepreneurs, armed with the latest technology and fired with the faith of the prevailing orthodoxy that "greed is good" launched attacks on state monopolies from the early 1980s. In Italy, Silvio Berlusconi, then merely an entrepreneur out to make more money rather than the owner of a soccer team out to improve his prestige, won the rights to televise the Copa de Oro competition played in Uruguay in 1981, with Italy being one of the competing countries. It was the first break in the Italian Broadcasting Service's (RAI) monopoly and the beginning of Berlusconi's takeover of Italian soccer through his privately owned television channel, Canale 5.

In 1977 the French Football Federation received about $100,000 from the state-run television channel. Ten years later, as a result of competition between Canal Plus, a subscription channel that was saved from bankruptcy only through televising live soccer, and the newly privatized TF1, it received over $100 million. Whether the game itself has benefited is another matter. The top clubs in France were often under the control of the local municipalities that owned the stadiums and appointed the teams' managers. Some saw through soccer a means of boosting the local region and their own prestige and profits. Between one and the other, the application of market forces and financial expansion beyond the sports world resulted in many clubs going broke or being threatened with bankruptcy. Powerful clubs in France had gone broke before the impact of television, but in the 1980s some individuals became so excited by the amount of money coming into the game that they ended up in jail or disappeared with a cloud over their reputations.

In the 1980s the competition from the new companies that broke up the cartels seemed only to increase the thirst for soccer coverage. In Italy the junkies could watch soccer on the small screen on Sunday from shortly after midday to midnight without a break, but they had to make do with a mere forty hours for the remaining days of the week. In Spain, as a survey by *World Soccer* reported (March 1995), in the twelve months beginning 1 August 1993 television channels showed 788 matches, of which 512 were live. Two state run channels compete with two private channels and one subscription channel, as well as a host of regional channels, where Catalan and Basque broadcasts—how Franco would suffer at the thought—enjoy particularly high ratings. Smaller countries that cannot keep foreign soccer broadcasts at bay have had to adjust their domestic programs accordingly. In Ireland the big games are played on Friday and Saturday nights to avoid the competition from television. Despite the saturation coverage, attendance at the English Premier League and the German Bundesliga has continued to rise recently: games in the Bundesliga in the 1994–95 season averaged 30,261, nearly double that of six years previously.

In Germany the money from the television bonanza is more evenly spread around the Bundesliga clubs, but this is exceptional. Commercial television was interested only in the star players and star teams, leading to ever more outrageous payments to the best players. The madness in regard to expenditures on players and desperate attempts to keep up with close rivals has affected even the game's greatest clubs, some of which have found themselves in serious financial trouble. Spain's Réal Madrid, still playing before large home crowds, was threatened with accumulating debts; Benfica in Portugal played games before 120,000 spectators in the Stadium of Light, but its players could not be sure that their paychecks would not bounce. On the other hand, Celtic in Scotland found itself in trouble by clinging too closely to the family dynasties that had been with the club for over a hundred years and was saved from bankruptcy only by the intervention of an expatriate Scot, the Canadian millionaire Fergus McCann. Napoli, which had paid a fortune to attract Maradona to the club and then to keep him there, was faced with bankruptcy when season-ticket sales dropped from 55,000 to less than 10,000 after he left the club for Seville in September 1992. It has to be said, however, that as in Celtic's case, maladministration was also to blame. A few books have come out in recent years denouncing this financial chaos, some using the current imagery of soccer in the title, as in Edwin Klein's 1994 publication detailing the problems in Germany, *Rote Karte für den DfB: die Machenschaften im Deutschen Profifussball* (Red card for the German FA: intrigues in German professional football) and French journalists André Bufford and André Soulier's *Carton rouge* (Red card).

Through it all Ajax of Amsterdam has pursued a policy of self-sufficiency, building on the long Dutch tradition of bringing their young players to maturity through extensive coaching schools, which do not neglect their general education. Few if any clubs have produced such a bright array of young talent as Ajax has in the last thirty years, allowing the club to keep itself comparatively free from reliance on sponsorship and television. It would be heartening to think, in view of Ajax's triumph in defeating Milan in the final of the 1995 European Cup with a goal scored by eighteen-year-old Patrick Kluivert, that this is the wave of the future. Heartening, but unlikely. Other giants of the game continue to confirm their hold on power and money: Barcelona, Manchester United, Bayern Munich, and above all Berlusconi's AC Milan. Berlusconi outstripped all his rivals without tarnishing his business reputation in a country whose soccer, like its politicians, has frequently been associated with bribery and corruption. He bought into the club in 1986, replacing two disgraced presidents, and under his administration AC Milan has gone on to rank with the great teams of all time, its 4-0 crushing of Barcelona in the final of the 1994 European Cup producing some of the finest soccer played by a club side since the glory days of Réal Madrid. Berlusconi made his fortune outside soccer and then used his star soccer players to boost his business interests, but he went on to astonish the world of politics and sports when he ran for the Italian presidency in 1994. With little political experience but controlling the country's main media outlets, he ran on the reputation of AC Milan and the slogan of the Italian national team: "Forza Italia." He succeeded at the polls and was elected president with the support of right-wing and neofascist parties.

Not far from Berlusconi, in the Mediterranean port of Marseilles, another millionaire and would-be politician built his reputation on ownership of a soccer team: Bernard Tapie of Olympique Marseille (OM). Some have called him a "Red Berlusconi," and his populism has placed him on the left of the political spectrum, although in the Socialist party and outside Marseilles he is seen more as an opportunist. The fates, however, have not been as kind to him as they have been to his Italian rival. He bought up lavishly to create a great team for the soccer-mad population of France's second-largest city, which includes large minorities of immigrants, mostly from North Africa, and in 1991 the team came within penalties of the European Cup, Red Star taking off the trophy. Two years later, however, OM beat AC Milan to become the first French club to win a European trophy. In 1994 Tapie entered the lists as an independent Socialist for the European parliament, but by then his and OM's involvement in a soccer scandal took up as much media space as his political ambitions. His club was found guilty of attempting to bribe players in a French league match in 1993, and OM was relegated to the second division, lost the right to represent Europe in the World Champions Cup, and was banned from European competition for a year. Tapie's career was ruined as he faced imprisonment; his majority share in the club was sold for a franc, while the weight of debt on the bankrupt club prevented it from accepting promotion back to the first division.

British soccer also came under the sway of the profiteers, and some millionaires found that business and soccer in Britain are still not synonymous. As in Europe, the worst financial excesses came with privatization and decentralization, along with the introduction of satellite broadcasting and cable television. In November 1987 BSB (British Satellite Broadcasting) made overtures to the wealthiest clubs in England, forcing the commercial television channels (ITV) and BBC to enter the auction to secure the rights to televise games. Seduced by the largess on offer, in 1992 the FA and some of the richest clubs broke away from the League to form a "superleague" called the Premier League. The coup was not as clean as they would have liked, and in the end the Premier League was no more than the old first division, but run by the FA instead of the League. It ended a century of uneasy cooperation between the FA and the League and a decade in which the richest clubs set out to ensure that they did not have to share their wealth with the weaker clubs.

The communist-bloc countries, in addition to enduring omnipresent political corruption, also had their own version of the capitalist disease. Hungary in particular had suffered from widescale corruption, but throughout the 1980s new financial scandals were regularly brought to light in Czechoslovakia, Bulgaria, and Poland, as well as in Hungary, with several players and officials sent to jail. The breakup of the Soviet Union initiated an exodus of star players with little return to the local game. Some financial sharks engaged in dodgy business ventures from the money they made in arranging transfers, and the game was brought to an all-time low; apart from the corruption and loss of skilled players, the stadiums lost the social function they served in the days of dictatorship, while the tensions of games against the now independent republics, which had used soccer for their nationalist campaigns, was gone. In Romania and Bulgaria, on the other hand, the lifting of controls seems to have released talent for the national teams, although whether the domestic game will benefit from their success in USA 1994 remains to be seen.

---

In the early 1960s Eric Batty saw too much money as a cause of the problems facing Italian, French, and Spanish clubs at that time, and three decades later soccer was still awash with money, while more clubs than ever were deep in debt. By then the FA had given up its long-held position as custodian of the game's high moral standards in England, while the "people's game" was being battered by the forces of raw materialism. Above all, its dignity continued to suffer as advertising signs invaded the playing arena and commercial graffiti disfigured the once-sacred uniforms of the players.

Soccer stadiums and soccer players have been associated with commercial ventures from the earliest days—even the first rules of the FA were printed by the sports equipment and clothing supplier Lillywhite, which bought the sole rights to publish them, and the most intransigently amateur clubs have relied on advertisers to cover publications costs. Long before television, stand roofs were plastered with advertisements, the maker's name was displayed prominently on the ball, and entrepreneurs in Britain sold meat pies, fried potatoes, and Bovril (a meat-flavored hot drink) to the fans entering the ground. Such culinary delights were looked on with some horror by the more delicate palates on the Continent, but there, too, the same entrepreneurial spirit prevailed. Newspapers ran advertisements that used the appeal of the game, and match programs had more advertisements than sports information. Some major soccer competitions, on the Continent more than in Britain, were sponsored by newspapers and commercial firms. All that television did was widen the market—by the commercial equivalent of a quantum leap.

Shirt and perimeter advertising made little impact when it was seen only by those at the game and in the occasional photograph, and the British press ridiculed the first advertisements to appear on the shirts of foreign teams in Europe. National broadcasters at first refused to televise games where players had these advertisements and either told the teams to change their uniforms or took their cameras away. After some resistance in the early 1980s, however, the television companies gradually gave in, insisting at first that advertising be limited to a particular size. In the mid-1960s teams from France, Austria, and Switzerland were among the first to put advertising on their shirts, and they have retained a standard of ugliness in sportswear ever since. In Germany, Eintracht Braunschweig first entered the field with the name of a local brewery in 1973, and five years later only Schalke and Köln of the Bundesliga clubs held out against the practice. A fee of £225,000 a year eventually broke them down. In England the non-League club Kettering was the first to carry shirt advertising, that of a local tire manufacturer, in January 1977, but the League told the club to remove it. Manager Derek Dougan refused but then compromised by agreeing to leave just the letter *T.* Shortly afterward the FA turned down an offer from Ladbroke, the betting firm, to sponsor the Home International competition, thereby upsetting the Wales FA, which thought that it should have been consulted. The chinks were beginning to appear, and the big clubs soon put money before tradition. Arsenal finally allowed commercial graffiti to besmirch their famous red-and-white shirts when a Japanese firm offered the appropriate sum of money. In Spain Catalan pride and a refusal to follow its Madrid rivals has left Barcelona as the only major soccer club with the dignity of a commercial-free uniform. Some other clubs and countries have maintained a level of decorum in succumbing to the new reality, but others seemed not in the least abashed about presenting their players as mobile sandwich boards chasing the ball around a supermarket.

---

At the same time as wealth undreamed of poured into some club coffers and the bank accounts of individual players and their agents, fewer people were attending the games in the 1980s. The problem of declining attendance was not peculiar to soccer, or even to sports, for churches and cinemas suffered from much larger losses, but in the 1980s paying spectators were still the most important source of income for most clubs, and their absence from the grounds threatened some clubs with extinction. Argentina and Brazil were still two of the world's great soccer giants at the national level, but chaos seemed to rule in the domestic game, encouraging star players to seek their fortunes elsewhere. In Argentina top clubs have fielded reserve teams in the national competition so that their first teams could earn bigger money in tours of Europe. In Brazil some clubs do not even own their players, who are controlled by agents whose only interest is in selling them for the cut they get in the transfer fee. Other irregularities in Brazilian soccer, none of which do the game any good, including changing the rules to aid particular clubs, have been protected at the highest level—in Brazil and even beyond. Club loyalties have declined, and of the Latin American countries Mexico is the only one with a healthy following through the turnstiles, averaging 20,000 and much more for the big games in recent times. The average salary for a Mexican player in the top division is $150,000, compared to $65,000 in Argentina, $48,000 in Brazil, and $36,000 in Colombia. In Uruguay at the start of the 1995 season twelve first-division clubs owed their players over $1 million, Nacional accounting for nearly half of the unpaid salaries.

In England average attendance at first-division football dropped from over 30,000 to 24,500 in the 1970s and fell by a spectacular 30 percent between 1980 and 1986, a drop of 8 million. In Belgium crowds averaged around 9,000–10,000, in France they averaged 5,000–7,000, and in Germany crowds at the top games averaged between 20,000 and 23,000 in the 1970s and were as high as 27,000 in the 1977–78 season. In Italy Milan was relegated to the second division in 1980 over a corruption scandal, and the game was afflicted by other off-the-field problems before Italy in the late 1980s could boast the best league in the world. In 1984 Napoli signed Diego Maradona, with a consequent increase in average attendance by 20,000 to 77,457. In 1985 average attendance in the Serie A was 39,000. Nevertheless, the top-drawing club in Europe—and the world—was Barcelona, which throughout the 1980s was drawing crowds of over 100,000 to all its home games; Réal Madrid averaged 70,101 in the 1984–85 season.

A popular club on a winning run has no trouble attracting the crowds, and the appearance of a genuine star player would always increase the gates—dramatically, in the cases of Matthews in the 1950s, Pelé in the 1960s, Cruyff in the 1970s, or Maradona in the 1980s (or Kamamoto in Japan). These were the players the fans happily paid money to see, and these were the players the sponsors wanted to carry their names. Despite the falling attendance, players' salaries—and not just those of the superstars—continued to escalate. At Napoli Maradona earned over £1 million with sponsorship money in his first year and then went on to triple that amount. The most highly paid players in Italy and Spain were all foreigners. In the 1990s the over-the-hill Maradona, burdened by his drug habit and a weight problem, missed more games than he played yet cost his new Spanish club, Seville, an estimated $288,461 per match. Paul Gascoigne, England's overenthusiastic young genius, was transferred from financially troubled Tottenham to Lazio for £5.5 million in June 1992 but missed many games through injury. *Corriere dello Sport* calculated that as a result he cost his new club £400 per minute. Clubs have been equally profligate with their expenditures on managers, where even those who fail can expect to walk away with a half-million pounds on termination of their contract. Such costs are subsidized mainly by gate receipts, admission prices having rocketed in Britain, where soccer was once a cheap entertainment. The ultimate cost, however, as Nick Hornby has warned in his fascinating autobiography of a soccer obsessive (*Fever Pitch*), could be in losing the young fans who once got caught up in the fever and carried their obsession into a mature age, following their club regardless of the fare being served up on the field.

---

The players at the center of the media attention have not remained unaffected by it, and the British, who once thought the open expression of joy over goals scored was the province of excitable foreigners, now play to the crowd and the television camera. In 1976 the FA was concerned about the "kissing and cuddling" that it feared was bringing the game into disrepute but could do nothing about it. These expressions of joy were often more honest than the studied indifference of another age, and they could be amusing, but some of the orgies of congratulation that greet a goal today are simply embarrassing. In Brazil elaborate dance rituals choreographed to celebrate goals had to be banned, for although they were aesthetic enough in themselves, they took up too much time.

Off the field the fans engaged in ever-more extravagant means of supporting their teams, from the massive banners lovingly created to catch the eye of the camera on the one hand to the savage displays of violence against rival fans that have increasingly disfigured the game on the other. Such partisan behavior took root above all in England. Throughout the 1970s and into the 1980s, English soccer hooligans inspired terror in innocent travelers and shoppers who crossed their path on the way to a game, forced the police to adopt new strategies to cope with the menace, and spawned a new academic industry to analyze the phenomenon. Not surprisingly, serious studies have located the roots of the problem in society, and some researchers insisted that there was more illusion than reality in what was essentially a "ritual of violence." This may have been so in some or even most cases, but the level of violence was still intolerable. Those who studied the problem at close range rejected the claim that the hooligans had no interest in soccer; on the contrary, love of the club and stadium could take the place of the family and home they never had. Nevertheless, the spectacle on the field often became secondary to abusing fans of the opposite team across the "no-man's-land" created to keep the two factions apart. For the more serious hooligans, military-style planning preceded attempts to eject opponents from their own "turf," and in the late 1970s the first of the middle-class hooligans, called "casuals" and distinguished by their designer clothing, made their much-publicized entry on the scene.

In the late 1970s, in a grotesque parody of the lead set by the British in soccer before 1914, Continental hooligans looked to the English as their model, tried to match them in thuggery, and adopted various English names to describe themselves: "boys," "lions," "panthers," "skins," and strange mixtures like "Pitbull Kop"—the Kop originally named after a hill in the Boer War but by the 1970s synonymous with Liverpool's most dedicated supporters. The English hooligans were less than impressed, however. French journalist Philippe Broussard spent time with some leaders of the "ultras" in Italy, Spain, and France, the "sidos" of Belgium and the Netherlands, and the "hooligans" of Great Britain, Germany, and Greece; in his book *Génération supporteur: Enquête sur les ultras du football* (1990), where he describes the experience, he says that the English hooligan leaders (like the men of the FA and the League earlier in the century) were contemptuous of the efforts of those who would be their disciples in the television age.

The Italians came to rival the English and produced highly organized groups of supporters who developed their own distinctive rituals involving colored flares, giant banderoles, and the humming of some of Verdi's best-known airs. Unlike the English hooligans, who tended to come together only at games, the Italian ultras spent much of the week together preparing their elaborate banderoles. It is not all in fun: banners at the San Siro in Milan in 1990 told the visitors from Naples that they were worse than blacks and expressed the wish that Hitler had done to them what he did to the Jews. Among themselves the supporters from the south were equally venomous, tensions between Roma and Lazio in the capital reaching crisis point in October 1979 when a young Lazio fan was killed by a flare fired by an opposing Roma supporter. In contrast to fans in Britain, where politics seldom features in club support (apart from the eternal exceptions in Glasgow, where Rangers have many Unionist supporters and Celtic has Irish nationalists), French and Italian supporters sometimes adopt political postures. At the end of the 1970s Roma was the first Italian club to organize its various factions into what became known from the beginning of January 1977 as the Cucs—the Commando Ultra Curva Sud, the "commandos" of the supporters who gathered in the south curve of the Olympic stadium, which they shared with Lazio. Italy at that time was racked by political violence, particularly from the Red Brigades, and the two big Roman rivals were said to represent different sides of the political spectrum, Roma being on the Left and Lazio on the Right. The somewhat shaky basis for this claim was that Roma was supported by all classes, whereas Lazio had a more middle-class support. There were factions within the support, however, and refusing to join the Cucs were the openly left-wing Fedayn and the right-wing Panthers, joined by the Boys.

In the changing alliances of the subgroups, the political ideology that emerged in the end was right-wing and often racist, with swastikas superimposed on banners and references to Hitler freely aired, often for shock value but never entirely in innocence. In Hungary MTK's Jewish past was resurrected, and Ferencvaros supporters assailed the team with antisemitic abuse. Broussard's Réal Madrid contact hankered after the days of Franco, his Greek contact Iannis worshiped the neo-Nazism of the British National Front (and Chelsea), and Roma and Lazio ultras yelling abuse at each other inside the grounds could find themselves marching together in political demonstrations in favor of the neofascist Gianfranco Fini. The Marseilles ultras, the only French hooligans who could rival the Italians, gave a peculiarly French touch to their team support; in addition to voicing hatred of Paris, they unveiled a banderole of record proportions (for France—it was ninety-one by twenty-one meters) that read: "One myth, one faith, one struggle. Marseillaise ultras, history continues," a curious mixture that could show the influence of Louis XIV, Hitler, and Trotsky in all possible combinations. In Strasbourg, when a popular coach was sacked in 1994 by the municipal council that owned the club, as is often the case in France, a banner proclaimed: "Socialism killed soccer and basketball at Mulhouse; is it going to kill our Racing?" In the communist bloc Czechoslovakia had some highly publicized hooligan escapades, and fans in the Soviet Union, in their rituals behind the goals and in their behavior to and from matches, could be seen to be following the example set in England. By then politics in the communist countries was a matter for confusion rather than a guiding light.

In Britain the racist National Front sought recruits among the hooligans. A Germany-England friendly set for 20 April 1994 at the Berlin Olympia Stadion had to be canceled out of fear that English fascists and German neo-Nazis would take the opportunity to celebrate the date, Adolf Hitler's birthday, with a display of thuggery in honor of the long-dead Führer. The English fascists had their most notable success the following year on 15 February 1995, when organized groups forced the abandonment of an Ireland-England friendly international in Dublin. Irish police failed to act on the warnings of their British counterparts, and less than a half-hour into the match missiles were thrown to chants of "No surrender," the battle cry of the Ulster and Unionist Protestants fiercely opposed to a united Ireland.

Many, if not most, of the young working-class soccer supporters came from a culture in which sexism and casual violence were facts of life and thus were susceptible to extreme right-wing politics. On the whole, however, it is unlikely that most hooligan groups had an ideology that went far beyond that of the Cardiff City fan reported by Paul Harrison in his 1974 article entitled "Soccer's tribal wars," whose confession that he wet his pants with delight at the thought of sinking his boot into another hooligan's head became almost as overquoted as the sayings of Bill Shankly.

Individual deaths in confrontations by rival fans in or near soccer grounds have been with the game for decades. One change today is that the clubs are less likely to claim that it is none of their business. In Italy on 29 January 1995 a Genoa fan was stabbed by visiting Milan fans before the start of the game, and when news of his death became known at halftime it led to serious rioting. The game was abandoned, and the Italian authorities took the unprecedented step of banning all Serie A games for the following Sunday as a mark of respect for the victim. This was the sixth fan-related death in or near a stadium since 1979. Shortly after the Genoa killing a player was killed in Paris after an amateur league game between two ethnically based teams; the Parisian minor league games were canceled for the following week. In England about the same time, and in full view of a national television audience, Eric Cantona, Manchester United's fiery French soccer genius, in a soccer version of the "man bites dog" story, attacked a Crystal Palace fan for abusing him as he left the field after yet another expulsion for indisciplined behavior. An indirect result of this was the death of a father of four on 9 April 1995 before these two clubs were due to meet in an FA Cup semifinal match. A dispute broke out in a pub between Manchester United and Crystal Palace fans allegedly over Cantona, resulting in bricks being thrown at the Crystal Palace fans as they boarded their bus for the game. One of them killed the Crystal Palace supporter. Since this killing took place some miles from where the match was to be played, neither club saw it as its responsibility.

Despite the ferocity of fan battles and the fearsome nature of some of the weapons, few deaths resulted. The media no doubt gave these hooligans more publicity than they warranted, and they were better copy than they were a serious threat to life and limb, but their behavior was a disgrace, an insult to the countries they visited, and a source of shame to their compatriots who did not share their loutishness. It was, therefore, as natural as it was unjustified that the tragedies of the 1980s involving English soccer teams should be ascribed to their hooligans.

The disaster at Hillsborough in 1989 came at the start of the Liverpool versus Nottingham Forest FA Cup semifinal. As is the way with British fans, many had waited until the last few minutes before entering the grounds, and because of the separation of the fans and an oversight in the allocation of tickets, the much larger Liverpool contingent was sent to the smaller Leppings Road end. Fearing trouble, for the crowds queuing behind the slow-moving turnstiles were growing impatient as the kickoff time drew near, the police opened the exit gates to let them in more quickly. It was then that the slow crush built up on the spectators closest to the fence, who had no means of escape. There were no side gates, the fence was built to withstand an army, and the small exit gates were pathetically inadequate. Absent was the one factor that had prevented similar tragedies in the century-long history of the game: easy access to the playing area. At the Valley Parade tragedy in Bradford in 1985, the fire was started by a lighted match or cigarette end dropped on rubbish that had been accumulating for over a decade. Even at the Heysel Stadium, although it is incontestable that Liverpool fans started the stampede that ended in disaster, the deaths were caused by a collapsing wall, and the situation leading up to it revealed remarkable incompetence. UEFA was blamed for scheduling the event at a below-standard stadium, and the separation of rival fans was clearly inadequate. To the extent that spectator fences were necessary to keep fans off the field or to keep them apart, then hooligans had their part to play, but it was a minor one when weighed against administrative incompetence and tragic errors of judgment. Nevertheless, the reaction of FIFA, which banned all English clubs from European competition after Heysel, was greeted with relief on the Continent and applauded in England.

Soccer has claimed the lives of more people than all other sports combined, but the most common cause of the deaths of these thousand and more fans has been poor crowd control, above all crushing in substandard stadiums, particularly against exit gates when a panic of some sort or another started inside the grounds. This was the case in the worst of them all, at Peru in 1964, and in other parts of South America, Asia, and Africa since then. The tragedy in Europe that occurred in May 1992 when fourteen people died and over a thousand were injured shortly before the start of a French Cup semifinal match between visiting Marseille and the local club Bastia, in Corsica, was caused by the collapse of a temporary stand installed to accommodate additional spectators. On the other hand, the most recent tragedy involving fans in Africa was simple hooliganism, fueled by provincial antagonisms, like that in Turkey in 1967 between Sivas and Besiktas. The African deaths came after the second game of the two-leg African Champions' Cup semifinal between ASEC Abidjan from the Ivory Coast and Asante Kotoko from Ghana, on 31 October 1993. The proximity of the two towns allowed thousands of fans to cross the border in coaches to see their team, running a gauntlet of abuse and missiles on the way, in scenes reminiscent of Belfast supporters of Glasgow Rangers traveling south to see them play in Dublin. At the second leg abuse turned to tragedy when an ASEC fan was killed in Kumasi and retaliatory violence against immigrant Ghanaians in Ivory Coast the following day resulted in twenty-five deaths. In Burma the separatist Karen guerrillas have used soccer to publicize their cause, most recently in October 1993 when they threw hand grenades into the crowds, causing seven deaths and injuring forty-five. Such deaths can hardly be attributed to soccer, any more than the so-called soccer war of 1969 between El Salvador and Honduras may be. No one has seriously tried to blame the Olympic Games for the deaths of hundreds of protesting students in Mexico on the eve of the 1968 Olympics or the slaughter of Israeli athletes by Arab terrorists at Munich in 1972.

Soccer has been branded as a game that inspires violence, but it neither is unique in this nor has a particular propensity to provoke violence. In French rugby before 1939, the extent to which players fought each other and spectators attacked referees was so great that the British associations refused to play in France. Cricket in India and the West Indies has been plagued with riots, and water polo has a violent record at the Olympics: at the 1932 games in Los Angeles, in the "naval battle" started by Belgium against Germany in front of the Führer at the Berlin Olympics, and the dramatically captured "blood in the water" encounter at the 1956 Olympics in Melbourne between the Soviet Union and Hungary shortly after the suppression of the Hungarian uprising. Ice hockey games in Canada have known deaths in the rink and riots in the stadiums, and in the United States the apparent absence of violence around sports events is in marked contrast to its reputation for violence in daily life. U.S. sports culture, however, is quite unlike that of the rest of the world. Spectators at U.S. football matches are people rich enough to afford the high entry charges, including many females; the cult of the traveling fan is absent, and games are conducted mainly with the television audience in mind. The worst fan-related incidents in the United States seem to be in postmatch "celebratory" riots, where much of the trouble is caused by thugs with no interest in sports taking advantage of the situation. In contrast, most soccer-related violence involves people who are deeply attached to the game.

The tally of deaths in and around the soccer stadiums of the world has to be seen in the context of the number of people playing the game and watching it. More to the point is the variety of cultures in which it is played, most of whose political and social systems are hardly models of "fair play." None of this tells us anything about the game; it suggest facts only about the people who play and watch it. Soccer's popularity by far surpasses that of all other sports. It is based on the game's simplicity, its economic democracy, and its appeal to the poor, the illiterate, the working-classes—those who cannot afford a polo pony, a yacht, a squash racquet, or a set of golf clubs; whose games take place on streets and beaches and spare lots, not in expensive leisure centers or well-manicured lawns; and who are more likely to settle their difference and express their grievances with blows rather than by recourse to lawyers and letters to the editor.

---

The great beauty of sport for most people is that it is an escape from the everyday problems of the world, a haven from politics and the day-to-day cares of earning a living. Sports historians have perhaps paid too much attention to the social role of sport, in large measure in reaction to the way many journalists have ignored it. But the two roles are different: journalists need to maintain friendly relations with the players and the management of the big clubs, and this has often made them captives of their profession rather than crusaders. Sports journalists have a right to claim that they are there to report the sport and leave to others the problems of society: the trouble is that the problems of society constantly crop up in the sport itself.

Glasgow Rangers exercised an unofficial policy against Roman Catholics for decades before the consciences of some Scottish journalists prompted them to campaign against this bigotry in the 1970s; racism in English soccer was a disgrace that most journalists and certainly television commentators tried to ignore in the 1970s; and

Brian Glanville was often a lone voice in his efforts to expose corruption in European soccer in the 1970s, above all in Italy, a country he knew intimately and with which he had a long love-hate relationship. On the other hand, soccer, unlike rugby and cricket, was never a tool of apartheid in South Africa, although FIFA under Stanley Rous did not have such an unambiguous record. Soccer's political overtones in postcolonial Asia and Africa, however, were something with which European reporters had trouble coming to terms. All sports have had to face some of these problems at some time or other; soccer has had to face all of them all the time. Today the sports press is generally more critical than it has been in the past, but television, with its reliance on sponsors and games that have become "commodities," is of necessity bland. Television commentators may be more willing today than they were in the past to criticize the racism and other crudities that besmirch the game, but they are never going to condemn the visual mess of commercial messages that pollutes the screen.

It was in the face of a largely supine press that a countermovement developed in Britain in the mid-1980s, spearheaded by generally younger soccer fans with literary pretensions who were appalled at the threat to the game by the hooligans on the terrace on the one hand and those in the directors boxes on the other. Using new technology they produced their own "fanzines" in which they gave an uninhibited criticism of the racism, sexism, corruption, and simple stupidity to be found in soccer. Some of these fanzines developed from photocopied sheets stapled together into well-produced glossy monthlies. These critics found a big market for their trenchant wit, and by 1990 it was calculated that 200 fanzines were selling a million copies.

The vast majority of the fanzines express left-wing views, and the idea of them caught on in the rest of Europe. In Germany smaller clubs were lauded for their efforts against more powerful neighbors, and a victory by Freiburg over Bayern Munich could be depicted as a defeat for capitalism. In Hamburg, St. Pauli, situated in the quarter of recent immigrants and academic circles, was seen as the team of the Left against the longer established, more bourgeois, and, some would say, "neo-Nazi" Hamburger SV. Most fanzines were against racism and came together in the Bündnis Anti-Faschistischer Fussball-Fan Initiativen (BAFF, the Alliance of Antifascist Football Fans). More generally they opposed creeping officialdom and denounced the attempts to install all-seated stadiums with the slogan "Sitting is for assholes" (Sitzen ist für'n Arsch!). It was perhaps hard to decide what a "left-wing" soccer club is: no money, few victories, or perhaps a past with working-class credentials. Despite this, Schalke supporters, whether of Left or Right, have simply been depicted as dumb. There were a few right-wing fanzines, such as *Supertifo* (Superfan), which came out monthly in Italian and tried to set up an international of soccer hooligans. It was no more successful than attempts to establish an international of soccer supporters from the other end of the political spectrum.

Nevertheless, and again with Britain in the lead, some success has been achieved in restoring the good reputation of the average fan. The Football Supporters Association was founded in England in 1985, shortly after the Heysel disaster, dedicated to educating the wilder fans and letting the ordinary supporter have a say in the corridors of power. In Denmark a cheery fan movement known as the "Roligans" ("peaceful fans") got under way at the same time, trying to treat the game more as a sport than an outlet for individual and nationalist aggression. Even the players began to exhibit the semblance of a social conscience, and the top clubs in Germany and Italy devoted a day in December 1992 to protest against that most odious of sports excrescences, racism. Following attacks on immigrant Turks in Hamburg in 1993, a match was organized between St. Pauli and Galatasaray of Turkey. Some clubs, especially in Italy, aware of the hooligans' devotion and the support they give the team on match days, have wisely entered into discussions with them, allowing them to use club premises to prepare their banners and trying to direct their energies away from violence and confrontation with the opposition.

It appears that not all the encouragement was positive, or the subsidies used in the best way. In the debate following the stabbing of the Genoa fan in January 1995, Italian clubs were urged to severe their connections with the Ultras, and the Italian parliament rushed through measures to clamp down on violent behavior and make it illegal for clubs to give free tickets to fan groups with a record of violence. In Argentina the links between fans and directors have more ominous overtones. According to the writer Amilcar Romero, clubs pay their most violent supporters not only to come and support the team at away games but to blackmail and threaten with violence players or others who do not do what they are told. So widespread is the practice that some players pay thugs for protection against this, writing it off as a form of tax on their income (Simon Kuper, *Football against the Enemy*). This practice was brought into the open in April 1994 when two River Plate supporters were killed by Boca fans after a derby match. Two months later José "El Abuel" Barritta, classed as Boca's "top hooligan," turned himself in to plead his innocence of having taken part in the murder. In Brazil, where life is cheap and guns

readily available to use in arguments, incidents of soccer fans shooting each other (or passing victims) do not even make the front page.
On the other hand, the stadiums of Brazil have not been taken over
by fans intent on going to war with each other, as is done in Europe.

---

Although soccer has had problems with hooliganism, and politics
is omnipresent in it, it has been freer than the Olympic Games from
overt political intrusion; above all, it has never had to face serious
boycott movements. This is in part because it is openly professional,
but it is also because at the administrative level soccer has been freer
from racism than most sports. Even in the stands, racism, like hooliganism, seems to be on the wane, especially in England, where most
of the fences erected in the 1970s came down after the Hillsborough
disaster and have not gone up again. It will never be eliminated, for
it seems to be a universal failing that people want to taunt someone
else, be it fans from the south of England mocking the unemployment
in the north by showing off their designer underwear or waving bank-
notes, those of Paris St.-Germain asking that the Liverpool supporters be decorated for their part in the Heysel tragedy, or fans in Nigeria throwing bread onto the field to mock the visitors from Ethiopia
(and in the return match the players who were alleged to have provoked a riot by pointing to their mouths and rubbing their stomachs).
Such sickness is of the psyche and has nothing to do with soccer.

Soccer's boycotts have been by particular nations over particular
grievances, above all by the presence of Israel and Taiwan, but the
claims of the Afro-Asian nations for more representation have also
prompted them. These boycotts have barely affected the major tournaments. The only time the World Cup had to face a potential boycott was at Argentina in 1978, in protest at the brutality of the Videla regime, which came to power in 1976 and embarked on a ruthless
program of terror epitomized in the "disappeared," the young men
who were picked up by the secret police and never seen again. This
was also the first World Cup since Italy in 1934 to be played with
blatantly political support. The Videla regime had inherited the 1978
cup competition from its predecessor but lost no time in trying to
show how it could organize a world-class event. It spent vast sums
of money to impress visitors, but whatever success it had in convincing visitors that Argentina was a modern nation, its success in raising the moral approval of the regime was slight. It was still possible
to separate politics from sports, however: despite the protests by left-
ists throughout the world, in Argentina itself guerrilla groups said they

would not upset the World Cup because it was a "feast of the people." Cesar Menotti, the team's manager, was no lover of the generals, and such was his power as the man who had guided Argentina to World Cup victory that he was able to criticize them with impunity for trying to usurp the glory. The Dutch runners-up, too, refused to shake hands with the Argentine dictator.

To the taint of politics in the 1978 World Cup was added that of corruption when Argentina secured its place in the final against a somewhat supine Peru team that was already out of the competition. Argentina needed to beat Peru by four goals to finish ahead of Brazil; it won 6-0, and Brazil went home the only undefeated team in the competition. Relations between Peru and Argentina improved with the gift of grain and the freeing of Peruvian credits in Argentina, and many were left to wonder at the more direct financial benefits to some Peruvian players.

The 1978 World Cup was the last to be played with sixteen finalists, as the increasing power of the Afro-Asian nations was recognized in the expanded tournament. The game had become truly global, although some of the smaller nations had trouble at times justifying their place in the elite. At Spain in 1982 CONCACAF was represented by Honduras and El Salvador, which finished at the bottom of their sections, but without any serious domestic consequences. Africa and Asia were also given two places each, although Asia had to share one of its places with Oceania. New Zealand filled one of these spots, qualifying after a journey of 55,000 miles and fifteen games, the last (against China) remaining in doubt until the last minute. Kuwait spent a fortune getting to Spain but managed only one point, in a draw against Czechoslovakia. The other newcomers did well: Cameroon never lost a game, but it scored only one goal and failed to qualify because although Italy also tied its three games, it scored two goals.

Algeria, the other African representative, played brilliantly but had the appalling misfortune to be eliminated by the collusion between Austria and West Germany in the most scandalous game in the tournament. For both European teams to qualify, only a narrow victory to West Germany would do; otherwise, Algeria would qualify. West Germany won 1-0 in a game where the players strolled around as though to a prearranged plan, and although Algeria protested, it was eliminated. West Germany was also involved in the other sports scandal of the tournament when its goalkeeper, Harald Schumacher, bludgeoned France's Patrick Battiston out of their semifinal game with a challenge on the edge of the penalty area that broke his jaw. Schumacher remained on the field, and Battiston never played again. Since Battiston had come in as a substitute, France could not bring on another player when the game went into extra-time. Germany did, and France fell before its opponent's superior strength; Germany came back from 1-3 down to tie, forcing the game into a penalty shoot-out, the first ever in the World Cup. The only support Germany got in the final against Italy was from Germans, and for months afterward lovers of the game heckled Schumacher everywhere he played. Italy recovered from its abysmal start to defeat Brazil in the semifinal and Germany in the final, with goals from Paulo Rossi that helped wipe out the memory of his conviction—along with seven other players—for accepting bribes, which had kept him out of the game for the previous two years.

Argentina's 3-2 victory over Germany in the 1986 World Cup final in Mexico was inspired by the genius of Maradona, who was irrepressible in a display not only of individual skills and deadly finishing but also of tackling and defense-splitting passes. The best game, however, was between Brazil and France, two of the most exciting teams from 1982, Brazil with its aging stars and France under the ever-developing magic of Michel Platini, the only player to rival Maradona at that time. France advanced to the semifinal on penalties, a means of deciding games that was becoming depressingly frequent. Of the underdogs, Canada represented CONCACAF but failed to score a goal, while Iraq failed to win any points, and South Korea managed only a draw against Bulgaria. Algeria lacked the fire it had shown in Spain and managed only a draw, but Morocco finished ahead of England, Poland, and Portugal in its group, only to be eliminated by West Germany on penalties in the quarterfinal.

The reputation of the "underdogs" was saved by Cameroon at Italy in 1990. Egypt played well, but South Korea and the United Arab Emirates failed to impress. Cameroon, on the other hand, was the star of the tournament, compared even to Brazil for the open-ended inventiveness of its play. Unfortunately its players also indulged in some crude fouls that cost them crucial free kicks and the expulsion of key players, which was how they lost to England in the quarterfinal, after outplaying the English in skill and imagination. In thirty-eight-year-old Roger Milla Cameroon had the player of the tournament; he was usually reserved until late in the game, when he would come on and score the winning goal. Most of the 1990 tournament, however, is best forgotten, above all the final. It did not augur well for USA 1994, but despite the fears of the soccer faithful, some of whom could not distinguish American sports culture from Disneyland and *Dallas,* and the doubts of the American media, USA 1994 defied the critics.

Some of the nations at Italia 1990 would never take part in the competition again, and some of the players who did so would play under the name of a new nation or a different regime. New nations lined up to enter FIFA and UEFA, many of them so small that added to others like San Marino, Liechtenstein, and the Faeroe Islands, UEFA could well create a superleague of the supersmall. The worst tragedies in the breakup of communism came in the former federal republic of Yugoslavia, as the independence of new states established more or less along ethnic lines degenerated into civil war. Croatians picked to play for what was still the Yugoslav national team were threatened with death if they did, soccer grounds became hospitals, and playing fields became graveyards, while players were sold to buy weapons. At the first feeble signs of peace in Sarajevo, a soccer match was organized in the main stadium in March 1994, between UN troops and a local select.

Unlike the Soviet Union, Yugoslavia had produced some of the finest teams at national and club level. It was entered in the 1992 European Nations Cup but had to withdraw, and Denmark took its place. To its own astonishment and the delight of all neutrals, Denmark advanced to the final stages, defeating the Netherlands in the semifinal and Germany in the final. It was a message of hope to those who like to see the romance of the game live on.

———

Team games like soccer will always have an interest that individual sports like golf and tennis, with all their charms, can never have. Individuals come and go, but teams live on from generation to generation; as a result, soccer players can embody the spirit of a nation or a locality, whereas golf and tennis, in the final analysis, are merely about individuals. Even with the commercial invasion of the 1980s, soccer has always been about much more than making money. When Japan lost by the narrowest of margins to South Korea in the final game of the Asian qualifiers for USA 1994, the utter despair that overcame each of the players was less for a lost personal fortune than for the destruction of a dream.

In some ways there is not much that has changed in the century and more in which the game has been played. In January 1887 "Observer," a writer for the *Scottish Athletic Journal,* condemned the alarming number of riots and injuries on the field and asked rhetorically whether the game was to become a source of good or evil. Dismissing the accusation that he was an old fogy who believed in the "superiority of olden times over those in which we live," he claimed that clubs were little better than "money-hunting organizations" dominated by a "win at all hazards" mentality. Their secretaries were concerned only about gate money and were "eternally scheming for filthy lucre." Thus speaks, of course, the critic of professionalism, but it must give pause for those today who see the game falling into the hands of the profiteers. It is also as true today as it always has been, however, that dreams of glory for an end beyond oneself, and not money, are the lifeblood of the world's great sports.

# USA 1994

In early June 1994 the eyes of the sports world, with the exception of the host nation, were turned on the United States, as the 24 teams that had qualified from the original 143 entries prepared to battle in the finals of the fifteenth World Cup. Even in the United States itself, as the competition got under way, the sports public of a country devoted to its own form of football could not remain immune to the fever that surrounded the competition. The *Los Angeles Times* was said to give more coverage to the tournament than did the London *Times,* and *USA Today* devoted two pages a day to it. The initial cynicism of the television companies proved unwarranted, and the sponsors were delighted at the audiences their products reached. For those at the games, and the millions more watching on television, USA 1994 turned out to be a festival of attacking soccer, major upsets, drama, and controversy, without the riots and displays of poor sportsmanship that have on occasions given the game a bad image. Unfortunately the fairy-tale final between the two giants of world soccer, Brazil and Italy, proved to be a crushing anticlimax, and those Americans tuning in to the final game to see what all the excitement had been about would have switched off their sets none the wiser. Elsewhere, 150 million Brazilians began one of their greatest carnivals ever, and in complete contradiction to the cynical notion that winning is everything, losing teams from the World Cup went home in 1994, as they had done on previous occasions, to a tumultuous welcome just for doing well.

The final of USA 1994 was destined to be a historic game even before it started, since one of the two finalists was guaranteed to become the first four-time winner. Unfortunately, it also became historic for the wrong reasons: the first drawn final, the first no-scoring final, and the first final to be decided by penalty kicks. For soccer fans it was an engrossing game, but the heat had taken its toll on exhausted players, and the defenses were on top, as the world's best strikers suffered from injury and tired legs. Brazil missed two clear chances, and a rare mistake by Gianluca Pagliuca, the Italian goalkeeper, which saw the ball slip through his arms and bounce off the post, almost sealed Italy's fate, whereas Roberto Baggio, Italy's savior in previous games, playing with a heavily bandaged leg, missed the only chance he was given. Had Italy won the penalty lottery, it would have been a travesty of justice, for Brazil would have won by any other of the suggestions to eliminate shoot-outs: counting successes in previous games in the final tournament or measuring one team's domination over the other in the final game itself in terms of corners, shots on goal, or the percentage of time the ball was in the defending team's half. Best, of course, is a replay, but that would have been too much to ask of players already subjected to an overly grueling tournament.

There can be no fair comparison with the pre-1966 competitions, and other competitions had their high points: the Italy-Brazil final of 1970 was incomparably better than the 1994 final, and no player dominated 1994 the way Maradona did in 1986, while the winning Brazil team was without the sparkle that had distinguished its three previous world-champion teams. Taken as a whole, however, USA 1994 was arguably the best World Cup ever. In addition to the high quality of the play spread throughout most of the twenty-four teams, never before had every game attracted so close to a sellout crowd, for even in soccer-mad countries like Italy in 1934 and 1990, Brazil in 1950, and Mexico in 1970 and 1986, the less-fancied teams often had to play before sparsely filled bleachers. The United States is more a continent than a country, of course, many of its states having populations greater than most countries. Moreover, although most Americans prefer to leave the Old World and its problems on the other side of the ocean, there remain many ethnic allegiances: the Irish and the Italians above all played before what amounted to home crowds, and the Latin American teams had the support of America's million and more Spanish speakers—nearly 92,000 people watched Colombia's game with Romania at the Rose Bowl in Pasadena.

The middle-class crowds (who else could afford the entry prices or the cost of travel?) were appreciative rather than fanatical, and there was little need for the security precautions, which in any case were kept in the background. A new color was given to multicultural America, but none of the Americans coming to soccer for the first time could be expected to forsake their own code of football, for that does not happen; just as some soccer fans claim that they would give up their spouse or religion before they would change support for their team, so football fans of whatever code retain an allegiance to the code with which they have grown up. U.S. sports reporters had a field day commenting on the idiosyncrasies of the game and its followers, usually with bemused good humor, occasionally with incredulous disbelief, always with comparisons to American sports heroes that were lost to non-American readers, and at times with the redneck parochialism that can be found in any country. Tom Weir of *USA Today* claimed that hating soccer is "more American than eating mom's apple pie," and in a special edition of *Newsweek* David Hirshey, deputy editor of *Esquire Magazine,* made a tongue-in-cheek confession about the derision he had faced for being a fan of soccer, a sport dismissed by his sports editor at the *New York Daily News* as a "game for commie pansies" (special issue, spring 1994). All were given the chance to see some of the features that justify soccer's being called the "beautiful game," and many came to some appreciation of why the game has captured millions of souls around the world.

The romance of soccer was there from the start, as the ragtag-and-bobtail team from Ireland beat the millionaires from Italy 1-0. Other underdogs came out with their tails up: South Korea was particularly unlucky, playing skillful football but failing at crucial moments in front of the goal, whereas fellow Asian representative Saudi Arabia secured a place in the second round with flashes of brilliance and one of the best goals in the competition. Morocco played well, and from sub-Saharan Africa Cameroon revived some memories of 1990 before its internal dissension showed up on the field and it collapsed facing Russia. Nigeria could well have reached the final; it played some of the best soccer in the competition, albeit in patches (and committed some of the worst fouls), but surrendered a one-goal lead to Italy in the last minute of its quarterfinal game and then lost in extra-time to a soft penalty. From the Balkan powderkeg came the explosive talents of Gheorghe Hagi of Romania and Hristo Stoichkov of Bulgaria, who shot their previously unsuccessful national teams to within an ace of the finals, disposing of former champions Argentina and Germany, respectively, on the way. Romania was eliminated on penalties in its quarterfinal match against Sweden, and Bulgaria proceeded to the semifinal only to be beaten by some bad luck and an Italian team under the influence of Roberto Baggio coming into form at the right time. The old cliché about every game being a difficult one is becoming true of the final stages of the World Cup:

Greece, rather lucky to be there, was the only nation that turned out to be a pushover.

In 1990 the U.S. team was dismissed as the simpletons of the competition and at 2,000:1 was a safe bet for the bookmakers. Four years later it was still an outsider, but the odds had shortened considerably: the young Americans had a new coach and a new approach to the game. They also had four years of intensive preparation, during which they notched up some notable victories. They were the host nation, normally a great advantage, although the hearts of many Americans were as likely to be with the team of their ethnic allegiance, for the vast majority of Americans remained unmoved by successes in a foreign game. Only a small percentage of Americans need to be won over, however, for the United States to have a massive following, and its team did as well as could have been expected of it. A clear win against early favorites Colombia, a draw with Switzerland, and a loss to classy Romania was enough to see it into the knock-out stage, where it was matched against Brazil on July 4. Few believed that an added dimension could have been given to that historic day, but as the Americans held out and the game proceeded scoreless into the second half, with Brazil a man short after Leonardo Araujo was expelled for a reflex short elbow jab that sent Tab Ramos to the hospital, the possibility of a giant-killing act became increasingly possible. A goal from José Oliveira Bebeto set up by Romário da Souza Faria in the seventy-fourth minute put an end to the impossible dream, and the exhausted U.S. players dragged themselves proudly from the field to the cheers of the onlookers at the packed Stanford Stadium.

No one had ever doubted that the Americans would run a well-organized competition, but even they had never had to run such a complicated event, with fifty-two games over thirty-one days being played in nine cities and three time zones and the additional complication of having to cope with a variety of languages. Whatever the foul-ups behind the scenes—the press had much to complain about, not least the limited access to facilities and over-officious security guards—they were kept off the field and the television screens. Conditions for the players were generally suffocating, but the atmosphere at the games surpassed all expectations. The opening ceremony (even more so the closing ceremony) is best forgotten, as was the opening game, which was the usual bore, but thereafter came some enthralling encounters, with spectacular goals, upsets, and thrilling plays that denied the heat and torrid conditions under which the players were performing.

It was the players who provided the actual spectacle, but the much-maligned FIFA must be praised for making it possible. After the peals of cynical laughter that rang around the soccer world when FIFA mentioned changing the game to make it more palatable for what it saw as American tastes, the final changes and instructions to referees were all positive. Awarding three points for a win instead of two discouraged playing for a draw, and the ban on the goalkeeper handling a back pass, introduced two years earlier, eliminated the most frustrating of the several ways of wasting time. That other bane of the soccer spectator's life, watching players roll around in histrionic agony at the slightest touch from an opposing player, was virtually eliminated by the use of stretchers to take them from the field to perform in private. One of the most delicious moments of the competition was when a Brazilian player leapt from the stretcher with Lazarus-like alacrity, only to be given a yellow card for feigning injury. Linesmen were told to ignore "passive" offside and favor the attacking player, which did not solve the eternal problem of the off-side rule but at least meant that mistakes were more likely to favor the attacker. Injury and time wasting were religiously recorded, so that most games went a few minutes beyond 45, although the South Korea–Bolivia game lasted 104 minutes—surely a record. Unfortunately FIFA did not proceed with the decision to introduce sudden death in extra-time to help avoid that most exciting but farcical way of deciding a game, the penalty shoot-out. Unlike at Italy 1990, however, only three games had to be decided this way at USA 1994.

It was FIFA's instructions to referees to protect the ball players, however, that had the most exhilarating consequences, for referees came down on foul play with a severity never before seen. The result was that key players like Romário of Brazil and Baggio of Italy did not have to suffer the outrages committed against the great players of previous tournaments, such as Pelé in 1966 or Maradona, who was a kicking-bag for cynical defenders throughout his career and who in 1982 was provoked beyond human endurance before finally striking back and getting himself sent off. Nor were there any of the on-field "battles" that had scarred the 1938 and 1954 competitions or the gross indiscipline that went beyond the referees' control in 1962 and 1970. Some referees were woefully incompetent and paid the price for it by being sent home early, but on the whole, and despite a questionable flourishing of red and yellow cards on occasion, they performed admirably.

More controversial was the use of the television camera to dispense justice for offenses that the referee missed. As always, television replays more often showed the referee to be correct, but when referee Sandor Puhl at the Italy-Spain game failed to see the Italian player's elbow that broke the nose of Spain's Luis Enrique in the penalty area, FIFA, acting on the video evidence, slapped Mauro Tassotti with the heaviest punishment in the competition. What it did not do, a controversial practice that has been used twice in Bundesliga games in Germany, was to have the game replayed on the grounds that Spain should have been given a penalty that would almost certainly have won it the game. Such a move would open up a veritable Pandora's Box, and even in the Bundesliga it was used only in cases involving a goal being scored. Since then FIFA has ruled out the use of video evidence to have a game replayed.

FIFA, however, has to be cautioned against getting too excited about its success in 1994 and introducing further changes for 1998. Wisely, it has decreed sudden-death extra-time, but less felicitously it has raised again the question of kick-ins instead of throw-ins. Most ominously of all, it has agreed to experiment with "time outs"—anathema to all soccer fans—in the Under-17 Youth Championship and the Women's World Cup. Apart from the pass-back rule, it was interpretation of the rules, not changes, that helped to make USA 1994 such a resounding success, the final game excepted.

---

Soccer shares with the Olympics the problems of its popularity and the power of television, leading to ever bigger and more showy spectacles. FIFA's move toward giganticism has been pushed by the pressure of the developing soccer nations demanding a place in the final, but FIFA under Havelange has willingly gone along with this. At France in 1998 there will be thirty-two teams in the final, twice as many as in 1978. Four weeks of intense competition in the middle of the day in stadiums that were like ovens made the outcome of USA 1994 in part a test of endurance. Summer games suit the European off-season, and playing at the hottest time of the day in the United States provided prime-time programming to European television audiences; these are realities FIFA has to come to terms with, but changes have to be made. Seven of the fifty-two games in USA 1994 were played late in the day, meaning that most Europeans had to watch them after midnight, but most were played when the heat was at its worst. This suited not only viewers in Europe but also the daily press that had to meet deadlines for the morning edition. At the end of the first round, when several games were played after midnight, European time, Italy's *Gazzetta dello Sport* had to prepare four separate front pages to account for the four possibilities that faced Italy in the last game of its group, where any one of the four teams competing at the same time could have ended up in any position from first to fourth. The paper could not afford to upset an Italian public whose nerves were stretched to breaking point from the tension of their previous games.

The problem of a final pool of twenty-four teams, and now thirty-two, is a more general problem arising wherever the finals are played. Although the increased numbers might please the smaller nations, and the players are always happy to take the increased money from television, there is too much pressure on the players, most of whom have just completed a strenuous league program. Somehow the finals have to be brought back to sixteen teams, perhaps by playing two semifinal qualifying groups of sixteen in two different countries in the year before the final: this would have the added advantage of allowing two additional countries to take part in hosting the world competition.

As the world game, soccer also shares with the Olympic Games the omnipresent problems of politics, some of which is part of the game, and some of which is not. The tragic slaying of Andres Escobar on his return to Colombia after his team's surprise elimination in the first round, ostensibly because of the goal he inadvertently scored for the U.S. team, had little to do with soccer and more to do with the drug and gambling cartels that seem to have entered the entrails of Colombian society like a deadly tapeworm. This society, which had the 1986 World Cup taken from it and where international games were banned after the killing of referees, has deteriorated to the extent that a Colombian killed a star soccer player. Throughout most of South America soccer players are usually so esteemed by the public as to be sacrosanct. When Romário's father was kidnapped shortly before the World Cup, he was soon returned, unharmed and without any ransom being paid: Romário simply said that if his father was not brought back safely, he would not play in the World Cup competition. The Brazilian underground soon got to work to ensure that Brazil did not go to the United States without its key striker.

Drugs are much less a problem in soccer than in track and field, and so the World Cup has been less disfigured in this way than the Olympic Games: artificial stimulants can create the extra muscle power and energy so vital to a runner, but no drug is capable of turning an ordinary player into a Maradona. Perhaps they can return a faded Maradona to a semblance of his former self, however, and so it was that Maradona, arguably the greatest soccer player of all time, caused the first major sensation of USA 1994 when he was banned for testing positive for what was described as a "cocktail" of drugs. He was immediately suspended and later banned from the competition, knocking the spirit out of an Argentine team that had promised so much under his inspiration. Maradona was born in one of Buenos Aires's shantytowns, but his dream of one day playing for his country was never farfetched. When he was barely out of his teens he had the world at his feet, a host of hangers-on in his train, and sycophants at his beck and call. The wealth and adulation proved too much; nevertheless, problems of discipline on the field and off, ending with a drug habit in Italy that had him banned from world soccer for fifteen months, did not prevent him from making an amazing comeback from a podgy sloth to an older version of the supreme athlete he once was. He led Argentina to victory against Australia in 1993 and so saved the nation from the embarrassment of not qualifying for a World Cup final. In the United States he led his team to two stunning victories, but apparently the support of his wife, his two children, and God, a trinity he frequently invoked, was not enough to sustain him. He left the game a tarnished hero, inevitably suffering in comparison with Pelé, the soccer genius from an equally poverty-stricken environment who is loved by soccer followers throughout the world. Pelé has been a vigorous opponent of all drugs throughout his life, in his playing days refusing to advertise alcohol or nicotine products despite the rewards this could bring. Pelé is the one soccer player known in the United States, and for the right reasons, for few can forget the image of sheer joy on his face as he leapt into the air after scoring a goal. In stark contrast lies one of the last images of Maradona, that of a half-crazed animal charging at the camera after he scored in Argentina's 4-0 thrashing of Greece in its first game in USA 1994.

The stars of the Olympics, like the stars of soccer, enjoy financial rewards today that were beyond the wildest dreams of their equivalents of even a generation ago, but the soccer stars usually have a much greater class gulf to clear. The soccer stars of the early days had to face the same problems of working-class youths enjoying wealth unknown to others of their class and adulation that could turn the coolest of heads, but the pressures on both counts is probably greater today, even with the help that a good agent or manager can bring. Since the advent of television we have seen George Best reach the ranks of the truly great but fall victim to drink; Johann Cruyff, on the other hand, whose mother was a cleaning women with Ajax, his first club, has ruthlessly carved out a fortune based on his soccer genius. Cruyff's contemporary and near equal on the field of play, Franz

Beckenbauer, was born into one of the poorest parts of war-torn Munich in 1945, where he played with a worn-out tennis ball until his bare feet bled, but he took on the role of captain and manager of Germany with all the aplomb of a born aristocrat. Eusébio came from Mozambique with a confidence unusual in a young African of the late 1950s, not only starring with Benfica and Portugal but setting an example of sportsmanship on and off the field that was equaled only by the likes of his contemporary, Bobby Charlton. The list could go on, showing that no soccer player is condemned by his social origins: the faults and frailties, as well as the courage and generosity, to which sport at the highest level gives rise can be found in all walks of life— which fact does not prevent us from admiring some athletes even more for the additional barriers that they have had to clear.

There are other problems created by soccer's immense popularity. Unlike the excitement of the Olympic Games' quadrennial festival of sport, which is usually limited to the weeks in which the games are actually hosted, the interest in soccer continues unabated in the intervening four years. During the four weeks in which the finals are now played, industry and social lives in many countries have to be adjusted to fit in with the playing schedules. In South American countries that have a team in the competition, workers are given time off on days when the national team is playing; the alternative would be mass absenteeism. In Brazil even that august center of learning, the National Library in Rio, has to fall in with the times: students and visitors were told that on days when the national team was playing in the World Cup the library would close at 3 P.M. In Argentina, Andrew Graham-Yool of the *Buenos Aires Herald* (30 June 1994) made so bold as to query why the nation should grind to a near halt when its national squad went out to meet "eleven other millionaires," using his criticism to challenge the government's assertion that Argentina is a modern nation. The business journal *Asiaweek* wondered whether any work was getting done in Asia, as workers in South Korea's Hyundai factory organized a three-hour strike that neatly coincided with South Korea's game against Bolivia, while in countries where games were televised in the early hours of the morning, governments warned industry about the precautions they might have to take to prevent problems caused by sleepy workers. In Bangladesh in 1990 a power station that broke down during the televising of the opening game was attacked by angry tele-viewers, and four years later students rioted in an attempt to have their exams rescheduled so as not to clash with the World Cup. In Thailand the minister of education gave pupils the day off following the final, which was played at 2:30 A.M. local time.

On the other hand it was reported from Israel that during the World Cup incidents of domestic violence were dramatically reduced, and in Ireland an unusual number of women had to seek birth-control precautions for their partners' unexpected love-making. In addition, it has been commonplace since the beginnings of the game that when the local—and presumably national—team is doing well, production increases significantly. Leading South American financial experts predicted that Brazil's victory would lead to substantial stock market growth, cut absenteeism, and boost production. If so, it was no real sacrifice when the government initially waived the $1 million due in tax that a brave and honest customs official wanted to impose on the nearly seventeen tons of dutiable goods that the victorious Brazilians brought back from the United States. Ricardo Texeira, president of the Brazilian football association (CBF), was quoted as saying that "Branco's goal was worth a hell of a lot more than a lousy refrigerator or a TV," and although this may have been true, it only served to emphasize that his country has separate rules for the superrich and the rest. As for the government, it knew that there were more votes to be won than lost in refusing to spoil the victory parade, but when the excitement died down public indignation forced the government to come to some compromise over the players' tax evasion (with the exception of Silvio Mauro's).

Other areas of business, especially those directly associated with the World Cup, had a bonanza. Television tuned in, and commercials were made with soccer as their theme, from the utterly entrancing clips of five year-old boys and girls from all over the world "preparing for World Cup 2010" to images of the Statue of Liberty playing "keepie-uppie." Cartoonists also had the statue variously holding up a soccer ball, the World Cup, or World Cup tickets in place of the torch of freedom or the book of law. Newspapers issued special supplements, and even business newspapers such as the *Asian Wall Street Journal* devoted whole pages to the tournament. One of the early fears of the organizers of USA 1994 was that it would not attract the big American television companies, and initially they were rather cool. After all, some Americans advertising executives have dismissed soccer as a "stupid game" because it has no room for commercials. Most soccer lovers want to keep it that way, however, and USA 1994 showed that it should be able to stay that way. Cramming commercials into an expanded halftime break was one solution; restricting the number of official sponsors and so adding quality to their reduced time was another. In South America a logo would appear for a few seconds on a corner of the screen, sometimes with a voice-over, occasionally taking over the full screen on such occasions as when a player was injured. Because South Americans understand the game, these interruptions were usually well timed and comparatively unobtrusive. Sports lovers can only decry all such intrusions and concentrate on damage control. So far soccer, above all the World Cup and major international competitions, has remained the game least affected by television's extraneous demands. USA 1994 was its greatest test in this regard, and it seems to have come through comparatively unscathed.

---

One of FIFA's main aims in giving the 1994 World Cup to the United States was to help win over the world's greatest sports public to the world game, although this was never a realistic goal. At the most soccer probably now enjoys a better understanding in the United States than it did before. It still faces the problem of creating a viable professional league that will encourage the youngsters who flock to the game at primary- and secondary-school level to continue to play when they leave school. Colleges still provide the traditional venues in which young Americans continue major sports, but a prosperous professional league could show that this need not be the case. Above all, American soccer needs to produce a homegrown hero, but this is an unlikely prospect at the moment. For any young American who loves the game and excels at it, the European leagues will still be the main goal. But even here a national professional league would be a useful stepping stone. The United States was the first country to be granted the finals without having a functioning national league, and one of the provisos was that one would be in place shortly after the World Cup. Translating the undoubted enthusiasm of hitherto uninterested Americans for a top-class world competition to a domestic league short on quality and based on ethnic allegiances is going to be difficult. The United States Interregional Soccer League, with seventy-two teams in eight divisions, does not augur well. Each division is playing by different experimental rules, all permitted by FIFA, from reasonable changes like running shoot-outs to nonsense like enlarged goals and no draws.

Soccer has survived wars and revolutions, dictators and capitalists, and it has gained more than it has lost from television. It has flourished without the participation of the United States, just as sport in the United States has flourished without soccer being of great significance there. If the two have come closer together as a result of 1994, as seems to have been the case, so much the better. If they have not, neither soccer nor the U.S. sports public will suffer. The tantalizing speculation remains, however, of how an American soccer team with all the wealth of American sports expertise and commitment behind it would perform on the world stage. In that unlikely event, we could well look forward to a World Cup final in 2006 or 2010 between the United States and Brazil . . . with Brazil the underdogs.

# Appendix

## Major Disasters at Soccer Matches

The following incidents are listed in order of severity.

| | |
|---|---|
| May 1964 | Lima, Peru: 318 killed, 500 seriously injured; victims were crushed against exit gates trying to escape when police fired on the crowd following disturbances toward the end of an Olympic qualifier between Peru and Argentina. |
| April 1989 | Hillsborough, Sheffield: 96 killed, 200 injured; victims were crushed against a security fence when police allowed uncontrolled entry to the grounds just before the start of an FA Cup semifinal between Liverpool and Nottingham Forest. |
| March 1988 | Katmandu, Nepal: 94 killed (some estimates say more); victims were crushed against exit gates trying to escape a freak hail storm during a match between Nepal and a Bangladesh XI. |
| June 1968 | River Plate Stadium, Buenos Aires: 74 killed, more than 150 injured; victims were trampled in a stampede when spectators in the stands threw burning papers on those below them at the end of a local derby between River Plate and Boca Juniors. |
| October 1982 | Lenin Stadium, Moscow: 69 killed, 100 injured; victims were among 15,000 fans crowded together in one part of a 100,000-capacity stadium. They were crushed in a fall down icy terracing in response to a last-minute Moscow goal at the end of a UEFA Cup game between Moscow Spartak and Haarlem of the Netherlands. (This disaster was kept secret from the public until July 1989, and in the speculation surrounding it, a figure of 340 dead was quoted.) |

| | |
|---|---|
| January 1971 | Ibrox Park, Glasgow: 66 killed, 100 injured; victims were crushed in a fall down a steep, narrow exit staircase, probably triggered by news of Rangers' late tying goal in an Old Firm derby with Celtic. In three other accidents on the same stairway in the previous decade 2 people were killed and nearly 100 injured. |
| May 1985 | Valley Parade, Bradford: 56 killed, 200 injured; most victims burned to death or asphyxiated in a final league match between Bradford City and Lincoln when rubbish under the old wooden stand caught fire. |
| February 1974 | Zamalek Stadium, Cairo: 49 killed, 50 injured; victims were crushed trying to get into the stadium before the start of a friendly between Zamalek and Dukla Prague. The venue had been changed at the last minute from the much larger Nasser Stadium, and fans were afraid they would not get in. |
| September 1967 | Kayseri, Turkey: 44 killed, 600 injured; victims were caught up in rioting following incidents on the field between visiting fans from neighboring Sivas and the home crowd from Kayseri. There were incidents inside and outside the ground. |
| January 1991 | Ernest Oppenheimer Stadium, Orkney, South Africa: 40 dead and 50 injured; victims were trampled to death when fighting began before a preseason friendly between Kaizer Chiefs and Orlando Pirates. |
| May 1985 | Heysel Stadium, Brussels: 39 killed, nearly 500 injured; victims (mainly Juventus supporters) were crushed when a wall collapsed as they tried to escape an attack from Liverpool hooligans before the start of a European Cup final between Liverpool and Juventus. |
| March 1946 | Burnden Park, Bolton: 33 killed, over 500 injured; victims were crushed when a wall and crush barriers collapsed in the first half of a FA Cup quarterfinal match between Bolton and Stoke City. |
| March 1988 | Tripoli, Libya: 30 killed, 120 injured; victims were crushed when a stand collapsed after a panic set off by knife-wielding fans during an international match between Libya and Malta. |
| April 1902 | Ibrox Park, Glasgow: 25 killed, over 500 injured; victims were crushed when part of new wooden terracing for standing spectators gave way early in the first half of an international match between Scotland and England. |
| November 1982 | Cali, Colombia: 22 killed, 200 injured; victims were crushed when part of a platform collapsed after a panic started by fans in the upper stand urinating on those |

|                  | below and throwing objects at them at a match between Deportiva Cali and Club América. |
|------------------|---|
| February 1981    | Karaiskaki Stadium, Athens: 21 dead, 54 injured; victims were crushed against exit gates during a local derby between Olympiakos and AEK Athens. |
| August 1985      | Soloniki Sports Palace, Moscow: 20 killed, an unknown number injured; victims were trampled in a panic when the lights failed during a World Youth Championship match between USSR and Canada. |
| November 1981    | Ibague, Colombia: 18 killed, 45 injured; victims were crushed when a wall collapsed before a semifinal between Deportivo Tolima and Deportivo Cali. |
| May 1992         | Furiani Stadium, Corsica: 15 killed, nearly 1,300 injured; victims were crushed when a temporary stand collapsed at the start of a French Cup semifinal match between local club Bastia and Marseille. |
| September 1979   | Meda Stadium, Indonesia: 12 children were trampled to death in a panic. |
| June 1985        | Estadio Azteca, Mexico City: 10 killed, 74 injured; victims were crushed in the crowd before a championship match between América and UNAM. |

The preceding figures for dead and injured are often estimates and do not include data for disasters at stadiums involving fewer than ten killed. Nor do they include deaths and injuries outside grounds in response to defeat or victory, as in the incidents in Colombia and Ghana referred to in the text.

## Tragedies Involving Players

| 1944 | The entire Chaux-de-Fonds team was killed in a train accident in Switzerland, including André Abegglen III, the youngest of the Abegglen brothers, who played for Switzerland. |
|------|---|
| 1949 | The entire Torino team (eighteen players) and support staff were killed when their plane crashed into a basilica at Superga, near Turin, on the way back from a benefit match against Benfica in Portugal |
| 1958 | Eight Manchester United players, along with three officials, eight journalists, and three others, were killed when their plane failed to take off after a refueling stop at the Munich airport, on return from a European Cup semifinal in Belgrade. |
| 1961 | Twenty-four members of the Green Cross club were killed in a crash in Chile on the way to a championship play-off |
| 1969 | Twenty-five members of the Bolivian champions, The Strongest, were killed in an air crash in the Andes. |

1979    Seventeen players of the Soviet first-division team Pakhtakor Tash-
        kent were killed, along with many other passengers, in a plane crash
        in Tashkent.

1987    Twenty players of Alianza of Peru were killed when their plane
        crashed into the sea on return from a championship match in Pac-
        ullpa. There were rumors that a terrorist bomb was responsible.

1989    Fourteen Netherlands-based professionals, along with many other
        passengers, were killed in a plane crash at Paramaribo airport on
        return to Surinam at the end of the season.

1993    Eighteen players and five officials, along with seven others, were
        killed when their Zambian Air Force plane crashed into the sea after
        a refueling stop in Libreville, Gabon. They were on their way to a
        World Cup match in Senegal.

## Major Soccer Grounds (1992)

Hampden Park, Glasgow, owned by Queen's Park Football Club, was the
biggest soccer stadium in the world until 1950. It has held British, European, and world record attendances:

April 17, 1937: 149,547 at a Scotland vs. England home international.
April 24, 1937: 146,433 at an Aberdeen vs. Celtic Scottish Cup final.
March 27, 1948: 143,570 at a Hibernian vs. Rangers Scottish Cup semifi-
nal (record for midweek game).
April 1948: A total of 262,926 people saw the 1948 Scottish Cup final, the
first game drawn, with the replay being played on the following Wednes-
day evening.
May 18, 1960: 127,621 at a Réal Madrid vs. Eintracht Frankfurt European
Cup final.
April 15, 1970: 133,961 at a Celtic vs. Leeds United European Cup semi-
final.

For safety reasons crowds were restricted to 134,000 from 1949, and after
the passing of the Safety of Sports Grounds Act in 1975, capacity was reduced
to 81,000. Reconstruction since then has reduced capacity even further.

London's Wembley Stadium is owned by a private consortium but has
guarantees that all the main English football matches will be played there
until the year 2000. It is used for purposes other than soccer, but it relies on
soccer for its main income.

April 28, 1923: 126,047, at a match between West Ham and Bolton Wanderers, the first English Cup final to be played there. This was the official
figure; up to 75,000 more are estimated to have forced their way in without paying. Beginning in 1950 attendance was restricted to 100,000.

Previous records for English Cup finals held before the inauguration of Wembley were as follows: 110,820 at the Crystal Palace in 1901 and 120,081 at the Crystal Palace in 1913.

Estadio Maracanã, Rio de Janeiro (officially Estadio Mario Filho), owned by the municipality of Rio de Janeiro, has been the biggest stadium in the world since 1950, when it staged the final of the World Cup, for which it was constructed. Its records are as follows:

July 16, 1950: 199,854 at a Brazil vs. Uruguay World Cup final (the figure is 205,000 when nonpaying attendance is included).
August 1963: 177,656 at a Flamengo vs. Fluminense match, a club world record (capacity was reduced to 165,000 and then to 125,000).

Based on FIFA's figures for 1990, the following are the world's largest stadiums. Unlike Hampden, Wembley, and the original Maracanã, where most of the spectators stood to watch the game, these are mainly seated, in some cases exclusively so:

Rungnado Stadium, Pyongyang, North Korea: 150,000
Estadio Maghalhaes Pinto, Belo Horizonte, Brazil: 125,000
Estadio Morumbi, São Paulo, Brazil: 120,000
Estadio da Luz, Lisbon, Portugal: 120,000
Krirangan Stadium, Salt Lake, Calcutta, India: 120,000
Senayan Main Stadium, Jakarta, Indonesia: 120,000
Estadio Castelão, Fortaleza, Brazil: 119,000
Estadio Arrudeo, Recife, Brazil: 115,000
Estadio Azteca, Mexico City, Mexico: 115,000
Nou Camp, Barcelona, Spain: 115,000
Bernabéu Stadium, Madrid, Spain: 114,000
Nasser Stadium, Cairo, Egypt: 100,000
Eden Garden Stadium, Calcutta, India: 100,000
Corporation Stadium, Calicur, India: 100,000
Azadi Football Stadium, Tehran, Iran: 100,000
Red Star Stadium, Belgrade, former Yugoslavia: 100,000
Central (now Republican) Stadium, Kiev, Ukraine: 100,000
First National Bank, Johannesburg/Soweto: 100,000–110,00

Most of the stadiums in Europe and Latin America were built specifically for soccer; in the other cases, soccer was the sport most likely to fill them. In Jakarta crowds of up to 150,000 are said to have attended games in the main stadium; 130,000 have been recorded in the Azadi Stadium in Iran; 127,000 at the Stadium of Light in Portugal.

# Membership of FIFA

| Date | Europe | South America | North and Central America | Asia and Oceania | Africa | Total |
|------|--------|---------------|---------------------------|------------------|--------|-------|
| 1904 | 7 | — | — | — | — | 7 |
| 1914 | 20 | 2 | 1 | — | — | 23 |
| 1924 | 24 | 5 | 2 | — | 1 | 32 |
| 1934 | 28 | 8 | 7 | 5 | 2 | 50 |
| 1954 | 34 | 9 | 14 | 5 | 18 | 80 |
| 1974 | 33 | 10 | 22 | 37 | 39 | 141 |
| 1984 | 34–35 | 10 | 23 | 40 | 42 | 150 |
| 1990 | 36 | 10 | 27 | 44 | 48 | 165 |
| 1993 | 39 | 10 | 27 | 44 | 48 | 168 |

Note: In 1994 membership had grown to 191, but is still in a state of flux with the applications from members of the new nations.

# Soccer at the Olympic Games before 1930

| Date | Venue | Number of Entrants | Final Standings 1st | 2nd | 3rd | 4th |
|------|-------|--------------------|------|-----|-----|-----|
| 1908 | London | 13 | Great Britain | Denmark | Netherlands | Sweden |
| 1912 | Stockholm | 11 | Great Britain | Denmark | Netherlands | Finland |
| 1920 | Antwerp | 13 | Belgium | Spain | Netherlands | [a] |
| 1924 | Paris | 22 | Uruguay | Switzerland | Sweden | Netherlands |
| 1928 | Amsterdam | 17 | Uruguay | Argentina | Italy | Egypt |

a. Czechoslovakia walked off in the final against Belgium because of the English referee's poor control of the game. No fourth place was awarded.

There was soccer played at all the Olympics previous to 1908, but these games were unofficial. At Athens in 1896 a Danish select beat an Izmir XI 15-0, and another game is said to have involved an Athens XI. At Paris in 1900 the English team called Upton Park beat a team calling itself France, 4-0. At Saint Louis in 1904 two teams from Saint Louis, Christian Brothers College and the St. Rose Kickers, and one from Canada played one another. The Galt FC team from Ontario won both its games and later received gold medals for its achievement. At the Interim Games in Athens in 1906, a Denmark XI had no trouble winning the soccer competition against three Greek teams.

The Los Angeles Olympics of 1932 were the only games where soccer was not played. Since then its importance has diminished considerably, for by 1936 most of the world's best soccer nations were professional.

# The Growth of the World Cup

| Date | Venue | Number of Entrants | Final Standings 1st | 2nd | 3rd | 4th |
|------|-------|--------------------|--------------------|------|------|------|
| 1930 | Uruguay | 13 | Uruguay | Argentina | Yugoslavia | U.S.A. |
| 1934 | Italy | 28 | Italy | Czechoslovakia | Germany | Austria |
| 1938 | France | 26 | Italy | Hungary | Brazil | Sweden |
| 1950 | Brazil | 23 | Uruguay | Brazil | Sweden | Spain |
| 1954 | Switzer-land | 34 | West Germany | Hungary | Austria | Uruguay |
| 1958 | Sweden | 49 | Brazil | Sweden | France | West Germany |
| 1962 | Chile | 50 | Brazil | Czechoslovakia | Chile | Yugoslavia |
| 1966 | England[a] | 53 | England | West Germany | Portugal | USSR |
| 1970 | Mexico | 69 | Brazil | Italy | West Germany | Uruguay |
| 1974 | West Germany | 90 | West Germany | Netherlands | Poland | Brazil |
| 1978 | Argentina | 94 | Argentina | Netherlands | Brazil | Italy |
| 1982 | Spain | 109 | Italy | West Germany | Poland | France |
| 1986 | Mexico | 109 | Argentina | West Germany | France | Belgium |
| 1990 | Italy | 113 | West Germany | Argentina | Italy | England |
| 1994 | U.S.A. | 143 | Brazil[b] | Italy | Sweden | Bulgaria |

a. This competition was boycotted by the Asian and African countries in protest at being allowed only one place between them.
b. Won on penalties.

# The Growth of Various Under-Age Tournaments

| Date | Venue | 1st | 2nd | 3rd | 4th |
|------|-------|-----|-----|-----|-----|
| | | \multicolumn{4}{Final Standings} | | | |

*The FIFA Under-17 World Championships*

| Date | Venue | 1st | 2nd | 3rd | 4th |
|------|-------|-----|-----|-----|-----|
| 1985 | China | Nigeria | West Germany | Brazil | Guinea |
| 1987 | Canada | USSR | Nigeria[a] | Ivory Coast | Italy |
| 1989 | Scotland | Saudi Arabia | Scotland[a] | Portugal | Bahrain |
| 1991 | Italy | Ghana | Spain | Argentina | Qatar[a] |
| 1993 | Japan | Nigeria | Ghana | Chile | Poland |

*The FIFA World Championships for Under-20s*

| Date | Venue | 1st | 2nd | 3rd | 4th |
|------|-------|-----|-----|-----|-----|
| 1977 | Tunisia | USSR | Mexico[a] | Brazil | Uruguay |
| 1979 | Japan | Argentina | USSR | Uruguay | Poland[a] |
| 1981 | Australia | West Germany | Qatar | Romania | England |
| 1983 | Mexico | Brazil | Argentina | Poland | South Korea |
| 1985 | USSR | Brazil | Spain | Nigeria | USSR[a] |
| 1987 | Chile | Yugoslavia | West Germany[a] | East Germany | Chile[a] |
| 1989 | Saudi Arabia | Portugal | Nigeria | Brazil | U.S.A. |
| 1991 | Portugal | Portugal | Brazil[a] | USSR | Australia[a] |
| 1993 | Australia | Brazil | Ghana | England | Australia |
| 1995 | Qatar[b] | Argentina | Brazil | Portugal | Spain |

a. Penalty shoot-out.
b. The competition was withdrawn from Nigeria at the last minute.

These youth tournaments were introduced to encourage the growth of soccer in underdeveloped countries. In the early years the established professional countries tended not to take them seriously, but that has changed over the years.

In 1992 FIFA decided that the soccer competition of the Olympic Games should be for players under the age of twenty-three. Spain won the tournament, with the other places going to Poland, Ghana, and Australia.

In 1991 the first World Cup for Women was staged in China. Six teams qualified from Europe, one (of three) from South America, two (Canada and the United States) out of eight from CONCACAF, one (Zambia) out of eight (with three withdrawals) from Africa, three out of nine from Asia, and New Zealand beat Australia and Papua New Guinea to represent Oceania. The United States beat Norway in the final, and Sweden beat Germany for third place. In Sweden in June 1995 a disappointed U.S. team had to be content with third place after beating China 2-0. Norway beat Germany (2-0) in the final.

# Glossary

AFC      The controlling body for Asian soccer.

CAF      The controlling body for African soccer.

CONCACAF      The controlling body for North and Central American soccer.

CONMEBOL      The controlling body for South American soccer.

Cup      The Football Association Challenge Cup, the longest surviving annual competition in the history of sport. Founded in 1871 as a knock-out tournament, it is often referred to simply as "the Cup."

cup-tie      A game in a competition for a "cup" based on the tradition of the FA Challenge Cup. These are knock-out competitions, usually single elimination, but sometimes played over two legs, home and away.

division      A grading designation in a league system, with the top teams in a first division, then second division, and so on. Recently, it has become common to call the top division the "Premier Division," or "Super League."

equalizer      A goal that ties the score.

extra-time      Originally introduced to break the deadlock in a tied cup game after the regulation ninety minutes. It involves playing an extra period of two fifteen-minute halves. Recently, a "sudden death" system has been introduced in which the first team to score in extra-time is declared the winner.

FA      The Football Association, the controlling body of English soccer, usually known by its acronym. Such was its historical preeminence that for a long time it virtually dominated world soccer. Unlike all other controlling bodies for association football, such as the Scottish (SFA), Welsh (WFA), or Irish (IFA) associations, it has never required the regional qualifier.

FIFA
The controlling body for world soccer, based in Zurich.

fixture
A match or a game.

Football League
The body founded to supervise the first soccer competition based on a league system, usually referred to simply as the League. The League and the FA, usually in harmony, sometimes in conflict, are the major bodies controlling English soccer.

goal-line
The line marking the breadth of the field of play.

ground
Where a soccer match is played; the term can mean the field itself, but more often it refers to the entire complex.

injury (or added) time
In soccer, time keeping is left to the referee, at whose discretion time is added beyond the regulation ninety minutes for stoppages due to injury or "time wasting."

knock-out competition
An elimination game, usually in a cup match.

league
See "division" and "League."

League
See "Football League."

leg
An elimination game played on a "home-and-away" basis is said to be played over two legs.

linesman
One of two officials, each covering a different half of the field by running close to the touchline, whose job is to assist the referee by flagging when the ball has gone out of play or when a player is "off-side." The referee is the sole official in charge of the game and can overrule the linesman's decision, but he can also consult the linesman in the case of incidents where the linesman is better placed.

match
See "fixture."

OFC
The controlling body for soccer in the Oceania region.

penalty
A free kick given for a serious foul committed in the penalty area, in which the attacking team nominates a player who tries to score from a spot twelve yards out from the middle

of the goal, with only the goalkeeper to stop the ball.

penalty area
The rectangular area around the goal; it measures eighteen yards from both goalposts and from the goal-line. It is only in this area that the goalkeeper can handle the ball without committing an infringement. Serious fouls committed by a defender inside this area are punished by a penalty kick.

penalty decider
A tie-breaker, usually in a cup-tie, in which each team has five penalties to decide the winner. In the event that each team scores the same number of goals in the "shoot-out," sudden death then comes into play. Although introduced in cup-ties, to replace the toss of a coin to decide which team would go into the next round, some countries have adopted the system even for league games.

pitch
The field of play.

pitch invasion
Spectators rushing onto the field, usually to interfere with the progress of the game.

"professional" foul
A deliberate foul committed on an attacker who has a clear run on goal. A free kick is awarded and the player who commits the foul is shown a red card (expelled).

promotion and relegation
In the league system the top team (or teams) in a lower division is promoted to a higher division and the bottom team (or teams) is relegated to a lower division.

red card
The card shown to a player who commits a foul so serious as to warrant sending off (expulsion).

referee
The official in charge of the game—he is never called an "umpire." See also "linesman."

replay
When two teams tie a cup game, and before a penalty decider is introduced, they play again, usually at the ground of the away club.

select (or XI)
Sometimes an "all-star" team, but not always, as such teams can be made up of players regardless of their talent.

sending off
Expulsion; players sent off cannot be replaced. See also "red card" and "yellow card."

stand
That part of the ground where spectators sit. In the early soccer grounds the vast majority of the spectators stood in the open (on

|                    | terraces), occasionally protected from the weather by a covered "stand." |
|--------------------|---------------------------------------------------------------|
| sudden death       | Means of deciding a tied game in which the first team to score after the regulation ninety minutes is declared the winner. |
| terrace/terracing  | The standing area of a ground, as distinct from the "stand." |
| touchline          | The line marking the length of the field of play. See also "goal-line." |
| UEFA               | The controlling body for European soccer. |
| yellow card        | The card shown to a player who has committed a deliberate foul, but not so grave as to warrant sending off (expulsion). |

# Bibliographic Essay

The serious study of soccer has almost been in inverse proportion to the game's popularity. Soccer was virtually ignored by academicians until the mid-1970s, when its study made intermittent and gradual progress. Recent years have seen a plethora of books and articles on its social and cultural importance, often the product of academic conferences where soccer was the main or even sole topic of discussion. Many of these works are in languages other than English, and most of them are listed in the bibliography to Bill Murray, *Football: A History of the World Game* (Aldershot: Scolar, 1994). Readers should consult that book for issues touched on but not dealt with in detail here, as well as for many of the sources on which this work is based.

There are various soccer encyclopedias with a genuinely international coverage. R. A. Henshaw, *The Encyclopedia of World Soccer* (Washington, D.C: New Republic, 1979), gives detailed coverage through to the late 1970s. A weakness in Henshaw's book is the comparative absence of players and personalities; this is the strength of Norman Barrett, ed., *World Soccer from A to Z* (London: Pan, 1973). Guy Oliver, *The Guinness Record of World Soccer: The History of the Game in over 150 Countries* (Enfield: Guinness Publishing, 1992), provides invaluable statistical coverage of the world game.

Of the earlier histories of soccer in English, one of the first to cover its global dimensions was the journalist Geoffrey Green's *Soccer: The World Game: A Popular History* (London: Phoenix House, 1953). For many years the only work in English by someone conversant with the game in Europe was that by the Austrian-born naturalized British journalist Hugo Meisl, *Soccer Revolution* (London: Phoenix Sports, 1955). The first venture into this territory by an academician was James Walvin, *The People's Game: A Social History of British Football* (London: Allen Lane, 1975). Although writing essentially about English soccer, Walvin shows how the game was carried around the world; an updated edition of this book is forthcoming. For a survey of the world game by a journalist with an unparalleled grasp of the European soccer scene, see Brian Glanville, *Soccer: A Panorama* (London: Eyre and Spottiswoode, 1968). A rather uneven collection of articles prepared for the World Cup in 1994 is John Sugden and Alan Tomlinson, eds., *Hosts and Champions: Soccer Cultures, National Identities and the USA World Cup* (Aldershot: Arena, 1994). Sugden and Tomlinson's work has major gaps, however; for instance, despite giving birth to the World Cup and being the host in 1938, France does not get a chapter in this book. Equally uneven, and barely living up to its title, is Stephen Wagg, ed., *Giving the Game Away: Football, Politics and Culture in Five Continents* (London: Leicester University Press, 1995). This book suffers from an uncertainty as to whether it is a work of history or sociology, while the content is patchy. Simon Kuper's *Football against the Enemy* (Orion: London, 1994) is a travelog of a journey across twenty-two nations on three continents in which the young journalist records interviews with players, directors, and fans, more or less indiscriminately, but with some fascinating stories well strung together. The story of British amateur teams taking the game on goodwill missions around the world is told by one of the participants in R. B. Alaway, *Football All round the World* (London: Newservice, 1948). Alan Tomlinson and Garry Whannel, eds., *Off the Ball: The Football World Cup* (London: Pluto, 1986), has two articles on the early spread of football: Tony Mason, "Some Englishmen and Scotsmen Abroad: The Spread of World Football" (67–82) and Alan Tomlinson, "Going Global: the FIFA Story" (83–98). Although absent from most bibliographies on soccer, W. Capel-Kirby and Frederick W. Carter, *The Mighty Kick: Romance, History and Humour of Football* (London: Jarrolds, 1933), covers the game throughout the world. Despite its title, Simon Inglis's *The Football Grounds of Europe* (London: Willow, 1990) contains a wealth of historical information. The attempt to "revise" the role of Britain in the spread of soccer is best summarized in Pierre Lanfranchi, "England's Most Durable Export? Recent Trends in Research on Football Development in Continental Europe," a paper delivered to the conference Sporting Traditions VIII, Canberra, Australia, July 1991.

For the founding of FIFA, see the organization's official publication, *FIFA: 1904–1984* (Zurich: FIFA, 1984). The history of the World Cup has been covered in innumerable popular histories. One of the most thorough is Brian Glanville and Jerry Weinstein, *World Cup* (London: SBC, 1960); Glanville has covered the story through subsequent World Cups.

There have been several histories of the European Cup competitions, the earliest of which is Roger Macdonald, *Britain versus Europe* (London: Pelham, 1968). Of the more recent, the best are John Motson and John Rowlinson, *The European Cup, 1955–1980* (London: Queen Anne, 1980), and Brian Glanville, *Champions of Europe: The History, Romance and Intrigue of the European Cup* (London: Guinness Publishing, 1991).

Among histories of the early game Montague Shearman's *Athletics and Football*, 3d ed., Badminton Library series (London: Longmans, Green, 1889), is written by one of its first enthusiasts; so too, but in a different sense, is the book by the archamateur N. L. Jackson, *Sporting Days and Sporting Ways* (London: Hurst and Blackett, 1932). Invaluable for soccer from the foundation of the FA to 1906, as much for its superb illustrations as for its comments on the contemporary game and its recent history, are the four volumes of Alfred Gibson and William Pickford, *Association Football and the Men Who Made It* (London: Caxton, n.d. [circa 1906]). Many of the first histories of soccer are based on the flawed but excellently documented work by Frances Peabody Magoun Jr., *History of Football from the Beginning to 1871* (Bochum-Langendreer: Heinrich Poppinghays OHG, 1938). Morris Marples, *A History of Football* (London: Secker and Warburg, 1953), is good on the game in England but otherwise weak.

Two official histories of the game's earliest institutions are Geoffrey Green, *A History of the Football Association* (London: Naldrett, 1953), and Geoffrey Green, *The Official History of the FA Cup* (London: Naldrett, 1949). The most recent official history of the FA is lavishly illustrated and contains a wealth of useful comment: Bryon Butler, *The Official History of the Football Association* (London: Queen Anne, 1991). The history of the Football League is covered with wit and style by Simon Inglis in *League Football and the Men Who Made It* (London: Collins, 1988). Providing a more critical view of the League's role, Braham Dabscheck has written extensively on players' rights. Many of these are listed in his most recent work, a study of the 1909 controversy: "'A man or a puppet'? The Football Association's Attempt to Destroy the Association Football Players' Union," *The International Journal of the History of Sport* 8, no. 2 (Sept. 1991): 221–38. The definitive study of players' rights is in John Harding, *For the Good of the Game: The Official History of the Professional Footballers' Association* (London: Robson, 1991). The best book on English soccer, covering the sport up to 1915, is Tony Mason, *Association Football and English Society: 1863–1915* (London: Harvester, 1980). The story is taken up to 1950 by Nicholas Fishwick in *English Football and Society: 1910–1950* (Manchester: Manchester University Press, 1989).

Scotland still awaits an academic history, although there have been some fine club histories and good articles on specific aspects of the game. The history of Queen's Park, which dominated the Scottish game in its first three decades, is covered by R. A. Crampsey in *The Game for the Game's Sake: The History of Queen's Park Football Club, 1867–1967* (Glasgow: Queen's Park Football Club, 1967). A history of Rangers and Celtic, which dominated it thereafter, is in Bill Murray, *The Old Firm: Sectarianism, Sport and Society in Scotland* (Edinburgh: John Donald, 1984; rprt., 1994). For an official history of the Scottish League, see R. A. Crampsey, *The Scottish Football League: The First 100 Years* (East Kilbride: Scottish Football League, n.d. [1990]). Soccer is a major theme in the collection of articles by Grant Jarvie and Graham Walker, eds., *Scottish Sport in the Making of a Nation: Ninety Minute Patriots?* (London: Pinter, 1994).

For soccer in Britain after 1914, but with a European dimension, see Ivan Sharpe, *Forty Years in Football* (London: Hutchinson's, 1952); Herbert Chapman, *Herbert Chapman on Football* (London: Garrick, 1934); Stephen Studd, *Herbert Chapman: Football Emperor: A Study in the Origins of Modern Soccer* (London: Peter Owen, 1981); Trevor Wignall, *Almost Yesterday* (London: Hutchinson, ca. 1946); David Jack, *Soccer* (London: Putnam, 1934); Charles

Buchan, *A Lifetime in Football* (London: Phoenix House, 1955); and George Allison, *Allison Calling* (London: Staples, 1948). For soccer in Britain after 1945, see Stephen Wagg, *The Football World: A Contemporary Social History* (Brighton: Harvester, 1984), and Peter Jeffs, *The Golden Age of Football* (Derby: Breedon, 1991). Percy M. Young's *History of British Football* (London: Stanley Paul, 1968) is readable and covers all of Britain. A collection of articles on the contemporary game in Britain is John Williams and Stephen Wagg, eds., *British Football and Social Change: Getting into Europe* (Leicester: Leicester University Press, 1991).

The best works on more specific aspects of British soccer include Richard Holt, "Working Class Football and the City: The Problem of Continuity," *British Journal of Sports History* 3, no. 1 (May 1986): 5–17, and Richard Holt, "Football and the Urban Way of Life in Nineteenth Century Britain," in J. A. Mangan, ed., *Pleasure, Profit, Proselytism: British Culture and Sport at Home and Abroad, 1700–1914* (London: Frank Cass, 1988), 67–85. John Hutchinson, *The Football Industry: The Early Years of the Professional Game* (Edinburgh: Richard Drew, 1982), has some excellent illustrations and a short but useful text. Stephen Jones published many works on economic aspects of sport before his untimely death; for soccer in England see his article "The Economic Aspects of Association Football in England, 1918–1939," *British Journal of Sports History* 1, no. 3 (Dec. 1984): 286–99. One of the best books on contemporary soccer—and one that gives a sympathetic view of the recent involvement of millionaire entrepreneurs—is Alex Fynn and Lynton Guest, with Peter Law, *The Secret Life of Football* (London: Queen Anne, 1989). Fynn and Guest followed this with *Out of Time: Why Football Isn't Working* (London: Simon and Schuster, 1994).

Before the 1950s biographies or autobiographies of players were rare things. Since then, however, they have grown exponentially, particularly through book clubs such as the Sportsmans Book Club. Many of them are fairly superficial, increasingly so as they rained down on the market, and to list all of them would be tedious. I would like to express here, however, my thanks to Sports House in Sydney for allowing me access to the most complete collection of such books—and others on soccer—that I have seen. Three books central to the threat of strike action in England in 1961 are James Guthrie, *Soccer Rebel* (Devon: Readers' Union, 1976); Jimmy Hill, *Striking for Soccer* (London: SBC, 1963); and George Eastham, *Determined to Win* (London: SBC, 1964). The dispute is fully covered in John Harding's previously cited history of the players' union, *For the Good of the Game*. There are several biographies of Stanley Matthews, but one of the most insightful articles on his career is Tony Mason, "Stanley Matthews," in Richard Holt, ed., *Sport and the Working Class in Britain* (Manchester: Manchester University Press, 1990), 159–78. Those interested in the role of blacks in British soccer should consult the insightful biography by Dave Hill, *Out of His Skin: The John Barnes Phenomenon* (London: Faber and Faber, 1989), which incorporates information from earlier books on the experience of black players by Al Hamilton and Brian Woolnough. For women's soccer see D. Williamson, *Belles of the Ball* (Devon: R. and D. Associates, 1991).

Much of the recent interest in soccer has centered on its hooligans, who have been studied and dissected like an exotic animal species. The most serious of these studies were conducted by sociologists from the University of Leicester; of their many works the most thorough is Eric Dunning, Patrick Murphy, and John Williams, *The Roots of Football Hooliganism: An Historical and Sociological Study* (London: Routledge and Kegan Paul, 1988). Their most recent work is Patrick Murphy, John Williams, and Eric Dunning, *Football on Trial: Spectator Violence and Development in the Football World* (London: Routledge, 1990). For an excellent participant-observer study see John Williams, Eric Dunning, and Patrick Murphy, *Hooligans Abroad: The Behaviour and Control of English Fans in Continental Europe* (London: Routledge and Kegan Paul, 1984; 2d ed., 1989). For a history of the more normal fans, see Rogan Taylor, *Football and Its Fans: Supporters and Their Relations with the Game, 1885–1985* (Leicester: Leicester University Press, 1992). For the fanzines, Phil Shaw's *Whose Game Is It Anyway? The Book of the Football Fanzines* (Hemel Hempstead: Argus, 1989) is a good introduction. An American perspective on hooliganism is presented in Bill Buford's *Among the Thugs* (London: Secker and Warburg, 1991). Although this book has been translated into other languages, it is rather superficial and does not bear comparison with Nick Hornby's autobiography of a soccer obsessive, *Fever Pitch: A Fan's Life* (London: Gollancz, 1992). This book has enjoyed unprecedented success and ranks with an earlier classic covering the game's hold on ordinary people, Arthur Hopcraft's *Football Man: People and Passions in Soccer* (London: Collins, 1968). Two books badly served, one by its cover and the other by its title, are gems of appreciation of the hold soccer has on its followers: Pete Davies, *All Played Out* (London: Heinemann, 1991), is a coverage of Italia 1990; Pete Davies, *Twenty-two Foreigners in Funny Shorts* (New York: Random House, 1994), was aimed at an American audience on the eve of USA 1994.

Soccer has not prospered in the English-speaking countries outside Great Britain, and this is reflected in the paucity of books on the subject. For soccer's failure in the United States, see Andrei S. Markovits, "The Other 'American Exceptionalism': Why Is There No Soccer in the United States?" *The International Journal of the History of Sport* 7, no. 2 (Sept. 1990): 230–64. For an account of some of its successes, see Sam Foulds and Paul Harris, *America's Soccer Heritage: A History of the Game* (Manhattan Beach, Calif.: Soccer for Americans, 1979); short and patchy, it has the advantage of including the memories of one of the oldest pioneers of soccer in the United States, who died only recently. Colin José offers an essentially statistical account in *NASL: A Complete Record of the North American Soccer League* (Derby: Breedon, 1989). For Canada, see Colin José and William F. Rannie, *The Story of Soccer in Canada* (Lincoln, Ont.: W.F. Rannie, 1982). Philip Mosely has written several articles on soccer in Australia, an indication to which are given in Philip Mosely and Bill Murray in the chapter on soccer in Wray Vamplew and Brian Stoddart, eds., *Sport in Australia: A Social History* (Cambridge: Cambridge University Press, 1994), 193–212. There is an official history of soccer in New Zealand: Tony Hilton, *An Association with Soccer: The NZFA Celebrates Its First 100 Years* (Auckland: NZFA, 1991). There is no major history of soccer in South Africa: for blacks and football in South Africa, see G. A. L. Thabe, *It's a Goal! 50 Years of Sweat, Tears and Drama in Black Soccer* (Johannesburg: Skotaville, 1983).

Most of the works on soccer in non-English-speaking countries remain untranslated, and works by English speakers on the game outside Britain are scarce. In addition to foreign-language works listed in the text and in the bibliography to my *Football: A History of the World Game,* see in particular *Actes de la Recherche en Sciences Sociales* no. 103 (juin 1994). The entire volume, entitled "Les Enjeux du football," is devoted to soccer. Articles in English in Sugden and Tomlinson's *Hosts and Champions,* of widely varying merit, cover Argentina, Brazil, Germany, Italy, Japan, Norway, Sweden, and USSR/Russia. The articles in Wagg, *Giving the Game Away,* cover areas rather than countries in a somewhat arbitrary manner: Africa (in fact Zimbabwe); Latin America (impressionistic with little history); North America (superficial); East Europe (i.e., the communist-bloc countries, but East Germany is omitted); northwest Europe; southeast Europe; Asia and the Pacific; and the Middle East (short but useful in view of the general neglect of this area). For Italy, see Stefano Pivato, "Soccer, Religion, Authority: Notes on the Early Evolution of Association Football in Italy," *The International Journal of the History of Sport* 8, no. 3 (Dec. 1991): 426–28, and Pierre Lanfranchi, "Bologna: The Team That Shook the World! A Football Team in Fascist Italy," *The International Journal of the History of Sport* 8, no. 3 (Dec. 1991): 336–46. There is nothing specifically on France in English. Siegfried Gehrmann is the foremost scholar on Germany. Part of his work can be found in English in "Football in an Industrial Region: The Example of Schalke 04 Football Club," *The International Journal of the History of Sport* 6, no. 3 (Dec. 1989): 335–55. For the early history of soccer in Germany, see Christiane Eisenberg, "Football in Germany: Beginnings, 1890–1914," *The International Journal of the History of Sport* 8, no. 2 (Sept. 1991): 205–20. On the England versus Germany game of 1935, see Brian Stoddart, "Sport, Cultural Politics and International Relations: England versus Germany, 1935," in Norbert Elias and Joachim Rühl, eds., *Sport History* (Niedernhausen: Schors-Verlag, 1985), 385–412. For that of 1938, see Peter J. Beck, "England vs Germany, 1938," in *History Today,* June 1982, 29–34. Jim Riordan's book *Sport in Soviet Society: Development of Sport and Physical Education in Russia and the USSR* (London: Cambridge University Press, 1977) devotes ample space to soccer. See also his article on soccer in his book *Soviet Sport: Background to the Olympics* (Oxford: Basil Blackwell, 1980). The best book on Soviet soccer, however, is Robert Edelman's fascinating history of spectator sports in the Soviet Union, where soccer is clearly shown to be the most popular sport: *Serious Fun: A History of Spectator Sports in the USSR* (New York: Oxford University Press, 1993). Duncan Shaw has written many articles on the game in Spain; for an example in English, see "Football under Franco," in *History Today,* August 1985, 38–42.

The first book in English on South American soccer came out in 1995, covering Argentina, Brazil, and Uruguay. Although short, this is a masterly interpretation: Tony Mason, *Passion of the People? Football in South America* (London: Verso, 1995). There are several good articles on South American soccer in Joseph L. Arbena, ed., *Sport and Society in Latin America: Diffusion, Dependency and the Rise of Mass Culture* (Westport, Conn.: Greenwood, 1988); see especially Steve Stein, "The Case of Soccer in Early Twentieth-Century Lima" (63–84); Janet Lever, "Sport in a Fractured Society: Brazil under Military Rule" (85–96); and Matthew Shirts, "Sócrates, Corinthians, and Questions of Democracy and Citizenship" (97–112).

Brazil has attracted several scholars who produced works in English, most notably the following: Robert M. Levine, "The Burden of Success: *Futebol* and Brazilian Society through the 1970s," *Journal of Popular Culture* 14, no. 3 (Winter 1980): 453–64; Robert M. Levine, "Sport and Society: The Case of Brazilian *Futebol,*" *Luso-Brazilian Review* 17, no. 2 (Winter 1980): 233–52; Ilan Rachum, "*Futebol:* The Growth of a Brazilian National Institution," *New Scholar* 7, nos. 1–2 (1978): 183–200; Peter Flynn, "Sambas, Soccer and Nationalism," *New Society,* 19 August 1971, 327–30. Janet Lever's *Soccer Madness* (Chicago: University of Chicago Press, 1983) is a sociological survey but has some interesting information. There are innumerable books on Pelé, but probably the most complete is the two-volume compilation of press extracts entitled *The Pelé Albums: Selections from Public and Private Collections Celebrating the Soccer Career of Pelé,* with an introduction and commentaries by Pelé (Sydney: Weldon, 1990). For Argentina, see Joseph L. Arbena, "Generals and *Goles:* Assessing the Connection between the Military and Soccer in Argentina," *The International Journal of the History of Sport* 7, no. 1 (May 1990): 120–30. Eduardo P. Archetti's works in English are somewhat anarchic.

There has been little written on soccer in Asia, but two handbooks that go well beyond straight statistics and that take Asian and Oceanian soccer to 1986 are Paul Moon and Peter Burns, *The Asia-Oceania Soccer Handbook* (Oamaru, New Zealand: authors, 1985), and Paul Moon and Peter Burns, *Asia-Oceania Soccer Yearbook* (Oamaru, New Zealand: authors, 1986). For information on the historic 1911 game in India, see Tony Mason, "Football on the Maidan: Cultural Imperialism in Calcutta," *The International Journal of the History of Sport* 7, no. 1 (May 1990): 85–96. Ken Knight's *Soccer in China* (N.p., 1991) is a desktop publication with the usual faults of these amateur productions, but it contains unrivaled material on the role of the Chinese in soccer in Asia.

There are several works on Africa in French and an official history of CAF in English: *Confédération Africaine de Football: 1957–1987* (Cairo: Nubar,

1988). There is a large gap between R. Clignet and M. Stark, "Moderniza-tion and the Game of *Soccer* in Cameroun," *International Review of Sport Sociology* 9, no. 3 (1974): 81–98, and Phyllis M. Martin, "Colonialism, Youth and Football in French Equatorial Africa," in *The International Journal of the History of Sport* 8, no. 1 (May 1991): 56–71. S. E. W. Akpabot's *Football in Nigeria* (London: Macmillan, 1985) is short but useful. See also Phillip Vasili, "The Right Kind of Fellow: Nigerian Football Tourists as Agents of Europeanization," *The International Journal of the History of Sport* 11, no. 2 (August 1994): 191–211. There is good material on Zimbabwe in the chapter on Africa in Wagg, *Giving the Game Away.*

Filling in the many gaps in the history of soccer is the publication *World Soccer,* which has been coming out monthly since October 1960. Of the academic sports journals, that with the most articles on soccer is *The International Journal of the History of Sport,* formerly *The British Journal of the History of Sport.*

# Index

BILL MURRAY teaches European history at La Trobe University, Victoria, Australia. In addition to books and articles on the French Revolution and Scottish history, he has published *The Old Firm: Sectarianism, Sport, and Society in Scotland* (1984) and *Glasgow's Giants* (1988), the centenary history of Rangers and Celtic. He is working on a book on France and the Nazi Olympics of 1936.

BILL MURRAY teaches European history at La Trobe University, Victoria, Australia. In addition to books and articles on the French Revolution and Scottish history, he has published *The Old Firm: Sectarianism, Sport, and Society in Scotland* (1984) and *Glasgow's Giants* (1988), the centenary history of Rangers and Celtic. He is working on a book on France and the Nazi Olympics of 1936.